David Lean

PHILOSOPHICAL FILMMAKERS

Series editor: Costica Bradatan is a Professor of Humanities at Texas Tech University, USA, and an Honorary Research Professor of Philosophy at the University of Queensland, Australia. He is the author of *Dying for Ideas: The Dangerous Lives of the Philosophers* (Bloomsbury, 2015), among other books.

Films can ask big questions about human existence: what it means to be alive, to be afraid, to be moral, to be loved. The *Philosophical Filmmakers* series examines the work of influential directors, through the writing of thinkers wanting to grapple with the rocky territory where film and philosophy touch borders.

Each book involves a philosopher engaging with an individual filmmaker's work, revealing how it has inspired the author's own philosophical perspectives and how critical engagement with those films can expand our intellectual horizons.

Other titles in the series:

Eric Rohmer, Vittorio Hösle
Werner Herzog, Richard Eldridge
Terrence Malick, Robert Sinnerbrink
Kenneth Lonergan, Todd May
Shyam Benegal, Samir Chopra
Douglas Sirk, Robert B. Pippin
Lucasfilm, Cyrus R. K. Patell
Christopher Nolan, Robbie B. H. Goh
Alfred Hitchcock, Mark William Roche
Luchino Visconti, Joan Ramon Resina
Theo Angelopoulos, Vrasidas Karalis
Alejandro Jodorowsky, William Egginton
István Szabó, Susan Rubin Suleiman
Jane Campion, Bernadette Wegenstein

Other titles forthcoming:

Leni Riefenstahl, Jakob Lothe
Bong Joon Ho, Anthony Curtis Adler
Chantal Akerman, Andreja Novakovic

David Lean

Filmmaker and Philosopher

Lydia Goehr

BLOOMSBURY ACADEMIC
LONDON · NEW YORK · OXFORD · NEW DELHI · SYDNEY

BLOOMSBURY ACADEMIC
Bloomsbury Publishing Plc, 50 Bedford Square, London, WC1B 3DP, UK
Bloomsbury Publishing Inc, 1385 Broadway, New York, NY 10018, USA
Bloomsbury Publishing Ireland, 29 Earlsfort Terrace, Dublin 2, D02 AY28, Ireland

BLOOMSBURY, BLOOMSBURY ACADEMIC and the Diana logo are trademarks of
Bloomsbury Publishing Plc

First published in Great Britain 2025

A catalogue record for this book is available from the British Library.

A catalog record for this book is available from the Library of Congress.

ISBN: HB: 978-1-3504-2931-4
PB: 978-1-3504-2932-1
ePDF: 978-1-3504-2933-8
eBook: 978-1-3504-2934-5

Series: Philosophical Filmmakers

Typeset by Deanta Global Publishing Services, Chennai, India
Printed and bound in Great Britain

For product safety related questions contact productsafety@bloomsbury.com.

To find out more about our authors and books visit www.bloomsbury.com and
sign up for our newsletters.

Contents

Figures

Preface

The filmmaker is David Lean (1908–91). Although interviewed on many occasions, he was lifelong reticent regarding anything approaching a philosophy of film. The task, to draw out philosophical issues from his work, will be in every sense exacting. Lean learned his craft in the cutting room. His reputation as a director flowed, as we hear in a poem by David Low of 1952, from his reputation as a cutter of almost obsessive precision and perfection.

> Look at that posture, surely caught
> As one of his own shots. Philosopher
> And artist, sensitive, dagger-hard
> To carve his picture.

Lean edited through the 1930s and began directing in the early 1940s, at first in collaboration with Noël Coward. Coward's influence as producer, scriptwriter, co-director, actor, songwriter, and great wit of the age cannot be overestimated. On his sixteen films, Lean worked repeatedly with actors like Trevor Howard, Alec Guinness, Celia Johnson, John Mills, and Ann Todd; composers like Malcolm Arnold, Arnold Bax, and Maurice Jarre; and writers, producers, and cinematographers like Robert Bolt, John Box, Guy Green, Anthony Havelock-Allan, Ronald Neame, Sam Spiegel, and Freddie Young. To name Lean must often then mean to name the entire team.

The book begins and ends with a motif running from the early, more domestic films locally situated in the English home to the later, more extensive epics of colony, commonwealth, and empire. The fidelity-infidelity relationship defined by marriage extends to the loyalty-betrayal relationship regarding countries playing at war and at peace. The relationship further extends to Lean's way of making films as works of a finely crafted art.

The book explores Lean's cinematic thinking in terms of music, although a music that is more broadly a musicality. Cutting, Lean said, is akin to how music flows in pictures. "I don't say that I'm writing music, Of course I'm not. But flow, music, creating images, it's in the same line of country." Lean's musical motifs are known worldwide: Lara's theme in *Zhivago*, the Colonel Bogey March in *Kwai*, Estella's motif in *Great Expectations*, Rosy's motif in *Ryan's Daughter*, Lawrence's motif for his adventure in Arabia, and of course Rachmaninoff's extraordinary chords in *Brief Encounter*. Yet, the motifs belong as much to the unfolding of the narrative and drama as to the film score. Many scholars address Lean's soundscapes with sometimes in-depth and sometimes passing descriptions. They rightly focus on the music *scored* for his films, how temporal and sound patterns find correspondence and articulation in verbal and visual design. I close in to investigate the sound, speech, and noise as *sourced* to objects of the world when the gramophone and radio were becoming indispensable furniture items for the home. Lean's films contribute to a furniture-art par excellence, an art with a touch of wit, so I want to show, rarely associated with this particular filmmaker.

If film, as a modern art, cannot do without its technological condition, then to pursue a philosophy of film music as simply continuous with a philosophy of music before film would be in error. For Lean, the continuities and discontinuities both matter. Behind his modern romance is a romantic aesthetic associated with a Beethoven paradigm that has long tested every expectation, great and small, under the rubric of *being true* to a work, a life, a person, a home, and a country. I have worked lifelong on this paradigm of (in)fidelity. So, too, in his cinematic ways, did Lean.

Lean's films make for a furniture-art because home is where he cut his keys of analysis. However, from home, persons may be transported or leave for periods of time for brief or more extended encounters. While the gramophone and radio make for one means of Lean's transportative art, the train, plane, ship, and automobile make for another. Trafficking in ideas, his films work through the modern reproductive and transportive technologies of sight and sound. *Cutting* — the term for the streaming of images — cannot do without *mixing* — the term for the streaming of sounds.

Cutting and mixing make for a *reeling perspectivism*, this being a good descriptive phrase for capturing the movement between places and times or between competing opinions and attitudes. The working-through makes for the *analysis* and for the *critique*. The book investigates how private and public arrangements of subjects and objects, persons and things, beliefs and moods are set and upset to defamiliarize home comforts. Engaging critique as a form of analysis means putting persons, places, and situations on trial to weigh and reweigh evidence. No film by Lean ever sits still on the sofa. For many, Lean is an irritating moving target; for others, a master of cinema's reeling and revealing moves.

The book does not consider the projects Lean seriously considered but did not complete. And while it surveys the critical reception of the films at home and abroad, it does not investigate every country where they have had an impact. Nor does it delve much into Lean's sometimes antagonistic relations with actors, scriptwriters, cinematographers, or producers, who were sometimes also his closest friends, lovers, or partners in marriage. (He married six times.) Nor does it include the British titles to refer to those who, like Sir David Lean, received such honors. It approaches Lean, accordingly, less through chronology, biography, and big business than through a micrological analysis that makes much ado out of a small detail, and, wherever possible, a musical detail that makes for a twist in the wit. Throughout, I take responsibility for my approach, although I draw constantly from a veritable archive of past and contemporary criticism and critical scholarship. There are already many good books on Lean. Like Lean's films, this scholarship repeats themes and reuses material. So, too, do I.

I chose to write about Lean given my own family home. My grandfather, Walter Goehr, is credited as the composer and conductor for *Great Expectations*. The crediting proved a contentious matter. Beginning the project after my mother's death in 2022 allowed me to recall my childhood in London after forty years of living in the United States and after forty years of working with the fraught history of

German philosophy and music. My memories drew me back to the double bills where my mother revealed a passion for cinema second only to her love of opera. *Brief Encounter* was one of her favorites. Finishing this book sadly coincided with the death of my father. He recalled very late in life his having briefly been considered by the Lean team to compose music for *Lawrence of Arabia* and how he had suggested using Hanns Eisler's techniques as a guide: clearly, the proposal didn't fly. I honor the paternal line of my family by pursuing the musicality and wit in Lean's films while dedicating the book to my mother—in memoriam.

Chapter 1 introduces motifs of music, marriage, and movement. The dialectic between fidelity and infidelity carries two senses of music: first, as worked through the film's furniture and technology *on display*—often in a family home; second, as worked through *musical metaphors* that turn old into new thoughts and new into old thoughts. Home emerges also with the sense of returning to source materials—novels, plays, and musical works. Lean's films were mostly *adaptations*. To suggest a work adapted, a character might carry a camera (*Summer Madness*), a musical instrument (*Doctor Zhivago*), a gramophone (*Ryan's Daughter*). A voice-over might read from the first page of a novel (*Great Expectations*), or cuts might be made by turning the newspaper pages of time (*This Happy Breed* and *In Which We Serve*). Lean made a cinema out of a history of the traditional arts. Through fidelity and infidelity to a past, his words, images, and sounds came to the screen as newly made for film as modernity's newest art.

Chapter 2 investigates the private adultery and public betrayal in *Ryan's Daughter*, as worked through the Beethoven bust sitting on the mantelpiece and the Beethoven symphony playing on the gramophone in the marital abode. The bust plays to the running motif of combustion. For individuals and countries, aged relations of domination and devotion threaten to blow the whole world to pieces. To prepare for the spin of Beethoven, the chapter begins with the Beethoven moment on the radio in *This Happy Breed*. What, in the 1940s, had this Beethoven moment to do with the film's Shakespearean invocation of the "sceptred isle," with the "fortress . . . [a]gainst infection and the hand of war?" Why had the fortress to be rebuilt in every home for each and every generation?

Chapter 3 forefronts accidental moments and meetings. It focuses on *Brief Encounter* and on the fact that Sergei Rachmaninoff's Second Piano Concerto happens to be on the radio. ("Rachmaninoff" will be spelled this way, hence, with a silent correction in quotations of other transliterations of the Russian script.) Written by Noël Coward and long regarded as one of the greatest films ever made, *Brief Encounter* became almost immediately *the film* to address the movement and music of war and peace in British society. But it was only one of several films by Lean (and Coward) on this subject. With a lighter touch, *Blithe Spirit* allows a husband to run through marriages until, dying in a car accident, he meets his comeuppance in a world of spirits: two dead wives. As a writer, the husband learns (like a filmmaker or a lover in an affair) that he can't control every event or mood, or, indeed, every judgment, as when a popular song is claimed to outlast a classical concerto. Because a Rachmaninoff record is already wittily refused in *Blithe Spirit*, might we find a comparable refusal in *Brief Encounter*?

Chapter 4 starts with *In Which We Serve*, where adultery would be committed were a sailor to prove more loyal to his family back home than to his ship. With its title drawn from the *Book of Common Prayer*, the film tells *the story of a ship*. Shown sinking, the British ship plays to the *forever of England* for each who serves. A sinking ship never truly sinks (given an old Socratic thesis) if the (musical) cables of the soul remain intact. The chapter further investigates a reception of *Brief Encounter* abroad, after which it shows how the film and the Rachmaninoff Concerto came together and separately to serve a British Cinema playing out its comedies and tragedies of middle-class English moderation on all the world's stage.

Chapter 5 begins with Lean's two Dickens adaptations: *Great Expectations* and *Oliver Twist*. The Dickens films are read for their complex soundscapes, for their themes of home, identity, and belonging, and for a raw politics bearing on anti-Semitism. Twists of great expectation sustain the overall method of analysis, while specific difficulties arise regarding the employment in Britain of foreign composers or the introduction of Jewish figures into films made in the shadow of the Second World War. Mastering a craft and making a home are juxtaposed with the craftiness of hand and step, of suspect reasons, justifications, and opinions. We see this then further in the comic-tragedy *Hobson's Choice*, where the marriage of three rebellious daughters is construed as a betrayal of the Lear-like father, until the father is given no choice other than to concur with his daughters' choices.

Chapter 6 opens with *The Passionate Friends* (US: *One Woman's Story*), where the contending parties travel between England and Switzerland to reassess a marriage and an affair situated, like *Brief Encounter*, around the Second World War. The chapter then reads *Summer Madness* (US: *Summertime*) for a reconstructed, postwar tourism in Italy. Situated in Venice, the film spans a bridge and a season of a suspect affair. A middle-aged woman from America's Midwest is drawn to a questionably honest Italian shopkeeper through the trading of a red goblet. Already a dream location in *Brief Encounter*, Venice is mapped as a landscape where truth is distorted by an economic abuse of beauty. The abuse amounts to a constant berating of Hollywood, given a souvenir to be taken home as a keepsake.

Chapter 7 continues with combustible motifs of music and technology. It focuses on the trials and tribulations in *Madeleine*, *The Sound Barrier*, and *The Bridge on the River Kwai*. The films share in constructing spaces of confinement. *Madeleine*'s Victorian murder trial ends with an almost smile, corresponding to the trial's famously unresolved verdict. Did the film fail in having ended likewise, with a question mark? *The Sound Barrier* questions the English family as an unbreakable unit through a wife's loyalty to her father, husband, and son. Both films ask what a woman owes herself. *The Bridge on the River Kwai* explores and exploits different modes of disobedience and sabotage as a bridge is built and then destroyed under caged conditions of hard labor.

Chapter 8 seeks the musical moments, often still comic, and the framing devices in Lean's *Lawrence of Arabia, Doctor Zhivago*, and *A Passage to India*. In *Lawrence*, an almost operatic allusion forefronts the making and unmaking of a myth: the myth of a man as a leader of a people as written by the man himself and then by the filmmaker. In *Doctor Zhivago*, the double love for a wife and a lover is worked out through the upheavals and complex family alliances of the Russian Revolution. The image on my book cover lies. A gloved Zhivago more carries than actually ever plays the musical instrument, the balalaika, that gives frame and form to a film about the gift of a parent who passes down a talent to make art. *A Passage to India* is about an English woman who, engaged to an English magistrate, brings an Indian doctor to trial with a false accusation of attempted rape. Here, a persistent echo puts an entire country, beyond any single individual, on trial.

Acknowledgment

Thanks to Ry Nafuma Smith for her editorial assistance and Julia Crockatt for the preparation of the images. Thanks to Jon Blair, Magda Bogin, Mitchell Cohen, Bernard Gendron, Phillip Hogh, Gregg Horowitz, Daniel Herwitz, David Huckvale, Simon May, Francey Russell, Mark Slobin, Gintare Stankeviciute, Wendy Steiner, Melanie Williams, and Margaret Jones. I am grateful to anonymous readers, students, and audiences with whom I tried out ideas. Thanks to Costica Bradatan for the invitation to write for his series and the editorial and production team at Bloomsbury Press.

Note on Text and Translation

In-text bracketing provides abbreviated references for quotations and suggestions for additional reading. Tense use varies according to whether references to scholars and writers are from this or past centuries. Italics stress motivic words and indicate direct spoken quotations from film and play scripts. Translations are sometimes silently modified.

Abbreviations

DL	Lean, David & Organ, Steven, ed. (2009) *David Lean: Interviews,* Jackson MS: University of Mississippi Press.
KB	Brownlow, Kevin (1996) *David Lean*, New York NY: St. Martin's Press.
MA	Anderegg, Michael (1984) *David Lean,* Boston: Twayne Publishers.
MW	Williams, Melanie (2014) *David Lean*, Manchester: Manchester University Press.
SS	Silverman, Steven M. (1989) *David Lean,* NY: H.N. Abrams.
PFR	Penguin Film Review
TL	The Listener

Chapter 1

Making the Cut
by Musical Means

Introduction to
the Films of David Lean

Chapter 1 introduces the domestic and social mobilities—the brief encounters and unexpected adventures—used to destabilize and restabilize normative structures according to principles of form: forms of life and forms of work. The many mobilities range from private adultery to public infidelity, disloyalty, and disobedience. A homefront may defend a marriage, a country, an empire. It connects to the idea of a frontier and to those sent to the front in war. From the idea of transport comes an aesthetic of mobility. The traffic of the train, plane, ship, and automobile that first invested modern time and space into the moving picture quickly sped up either passages formerly taken by foot or incidents caught by the once more static camera. Along the moving tracks, the camera revealed the sounds and noises of postwar nations running out of time to extend their aged colonial limbs. An extensive literature records the development of cameras and microphones that once traveled with filmmakers, documentary makers, and so-called foreign correspondents. Once the province of letters, correspondence in cinema became a new way of fishing for news, a casting, as in radio broadcasting, by a modern technological means.

David Lean was trained in the cutting room when the golden era of silent movies was transitioning to fully synchronized music, sound, and noise. Employed by the Gaumont-British Picture Corporation, he learned his craft in an atmosphere of newsreel documentary and, increasingly, wartime propaganda. The history of the Gaumont Film Company reveals a competitive atmosphere in which Movietone, Pathé, and Paramount also played their parts, not least by showing how studio sound could revolutionize broadcasting. Lean recalled how bringing in the soundtrack was at first "bloody cumbersome" as it slowed down the cutting (KB: 84; MW: 10). Cutting daily newsreels made time of the essence. Some suggest that Lean was tempted to leave the integration of sound to others. Not so, however, the more he realized that becoming integral did not mean giving up on how sound, like early color-tinting, had been used in silent and monochrome films before the integration. The films made in black and white, when color was possible, came with a concentrated internal display of what new technologies of music could newly mean for the world and for film.

A book with a broader focus would investigate film as part of the agonistic history of the arts, the competitive claims made by the differently constitutive media, after which it would turn to the emergence of film out of photography. A related inquiry would engage the vigorous debates in the history of opera, operetta, song, programmatic music, and the modern emergence of what was called a *use-* or *functional-*music. Here, already, soundscapes were rarely reduced by the presence of a visual landscape or a text to the status of *mere* duplication, copying, or accompaniment. So why repeat all the arguments when it came to assessing music's place in film? Crudely denigrating the often subtle art of the musical cartoon, Mickey Mouse fast became the reference point for the sort of cheap duplication that found in the soundscape nothing "extra" or "more" by way of meaning beyond what was already given by the moving camera. Yet, why even suspect the presence of a mimicking mouse when so many were promoting film, from its very first days, as the true and natural successor to opera, with its musical capability to be a *total work of art*? What was this musical capability, and how did it connect to thoughts about *mimicry* and *mimesis* as these terms were shaping critical discourses regarding the rise and fall of cultures and empires? (Hinton 1989; Hansen 1993; Bhabha 1994; Goehr 2008: ch. 7)

One early critic to slap down the *mimicking mouse* was the first director of the British Film Academy, Roger Manvell, and just when praising what the composer Richard Addinsell had achieved in Coward and Lean's *Blithe Spirit*. Here was a music that did not merely mimic, he said, but, instead, perfectly reflected a world where a "vibraphone and trumpet" were *called for* to *call* the "eccentric" Madame Arcati to her task: to take a "perilous" bicycle ride through a village in order then, on arrival at a modern middle-class home, to prepare for a séance (1955: 65–6; also Mazey 2020: 37–8). The séance proved yet more revealing. Readying the room, she sought a suitable music for the record player. Not Rachmaninoff, she said, but a popular song. And what a song she chose to turn the tables (in every sense) on what it meant in 1945 for one sort of music better to suit than another cinema's transformative purpose. There will be lots to say about the wit of a furniture that, being rearranged along the lines of musical chairs, reevaluates traditional values.

Lean rejected "mickey-mousing" explicitly if it rendered music in any way subservient to film. He described how music could be used to test cinematic errors: how, by its presence and then absence, it could reveal a camera shot to be necessary or unnecessary. He mentioned a case where a critic had missed a cinematic point by charging some music by Maurice Jarre as simply "loud and obstructive." Jarre won three Academy Awards for three of the four films he made with Lean: not for *Ryan's Daughter*, but for *Lawrence*, *Zhivago*, and *A Passage*. "I always give directions for the music," Lean explained. "When the composer starts getting involved—you'd think I was married to Maurice Jarre—I show him the script. . . . I tell him the mood. . . . You have to work very, very quickly, and you can make huge mistakes. Or you might forget things. Music helps fix those lapses" (DL: 40–1, 56, 111).

Of directing, Lean said: "The old-fashioned film director believed himself a kind of celluloid emperor, but this has now become a music-hall joke. Today we directors belong to a well-respected profession. At our head is Charlie Chaplin. He writes his own stories. He directs them. He acts in them and he even composes the music" (KB: 313). An American director living in Britain, Alexander Mackendrick (1954), almost said the same thing: "Chaplin did it, [all] . . . and he is the best. He produces, writes, directs, acts, and composes the music." But the "even" in Lean's "even composes" stands out. Lifelong adamant about directing every aspect of his filmmaking, including the music, Lean, unlike Chaplin, had no practical know-how of the art. Offered lessons by Malcolm Arnold, he professed interest, but that was it. Still, he recalled the weekly music appreciation lessons of his childhood—the "wonderful precision" of the "HMV Gramophone" with its "mahogany horn" and "bamboo triangle" needle, and the "rather outrageous modern music" of the young Richard Strauss. Apparently, had his talent been different, he'd have lived the "wonderful" life of a "jazz pianist" (SS: 19; KB: 45). One wouldn't guess this. He made his films not from jazz but, given Coward's influence, from an overall non-improvised romantic-classical music constantly challenged by witty servings of popular song.

Lean knew that music could prepare an audience for a certain action or mood or that it could distract an audience from the *realism* of a scene. Here, one might think of Alfred Hitchcock's witty refusal to use an orchestral soundtrack for his film *Lifeboat* (1944) about the survival of a shipwrecked group at sea: whoever finds an orchestra on the open sea! (Goehr 2008: 217). Already, however, in their shipwreck film of 1942, *In Which We Serve*, Coward and Lean used a music at sea: first to sing out the rule of Britannia's waves for its people never to be slaves and then to flash back to a home where an orchestra could ripple through the radio with news, say, of a shipwreck. "I try to write sound and music into a script," Lean would remark: "I'm always telling the sound people, 'Don't be realistic with sound. The audience has got to think it's realistic, but use it like an orchestra'" (DL: 76). Evidently, new sound technologies could orchestrate the "reality effect" to a convincing-enough degree.

Lean often silenced the orchestra to orchestrate soundscapes of natural and unnatural noises for urban and rural landscapes. Roger Manvell particularly liked the orchestral music dissolving into the soaring sound of an aircraft in *The Sound Barrier* and how, in *Hobson's Choice*, the music plays "ironically over the display of shoes . . . before the door bursts open with a gust of wind" to let the drunken Hobson enter with a "titanic belch" (1955: 66). Forty years on, John Thornley (1989) selected *Great Expectations* for the "gusts of wind" that seem "almost" to have been "written down on music manuscript paper," and how, to open *Brief Encounter*, "the whistle and terrifying swoosh of a passing steam train" dissolves into Rachmaninoff's first "ominous, looming piano chords." Usually, critics would name the composers for the films. Here, however, it was Lean whom Thornley congratulated for "composing" the soundscape in a much broader cinematic way.

Film's mechanized technology for producing sound and image encouraged Lean and his team to perfect their craft, to make *cuts* both great and small, passing and extended, between place and time, action and intention, voice and body. Voice-overs, close-ups, and long-shots, like patterns of music, noise, and silence, served every literal and metaphorical mode of transport: Laura's remembrance of her affair in *Brief Encounter*; a Midwesterner's arrival in *Summer Madness* amid all the hustle and bustle of Venice; an English women leaving a cold climate in *A Passage* to arrive in an India of intense sound and color. "I'm terribly conscious of the sound track," Lean once remarked, "which is almost as important as the pictures" (DL: 95). Does the "almost as important" belie my reading of Lean's films through all their bangs and whistles? Not if we attend to the play of music as mixed up with creaking posts or gusts of wind, dissolved then by voice-overs to produce a soundscape, wherein the music cannot be separated from the rest. And not if we pursue music and sound as furnishing the film for a family that feels at home, or for a family that remakes its home away from home, as in the camp in *Kwai* or in the British clubs in India and Arabia.

Scholarly literature regarding film music is extensive and provocative. Arguments range from denying the very use of the term "music" for what happens in film to embracing every sort of music to support what film offers, also through text and image, to produce a world *viewed*. In diegetic and non-diegetic patterns, music and sound stand in parallelisms or counterpoints with text and image. Early theorists described music as variously *integral*, *featured*, *incidental*, or *for the news*. They asked how far music *in* or *for* film, or a hyphenated film-music, could or should carry traditional attitudes and classical tastes forward (London 1936; Eisler & Adorno [1947]

2007). Like scholars today, they addressed the alleged discomfort of the "less educated" audiences who experienced music separated from its instrumental or technological source. Opera-, church-, and theater-goers were of course already accustomed to a music hidden by a stage or screen. Filmmakers often displayed a live orchestra or soloist or closed up on a gramophone or radio. But what then was achieved by letting music drift away from the source, only to return? Scholars note how a music's being experienced as close to and far from its source production might match how melodies leave and return through modulation and counterpoint to a composition's key, which, in turn, might match how people leave and return home either because they dream or because they're sent overseas on some sort of military or religious mission (Richards and Sheridan eds. 1987; Gorbman 1987; Flinn 1992; Buhler 2013).

Many scholars approach painting and film as a *visible music* for the eye, for frame and form, and for the graphing and mapping of narrative and meaning. The radio or gramophone that broadcasts a music or voice was often placed in rooms where large public events were channeled to impact even the most private of family relations. The more the public domain infiltrated the private home, the less it could do without the news that came through the daily newspaper or radio broadcast. The news replaced the *Book of Common Prayer*. Many named the radio play and documentary broadcast as the immediate predecessors to cinema in the moment of its turn from *silence* to *sound*. Radio's *radiation* was a *tuning in* for information and entertainment or an experiment for programming a *music while you work*. Complaints soon rained down about a mechanized music delivering a product that would no longer be listened to: a music *misused*, *unnoticed*, or *backgrounded*. Working with Coward, however, Lean upended many such complaints through subtle and often witty rearticulations of music's use and display.

I am nowhere claiming music or sound's priority in (Lean's) films, nor an approach to film music never before heard or seen. Nor am I denying the pathbreaking use of technology in, say, opera before film, as in the production of the first radio-operas (Murray-Schafer [1977] 1994; Rehding 2006). Nor am I claiming that marriages between Lean as filmmaker and his composers were always made in heaven. Instead, I am weaving the *mixer*'s art into the *cutter*'s art to forefront film's display of a technology branded as modernity's *furniture-art*. The more we notice sound's display, the more we comprehend the formalist and realist tendencies in the history of thinking about opera, theater, photography, and film. Much theory pits formalism *against* realism, but, in productive and witty counterpoints, each side works to supplement the other.

The dominance of the British Broadcasting Corporation (BBC) emerged with the institutionalization of British cinema and with the consolidation of roles such as writer, producer, director, and editor. Crediting the composer often proved far more contentious than crediting the sound mixer, sound producer, sound engineer, or sound recordist. *Great Expectations* inaugurated the use of the new "recording rooms" and "sound-booth" at Denham (Huntley 1947: 17). The role of film editor as worthy of credit stemmed back to around 1910, though it took decades before the mobility of roles assumed any fixity of labor relations (Perkins and Stollery eds. 2004: 61–91; Lean 1947a). Whereas some saw in the solidification of roles a loss of freedom (and women acknowledged) in the emerging form, others praised a new cinema (and boy's club) acutely conscious of shaping opinion. Many early commentators demanded a *new deal* — and first off for the scriptwriter. "In no other art form," Sydney Box wrote in 1947, "is the writer regarded as subsidiary to the technician and the interpreter. For the sake of the medium, as well as that of the writer, this position must be reversed." When he asked his readers to check the films to see if the writer had been adequately credited, he listed Coward and Lean's films first.

To trace the changing reception toward Lean, I looked at academic literature and popular journals, magazines, posters, and trailers. I plowed through *The Listener* to get a sense of Lean's radio reception and the *Penguin Film Review* to find Lean's name increasingly coming to stand for the expected mastery of the cutter's art with all the benefits of its concentration and all the risks of its excess. Given the husband's concentration on his crossword puzzle in *Brief Encounter*, one can only smile when, decades later with Lawrence's accidental death in mind, *The Listener*'s crossword for January 3, 1974 made *David* of David Lean the answer to the clue: *Crashing, beginning to swerve, but without mishap*. Outliving

Lawrence, Lean almost also outsmarted him—when (to adapt Steven Spielberg's words) Lean captured "the entire scope of the Arabian Desert" in a single cut (DL: xi).

Made increasingly in *foreign* locations, Lean's films affirmed and cracked what Raymond Durgnat in 1970 titularly described as *A Mirror for England*. Lean contributed to the nationalization of a film industry while negotiating a dependency on US sponsorship, licensing, and censorship in matters of production, distribution, and reception. When newscasting was almost just *war-casting*, Lean could hardly ignore the allied promotion of values against the enemy, just as, postwar, he couldn't ignore the international Red Scare and (Hollywood) Blacklist impacting the content of his films and the persons with whom he could work. Broaching individual authorship versus collective production, one finds Lean embroiled in the contentious crediting, discrediting, or under-crediting (of) the labor of others.

From a comparable sociological perspective, many commentators ask whether, in moving abroad, Lean became a British director in name only, especially when some, like Michael Balcon, declared Lean a director deserving of "international calibre" (1951: 37). Gerald Pratley, contrarily, placed Lean within a heritage of British Romanticism: "A romantic in all respects," Lean "is to the cinema what Dickens is to literature, Gainsborough to painting and Vaughan Williams to music" (1974: 13). Shadowing what it meant to *be British* was always the question of what it meant more specifically to be *English*.

With social labor relations solidifying the idea of cinema, Lean assumed an authoritative hand over the teamwork to produce what, decades later, was branded *the director's cut*. How different was this from when, centuries earlier, opera was first directed on the theater's stage? The *director* who cut and edited also shaped, selected, and orchestrated somehow *alone*, as Lean was regarded variously as a ring leader leading a traveling circus, a general of an army, or an orchestral conductor of a thousand musicians. Lean demanded a loyalty both praised and resisted—by actors or by the producer, who, overseeing the project, often felt more deserving of the *best picture* award than the director, who was assumed to be in charge only of what in a film made for the art. Always conscious of his authorial charge, Lean would invoke Shakespeare and Beethoven to note that film hadn't yet produced anything like that or them in the movies (MA: xii). Was this a conceit or a reflection of his emerging reputation, when knowing a film was *made by David Lean* began to carry more weight than either the producer's or a lead actor's name? *Mobilizing* Shakespeare carried the weight of England as motherland (Puckett 2017: 87f.), while invoking Beethoven fathered in the German work-concept for "classical" musical works (Goehr [1992] 2007).

Lean drew from the traditional musical genres of the concerto, symphony, and opera. Before the paradigmatic Beethoven symphony, the symphony already accorded with the preparatory use of an overture. His later "epic" use of orchestral overtures preceding the credits recalled how the opera took over the introductory symphonic sampling of melodies as anticipating a drama's motivic unfolding. To sample the melodies and motifs sustained the unifying drive and internal patterning of the (Wagnerian) music-dramas that later, by technological means, came to capture an aesthetic *seamlessness* toward which Lean so consciously strived (DL: 62).

Truth to a work (*Werktreue*) was the traditional concept for capturing a formalist aesthetic premised on Lean's lifelong commitment to cutting a romantic ideal doubly: by *the real* and *the reel*. Here, Lean was aware of pressing questions at home and abroad asking after film's relation to the tradition: whether film could achieve the status of being an art wherein form and content were brought to the dynamic unity demanded for aesthetic semblance. Appealing to the traditional rubric of the aura, many early film theorists were tempted to deny film's claim to seamlessness as a technological and even ontological impossibility. But why fear the cut or a technological dependency if a filmmaker could use film's condition not to destroy art's illusion but to produce it with a modern self-reflexivity? (Hansen 2008). With cutting scissors in hand, Lean fought for a formal coherence recalling a once Romantic *connectedness* (in German, *Zusammenhang*).

Coming from theater, Noël Coward told Richard Attenborough in a BBC interview in 1971 that he hated the word *cut*. What did he hate more: editors recommending cuts to his scripts or the surgical cutting that constantly interrupted a live action: take 1, 2 . . . take 22? For Coward, the hate was really his own "strong prejudice," as he described it, "against the moving picture business" (Aldgate and Richards 1986: 193). Cutting was always part and parcel of the rehearsal on the theater's stage. Why not see film as having a rehearsal, a preparation then experienced in the final product? Why was cutting so generating the anxiety that a crime was being committed against art, as Chaplin broached the issue in his silent film of 1914 *The Face on the Barroom Floor*, and Ernest Borneman, later, in his 1937 murder mystery *The Face on the Cutting Room Floor*? Looking back, Lean recalled Coward's "wonderful natural instinct" for the movement of actors, a sense of rhythm, even if he "hated" the word "rhythm" for its potential abuse. He thought it had been "used in so many wrong ways" (SS: 47). But what if "rhythm" found a good use for the right sort of "choreography," "cutting," and "staging," a rhythm without which film cannot do?

"Cutting" covered *the rough cut*, *match cut, cross cut, jump cut*, and *the cutaway*. And then the *invisible or smooth* cuts for *transitional, dissolving, fading*, or *seamless* movements. In drafts of scripts, Lean often used the word "dissolve." All sorts of cuts, smooth and broken, were being tried and tested by the most avant-garde of surrealist, constructivist, and cubist artists as well as by those less inclined to radical experimentation. Visual cutting came then with audio splicing as Sergei Eisenstein and friends explained in 1928 in their "A Statement on Sound": to show how "montage" could produce a unifying (musical or rhythmic) effect, this being "the indisputable axiom on which the worldwide culture of the cinema has been built" (Mackenzie ed. 2014: 565–8; Metz 1991: 53–4).

From the woodcut on, cutting drew on the oldest analogies between pen and sword or pen and knife to draw out a society's civilizing and barbaric tendencies. Walter Benjamin knew this when describing film as an art *of* and *for* exhibition under the modern surgical condition of technological reproducibility. Cutting was feared because technology was feared. Gazing back to the German poet Novalis in 1939, Benjamin found a "Blue Flower in the land of technology," a sense of the *real* coming over with an *immediacy* both despite and because of the *reel's* extreme artifice, as though the hands-on touch of the director had no need of a technological device (2003: 263; Hansen 1987). Benjamin brought the truth and lie of artifice to an emancipatory cause, to serve not an aestheticization or cover-up of (political) life but an art that could break through the maneuvers closing down all critical self- and world-reflection. He was not alone in this cause. But was Lean a fellow traveler?

Many confront Lean as an apolitical filmmaker. Still, because political momentum is not always worn on the sleeve, our analyses must unravel the orders of meaning that his films give off at first sight. The idea of a *reeling perspectivism* captures how the cinema moves between different social attitudes or political opinions without pinning a given film down to a single standpoint. It captures the point-counterpoint relation for someone who, transposing the art of writing, composing, and painting to cinema, wants even the most finely-cut products to retain an openness or productive ambiguity of meaning, expression, or point of view. For standpoint critics, ambiguity is irritating and condemned as a mode of avoidance. For others, it sustains claims of art's modern double-sided or relative autonomy, a way for art to be *true to* art and *true to* a freedom of thought about the world without capitulating to a single ideological or overriding order of knowledge. As Stanley Cavell asked in 1981 of the Hollywood comedies of marriage and remarriage, I will ask after the existential tapestry that emerges from the films by Lean that were sewing seams constantly anew in the face of modernity's relationships coming apart.

The thought of a *reeling perspectivism* comes from my watching Terence Davies and Jon Spira's 2022 *Reel Britannia*, a witty documentary on what made British film British. Beginning in the 1960s, it bypasses postwar film of the 1940s and 1950s to forefront an experimental filmmaking in and about London as the hotspot for sex, drugs, and rock and roll. Then it turns to the often Oxbridge comedy that took everything to scatological extremes. Lean, consequently, gets only a passing mention and then only to his "epics": "British cinema had never really done epic, with the notable exception of David Lean" (Figure 1).

Robert Murphy's impressive four-volume anthology *British Cinema* also somewhat brackets Lean despite the publisher's advertising that promises "an indispensable one-stop resource on

Figure 1 David Lean by Paul Loudon, from Terence Davies/Jon Spira, courtesy of *Reel Britannia.*

the major periods . . . (including immortals such as Alfred Hitchcock, David Lean [and on]).” Even the few and good discussions of Lean do little to mitigate the tension one feels today between Lean's unquestioned reputation and a contemporary desire to disregard him.

Vinod Mahindru and Robin Dutta's 2018 documentary “Who Killed British Cinema?” begins its exposure of “shocking truths” with Lean at an award ceremony pleading for money for as-yet-unknown directors so that they can take the risks he took. Here, his father figure status does not lessen the love-hate relationship of critics toward his films from the start. Ever more strident and extreme, the criticism eventually led him to suspend filmmaking for enough years to inspire the biblical allusion to his wilderness years of exile (KB: ch. 4). Between *Ryan's Daughter* in 1970 and *A Passage to India* in 1984, Lean made no major film.

Today, his films come over as textbook in their display of every political *incorrectness* or *suspicion* regarding sexual and gender dynamics, colonialism, nationhood, and class warfare. Thorny questions constantly arise regarding the representations between fact and fiction that offend: of Arabs, Jews, Indians, Italians, and Russians; wives, mothers, and daughters, husbands, fathers, and sons; the working versus middle versus aristocratic classes; child labor and criminality. What to do? Trash films? Brought under the rubric of "the movies," the films get condemned at home and abroad as box office sellouts to Hollywood. Seeking an "Anti-System" in 1957, Lindsay Anderson of the British New Wave bemoaned the number of (foreign) films denied distribution in favor of films like *Kwai*. Even if rationing was necessary, he asked, why choose "a huge, expensive chocolate box" that had so little to compare it to Lewis Milestone's much-appreciated 1930 *All Quiet on the Western Front*? Clearly, less was sometimes more.

When Melanie Williams contributed to the series British Film Makers in 2014, she declared her monograph "the first full-length study of all the director's films to originate from a British author and press," and, hence, the first book by an author to give David Lean "his due." She began with a quotation from 1985: "The curious thing about Sir David Lean is that everyone likes him except the critics" (MW: 1–4). She went on then to offer a most productive feminist reframing that would allow Lean's films to be read with a sort of then-and-now of British filmmaking, with a deep awareness, that is, of changing artistic tastes and political attitudes. Wanting to rescue Lean, she wasn't alone. Beginning in the 1940s, and increasingly thereafter, feminist theorists looked inside "women's pictures" to assess how far actors like Celia Johnson or Katharine Hepburn were subtly acting out against the conventionality and censorship to which (successful) films bound them (Haskell 1974; Kaplan 1978, 1990; Koch 1985; Kaja Silverman 1988; Shepard 2003; Dessem 2007; Thompson 2008; Bell and Williams eds. 2009; Basinger 2012). Williams joined these forces, while yet warning against subordinating British cinema too quickly to a gold standard of filmmaking and criticism as *made in America*.

Nor, indeed, could one simply assume that rescue strategies always succeeded in rescuing the films. That Lean's films proved so highly charged makes their critique more compelling, and not less, as the critique reevaluates the values brought to bear on the films' criticism. Critique as a philosophical pursuit departs from the immediacy of the thumbs-up-or-down criticism that has been assumed to rule the roost of the culture industry. Lean remarked that critics only tend to give filmmakers "the benefit of the doubt when (they) are obscure." And elsewhere: "The critics are the intellectuals. I'm always frightened of intellectuals" (DL: 54 & 60; MW: 2). By eschewing obscurity or by circumventing the world of intellectuals, however, he offered no comfortable clarity of mood or meaning.

Some theorists contrast films interpreted in the regular course of things with those that, more puzzling or opaque, invite interpretation (Wartenberg 2006). Critique takes further steps: to seek something exemplary that yields insight into the social and artistic premises that sustain the argument for film and its call for criticism more generally. To investigate Lean's films as a philosophical task is not, therefore, to hate them or to love them. It is to seek the characteristics that clue us into the premises that put film as art on trial.

Lean put film on trial by setting traditional claims of the real, the true, and the original into a broad field of fidelity, where fidelity began with the truth that he demanded of his work as a cutter's art.

Cavell compared the conditions of film's aesthetic power to the exercise of any human power, where the conviction in the exercise and the ordering of concepts, because not known in advance, structures "the architectonic of the critique" or makes sense of the demand for criticism and hence philosophy's intervention in each case ([1984] 2005: 120). The more the intervention, the more a critical analysis defamiliarizes a film's premises rather than leaves them safeguarded in place. The antagonistic output of critique tallies with reading Lean's films against the grain. Critique pursues the relevance still today of philosophical questions of the tradition regarding intentions, or a filmmaker's aesthetic and social commitments. It engages what came postwar to be known as "auteur theory," where, as part of the "politique des auteurs," critics took on the authority invested in the allied victory of postwar British American film (Kael 1963; Sarris 1970).

Lean was influenced by earlier and contemporary filmmakers: Chaplin, Hitchcock, King Vidor, Carol Reed, Orson Welles, Marcel Carné, D. W. Griffith, and the early Irish director, Rex Ingram. Lean, in turn, influenced many. For the latter, one might compare

Brief Encounter with Steven Spielberg's *Close Encounters of the Third Kind* (1977), with the latter's references to the pilots from the Second World War, to an ordinary life turned upside down, and to an exploration of a mothership. In 2006, for the *Irish Times*, Donald Clarke stretched the comparison. With the title "Close Encounter of the chaste kind," he recalled the initial ban of *Brief Encounter* in Ireland despite the most modest representation of adultery. What would the Irish make of a third encounter, he then asked perhaps with Coward in mind, if two men sharing a flat were suddenly interrupted by a heterosexual couple wanting, in Lean's words, to "screw like rabbits." Lean, apparently, didn't want to show any screwing at all.

With a different twist, Mel Brooks claimed in 1987 of *Spaceballs* to have redelivered *Lawrence*'s long shot and *Kwai*'s Colonel Bogey March, as dishes of "insanity," in preference, that is, to remaking *Brief Encounter* as "Jewish." Had he remade *Brief Encounter*, he explained, he would have had to shorten the noses, not to snub the original but to disguise the copying!

If, next, in *Brief Encounter*, we are made never to forget the radio, and in *Ryan's Daughter*, the combustible climate, so, comparably, in Spike Lee's *Do the Right Thing* (1989), the extreme heat, the radio, and the boombox determine the course of the day. If the one film questions the persistence of a tearoom or living room morality after the war, then the other interrogates an Italian pizza joint at odds with an African American community. Furnishing spaces matters for the form and content in both films. Delivering the "David Lean Lecture" in 2018, Spike Lee proclaimed one of the "greatest endings" in British cinema the bridge blown up in *Kwai*. That was "Lean's joint"—the "one take" they "had to get"—"that was how bad David Lean was."

Stanley Kubrick's *2001: A Space Odyssey* (1968) was said to be modeled, with a musical and commercial eye, on both *Kwai* and *Zhivago*, after which Kubrick's film was celebrated as more radical than anything Lean ever achieved when recycling popular and classical music into spheres far distanced and formerly unknown (McQuiston 2013: 29, 133).

Reviewing Spielberg's *Empire of the Sun* of 1987, Richard Combs found a "rediscovery of the cinema" not in direct quotation but in a shared sense of a hero who, as in *Kwai*, keeps forgetting which side he is on. Comparably, for Combs, heroism under a hot sun was tested (with the shared scriptwriter, Robert Bolt) equally in *Lawrence* and Roland Joffé's 1986 British film *The Mission*. But Lawrence as figure and film would win out as the "archetype" for postwar, colonialist cinema worldwide.

Cinematic influence and borrowing are keys for my argument, though mostly I keep my eyes and ears peeled on Coward. This way, we will see Lean's use of music, both classical and popular, sticking fairly close to Coward's way of placing large philosophical thoughts on tables or chairs, so that those with a seven-year itch might suddenly choose to pursue a brief four-handed encounter at a piano. *Extraordinary how potent cheap music is*, says a wife in Coward's *Private Lives*, but only because one of her two husbands doesn't want to listen to a *[n]asty insistent little tune*. No one thinks of Lean as a master of the comic, but seeking a Coward-like comic touch might deliver something we want and need to find.

Lean's films were almost always adaptations of older or contemporary works of which some, if not all, are still regarded as "classics"—by Charles Dickens, Boris Pasternak, E. M. Forster, and T. E. Lawrence. Some were more loosely modeled on prior works, as with *Ryan's Daughter* on Gustave Flaubert's *Madame Bovary*. Some of the adaptations became "classics" on their own terms and in Lean's lifetime, even surpassing the original—as *Brief Encounter* was said (wrongly, I think) to leave Coward's pre-war play of 1936, *Still Life*, far behind. The adaptations carried the new and the old, to forefront the mobility between media when a novel or play was remade into a film script or when a classical musical work was remade as a music scored for film. In this book, I attend to the originals mostly when they clue us into philosophical matters pertaining to music and wit.

With a film Lean had edited in mind, *Pygmalion* (dir. Anthony Asquith and Leslie Howard 1938), an early debate turned on whether adaptations benefited or suffered from the prior success of the original work. The *resting on Shakespeare syndrome* asked what *more* the film added: too close or faithful, the adaptation felt redundant; not close enough, then what? Some thought Lean's *departures* from the original more telling than his *fidelity*, not least in showing, in Michael Anderegg's words, a film's ability to bring out what was "proto-cinematic" in literature before 1900. A productive destruction of the literary text would, with perfect paradox, *re-create* a *new* work (MA: 38). Writing about *Oliver Twist*, Maria Christina Paganoni finds a "Janus-faced" artifact capable of delivering a "defamiliarizing lens" on the present "by revisiting the past" (2010: 309). Here, one cannot ignore the already Dickensian vision of a young man named Twist twisting perspectives on modernity's conventions and expectations.

Sergei Eisenstein explored adaptation as how a written text assumes through film a new plasticity of form (1944: 208). André Bazin described the effective aesthetic difference between reading the novel's language and experiencing the image material in a "darkened cinema." A different difference then followed from experiencing a musical work in the concert hall contra reading a score or listening to a *long-playing* record at home. (Long-playing records were introduced in 1948.) "The real problems" of adaptation, Bazin explained, "do not belong to the realm of aesthetics. They do not derive from the cinema as an art form but as a sociological and industrial fact . . . the drama of popularization." Adaptation and the consequences for the "hybridity" or "impurity" of film had everything to do with the quarrel over film's aesthetic versus sociological status as a high or popular art ([1967] 1971: 65–7).

In 1966, when addressing film's transparency as a materialist hand-down, Theodor W. Adorno described the loss of an imaginary or fictional potential in literature when the typeface of a written sentence became full-bodied on the screen ([1966] 1981: 200). But Siegfried Kracauer had already made the point in 1943 when considering the recent releases of Coward and Lean's *In Which We Serve* and Tay Garnett's *Bataan*. The more cinema encourages an explicit "Hollywood" spectacular, he had said, the more the *original* novel with its "inner action" is reduced to something *merely* preparatory for film (2012: 148).

Adaptation or, as once described, "picturization" meant a carefully negotiated license to change the title, words, characters, or music, the beginning, middle, or end. What got changed and what stayed the same spoke a thousand words. Sometimes, an adaptation by anyone was outright resisted, as by E. M. Forster and T. E. Lawrence, or, as with Arthur Laurents for *Summer Madness* or Pierre Boulle for *Kwai*, the authors objected to Lean's particular changes. *A Passage to India* was Lean's last film. He would have made another had he not died: his adaptation of Joseph Conrad's *Nostromo* was ready to go. Still, this has little prevented critics from reading a finality into the Forster film, an achievement even of something philosophical. But what? Perhaps a fidelity born from infidelity—meaning that, with all the anxiety of influence in hand, Lean rescripted the medium, mirror, and message in a cutting room that, lifelong, he wanted to make his own.

For *Time* in 1984, Richard Schickel praised Lean's *Passage* for having "no such thing as an idle shot," for allowing nothing to survive in "the final cut merely because it (was) striking in its beauty or novel in its impact." The thought of anything like an "idle shot" in Lean's films is almost impossible. The concentration of his labor, his perfectionism, fed a slogan where *doing a Lean* came to mean, with a sometimes mean spirit, that the director was taking or making too many shots, risks, or cuts (Sragow 1985: 21). For Robert Mitchum, being directed by Lean was "like being made to build the Taj Mahal out of toothpicks" (MW: 4). For Richard Combs (1988 and 1984), it meant a "love's labour" getting "lost" in "the overfingered" landscape. For Clive James (1971), it meant "disappearing" into a jungle to "get some David Lean-type footage of the pitiless waste." For Phil Hardy (1987), it meant arriving in Hollywood with colossal costs and grand visions: "it's as if David Lean made a Western." For Anne Karpf (1990), and for countless others, it meant aiming for anything and everything "epic."

Lean's focus on (in)fidelity brings us to the morality in the term "adultery," as derived from the adulteration or corruption of a natural, desirable, or dutiful state. Here, Lean, with Coward, looked back to the Victorian age that had inspired John Ruskin in 1865 to describe the home's "true nature" as revealing an Elysium of appointed tasks, as a "place of peace" and "shelter" from all "injury . . . terror, doubt, [and] division" (cf. MW: 60). Ruskin saw the home threatened when set on fire by a hostile "outer world" or when a husband or a wife overstepped "the threshold." Crossing the threshold preoccupied Lean given how, after the two great wars, the world seemed to have changed beyond recognition. What was he to do: construct a new sense of home, reconstruct an old one, or pit the promise of

Elysium against the ongoing battlefield of needs and wants? Ruskin had described the battle at home as an undesirable condition of superiority and subjection. Lean measured the high moral stakes against desires, conscious and repressed, for passion, freedom, change, and excitement. He weighed adultery as a public crime against the right to a privacy of one's chosen affections. He seemed drawn to the biblical thread that had made forbidden love desirable just because it was so forbidden.

Scholars stress bits of biography, one large bit being the Quaker upbringing of a young boy who, by being denied access to the cinema for the alleged harm and distraction it would bring, learned about cinema through descriptions delivered to him in secret. Lifelong, Lean seems to have carried the camera with all the guilt of making his art against his family's faith. Another tidbit bears on his fidelity regarding his more mature relations. Married six times, he confessed to treating each marriage more like an affair, as an adventure with a decisive beginning and ending. He regarded his marriages by their ends as closed books, assuming, like films, the form of finished works or performances of art: "Anything that is finished is finished. . . . Once you've made that decision, you've just got to cut people out of your life" (KB: 81; MW: 17). His sixth wife, Sandra Lean, reported his memory of how, when his parents separated, he stayed at the train station to avoid going home and how, later, he wanted to live as a nomad (2001:12). But staying away and going away are both ways of thinking about home, as each marriage, like each new film, comes, for better and worse, sometimes to feel just like a remake of an old one.

Pursuing the allegory between life experiences and the work of the cutter's art, one cannot bypass Georg Simmel's essay of 1911 on the *adventure* (*das Abenteuer*) with his declaration of the

> profound affinity between the adventurer and the artist, and also, perhaps, of the artist's attraction to adventure. For the essence of a work of art is . . . that it cuts out [*herausschneidet*] a piece of the endlessly continuous sequences of perceived experience, detaching it from all connections with one side or the other, giving it a self-sufficient form as though defined and held together by an inner core.

Reading these words, one might string up Lean's films according to a form that masters its content. Or, for Simmel, as "adventurers of the earth," our lives are "crossed everywhere" by "tensions" that, becoming ever more "violent," incline us to master the adventitious and accidental material completely. This way, an adventure or encounter assumes "the mysterious power to make us feel for a moment the whole sum of life" ([1911] 2002: 223).

Closed by a mastery of form, Lean's adventures were of necessity set against the before and after. How they accidentally or purposively began or ended clued us into the life from which they were cut out, the reality they left and to which they returned. When, then, the technological dependency met the romantic impulse, the *cutting out* of the adventure became also a *cutting off*: as when, by radio or phonograph, a musical transmission was severed from its live performance, or when, by plane or train, someone broke out or away for a brief while. Rarely, however, despite his use of monochrome, were Lean's cutouts so black or white. A radio transmission cut off from a live performance could still broadcast a performance as live. And when abroad, something of home was always carried in the luggage.

A Kiss in the Tunnel by G. A. Smith is captioned in the BFI National Archive: "The steamy romance between British film and the railways began with a brief encounter in 1899." Transport begins and ends nearly every one of Lean's films. "Why do I love these trains so much?" (DL: 105). Or "I often think of a film as a train journey. The permanent way, the rails, are the story line" (KB: 648). Here again, Coward was already on board: he traveled lifelong while never forgetting home. Behind the storylines, the tracks of modern technology, of scientific construction and achievement, spread far and wide. Lean would build his own tracks for the movement of the camera. There is a wonderful scrapbook history by Susan Briggs (1981), *Those Radio Times*, full of material about how radio broadcasting became timetabled in the manner of train schedules, or how, as in *Brief Encounter*, the wires of radar transmission came to carry all the trials and tribulations of romance. I imagine a title for a book about Coward and Lean: *From Radar to Romance*.

Allied ships and trains, contra enemy planes, make for the drama in *In Which We Serve*. Trains and tracks give form to *Brief Encounter*, *Summer Madness*, *Kwai*, and *Zhivago*. An underground train for a threatening suicide ends *The Passionate Friends* following a hopeful plane at the start. A plane of aspiration opens *The Sound Barrier* as it attempts to surpass the speed of sound. *Lawrence* begins with the motorbike ride that killed T. E. Lawrence in England and ends with the imagined car that speeds Lawrence home and away from his misconstrued heroics in Arabia. *A Passage* begins with a boat, then a train, and then a car speeding the English through the town, only to knock an Indian doctor off his bicycle. Looking back, nineteenth-century coaches and horses move between rural and city landscapes in *Great Expectations, Oliver Twist*, and *Madeleine*, to ask whether, in knowing where you are going, you need first to know from whence you've come.

Increasingly in Lean's films, the *encounter* or *adventure* draws on transport to support a modern tourism in places far away from home. Lean recalled his need to escape a stifling and cold country. Through his transport, the visual land- and soundscape rendered the foreign familiar and the familiar foreign. His landscapes questioned homes of safety and colonial settlement, while his soundscapes—silent to screeching—echoed broken dreams and promises. His later transport recalled the earlier Coward-inspired patterns of "thick and thin" family relations torn apart and sewn back together. "Thick and thin" relations find their way into philosophical analyses of public and private betrayal. "In a tricky and unstable world," wrote Judith Shklar, "fidelity may be in such short supply that betrayals become the norm. That does not excuse them, perhaps, but if disloyalty is expected, betrayal must lose its primitive horror" (Shklar 1984: 146; Margalit 2017).

The modern consciousness of technology's new tracks put early film's status as a *fine* or *noble* art, as photography before film, into question. Writing "The Seven Pillars of Hollywood" in 1946, Emil Ludwig made each pillar stand for a social role within the industrial production of a new state that, in a "bloodless revolution," was being added to the already "forty-eight" states of America. A decade earlier, Martin Heidegger named "[a]irplanes and radio sets" as what "nowadays" in the world of "things" strike us as "closest," so that he could describe the alienation of a false closeness that actually distances one from a home where matters of life and death ought to matter more (1971: 21). Analyzing the culture industry in 1944, Max Horkheimer and Adorno listed automobiles, bombs, and radios to articulate film's need to deceive a highly administered public. Aware of every modern transport, they heard and saw music and people spreading *everywhere* while traditional meaning had *nowhere* anymore to go. They saw upright pianos and barrel organs casting a street music voided of shadow and echo ([1944] 1981: Vorrede, 129–30). To the complaints, again, Coward and Lean answered back.

A modern idiom impatiently asks for clocked time to *cut to the chase*. Sourced to the 1920s silent film, the idiom demanded a final pursuit of a lover or criminal. It allowed the high speed of a car or train, and by extension modern times, to be *caught on camera*. Then came the chase to the end in the first music recordings as the vinyl was cut (as in *Ryan's Daughter*) to the last groove. To groove is to move, to choreograph patterns on the floor. The internal rhythm and the temporal gestalt that the camera follows through with its many angles match the common time of the pacing in the drama once known as the *alla breve*. Common time measures the beat of an army, as when, in *Kwai*, the English soldiers whistle the Colonel Bogey march in an uncommon circumstance. Lean engaged less the car chase than the transportation that, in the cutting room, brought mobility to his *footage*. The very idea of "footage" drew from the early measure of feet or *Faden* that once allowed ships (of fools) to survive or sink on the high seas (Goehr 2021: 470–1). Then there was the *decoupage*, the old decorative cutting out from pieces of paper, that, in cinema, turned and moved with every reel, frame, and strip. All these terms carried the long history of the traditional arts into a new art of cinema premised on *modern* times.

Lean's characters sometimes hang from trains, want to jump under them, or blow them up. Many look at and through panes of glass as windows of self-reflection, or, as in *Hobson's Choice and Lawrence*, at puddles and pools of water. Through the looking glass, persons reckon with their desires, as in the father-son birds-and-bees talk in *This Happy Breed*; the father-daughter discussion of *invention and adventure* in *The Sound Barrier*; the confrontation of soldiers in *Kwai*; the marital rift in *The Passionate Friends;* and Pip in *Great Expectations* as he stares as and at the gentleman of unwarranted prejudice he has become. While an express train may leave one with a little piece of grit in one's eye, as in *Brief Encounter*, getting something in one's eye, as in *Summer Madness, Ryan's Daughter*, and *A Passage*, comes more generally to betoken the internally related beginning and ending of an adventure.

The term "plane" connotes how space is cut through to achieve a *mise en scène*. The film-formalism tracks the movement of eyes and ears as a Dickensian observation of how people move through city streets and crowds. Anderegg stressed the poetic license and lyricism that came from cheating the science in *The Sound Barrier* when a plane is heard before it is seen—because the issue was for the plane to "fly faster than sound" (MA: 74). David Bordwell and Kristin Thompson mention *Lawrence* to illustrate the "stereo reproduction" that could help "specify a moving sound's direction": how "the approach of planes to bomb a camp is first suggested through a rumble occurring only on the right side of the screen. . . . Then, when the scene shifts to the besieged camp itself, the sound slides from channel to channel, suggesting the planes swooping overhead" (2010: 293).

Belá Balázs described the composite image and geometrical picture plane as made from the conjoining of spectatorial and camera viewpoints (1931: 208). André Malraux comparably sketched the terms for how modern cinema as a "means of expression" was born out of the destruction of, and liberation from, a circumscribed or fixed space, from the era when the cutter envisaged the division of his narration into planes. To illustrate, he placed the radio broadcast in strategic counterpoint to the photograph ([1939] 1958: 320–1). Overall, transport plays to the art of broadcast and displacement as well as to the fear of deception, so that, when put on trial, Lean's cinema helps us to review the trust we put in screened evidence.

Lean's films rarely yield philosophical generalizations. More, they ask us to seek what early theorists pursued as an unconscious optics, a micrological, micro-physiognomic, or stereoscopic analysis of cinema's innuendos, pathologies of wit, and woodcut grains. "Fidelity," insisted the novelist, Walter Besant, "can be only assured by acquiring the art of observation, which further assists in filling the mind with stored experience" (1894: 23). Without making psychoanalysis an explicit theme, Lean called for Freudian and Socratic couches to unsettle his characters' loyalties. In *The Sound Barrier*, when a woman, as wife, mother, and daughter, runs to the movies to escape her anxieties at home, we are brought to a double analysis of a world where new dreams of cinema and science confront the destruction of everything formerly believed. Tests and trials saturate his films. Between his *adventures* and *daily life* lie all the troubled paths of prohibition and allowance.

Between fact and fiction, realism and idealism, documentation and desire, documentary and propaganda, Lean's films invite us to a reeling perspectivism of private and public relations. The attitudinal stances of politics and morality move through a musical movement approximating a "visual accordion" (Deleuze 1986: 13). A technique of flashbacks turns old endings into new beginnings and old beginnings into new endings. With memory put on trial, we see that not all can be recalled, said, displayed. Absence, muteness, and silence cannot do without the camera's direction. What, regarding music, is foregounded and what backgrounded becomes as enigmatic and concealed as the history and motivations that lead persons to betrayal and infidelity.

Concealment sustains the tension between the aesthetic pleasure or beautiful form of land and soundscapes when, beneath the seamless surface, brutality and violence are hidden. Does concealment, by the power of suggestion, bring the violence more (consciously) to the surface? Lean claimed that violence becomes "much more frightening if you leave it to the viewer to imagine" (KB: 241). Critics duly note how little he made of *explanation*, that the whys and wherefores of his characters suggest a masking that rarely yields an explicit articulation of the human condition. To what extent the ordinary or real world is left over intact becomes, finally, the once Aristotelian question that leaves his films with the unresolved impression of a denouement. With this comes the hermeneutical remainder, the deliberate sense of an ending not being as closed as the completed form of his films suggests.

Chapter 2

Beethoven and Bust

This Happy Breed (1944), *Ryan's Daughter* (1970)

Beethoven's bust is the supreme bust of fidelity, bar none. A photograph of such appears on the original cover of my book, *The Imaginary Museum of Musical Works*. That book described the Beethoven paradigm that crystallized the romantic work-concept and the ideal of truth-to-a-work (*Werktreue*) in the theory and practice of classical music around 1800. A Beethoven bust sits on the mantelpiece in one of Lean's films as the prized possession of an older Irish husband whose younger wife, comparably prized, enters into an adulterous relationship with a decorated but disabled English soldier. Released in 1970, *Ryan's Daughter*, about betrayal, was strongly condemned for betraying the cultural promise of cinema in its own time and its historical subject matter: when, during the First World War, an Irish village, aided by a German shipment of weapons, took action against the occupying English army.

The setting was the aftermath of the 1916 Easter Rising. A father, the village publican, Thomas Ryan (Leo McKern), betrays his country and his daughter, Rosy (Sarah Miles). He sides with the Irish rebels, led by Tim O'Leary (Barry Foster), while informing on them to the English. Rosy has an affair with Major Randolph Doryan (Christopher Jones), modeled on Flaubert's Rodolphe Boulanger. She is cared for by a mute fool, Michael (John Mills), by a priest known as Father Hugh Collins (Trevor Howard), and by her husband, Charles Shaughnessy (Robert Mitchum), modeled on Flaubert's Charles Bovary, but also on the school teacher who first taught Lean about music and the gramophone (KB: 35). Neither the music on the gramophone nor the triangle of care saves Rosy from a violent public punishment when the villagers construe her adultery as a sleeping with the enemy.

The events join the political to the personal. The English major-lover, having lost Rosy, blows himself up in repetition of the trauma he has already experienced on a distant battlefield. His final lighting of a cigarette match cuts the scene back to an anxious Rosy at home, while, as a "match cut," it recalls from Lean's earlier film how Lawrence was transported from a military office in Cairo to the desert in Arabia. There, the cut marked the adventure's beginning, while in *Ryan's Daughter*, it marks its end. Asked about the repeated cut being "strikingly effective," Lean surmised: "maybe it should all be staccato. You have to choose your technique—you may want the thing to have a sort of sensual flow to it. . . . I often think of scenes in musical terms. They build up to a climax, then hover for a moment, and then . . . bang!" (DL: 92).

Doryan's suicide ends an affair that the lovers have already decided upon, allowing Rosy to return in some way to her husband. *It's busted, Charles. I busted it*—she cries out as though the rupture in their marriage was not foretold from the start. The *it* that was *busted* corresponds to a marriage shaped by the Beethoven bust that Charles prizes second only to his gramophone—while busting loose is what happens to the rebels' cargo when the weapons and explosives land on shore scattered by a powerful storm: *They've gone! Busted loose!* When the adulterous Rosy is named the informer, the village mob-leader tells her: *You've been tried and found guilty.* Her return stare of disbelief is met with a skeptical comeback: so you're *busting at the seams with innocence*! When Charles and Rosy finally leave the village at the film's end, they refuse the villagers the satisfaction of knowing that they have decided to separate: *I'm not*, Charles says, *for letting any of that lot know we've busted up.* Keeping up a front is Charles's way. Seeming to anticipate Doryan's death by fire, he tells Rosy that he thought he *could stand by*, waiting for the lovers *to burn* out their desire, but he'd come to see the flame as inextinguishable: that the lover would always stand between them *like a ghost about the place*—(the theme earlier of *Blithe Spirit*). Rosy takes the blame for the marriage *bust* even if it is Charles's fidelity to the Beethoven bust that prevents his expressing a passion that would have stopped her from looking elsewhere. Will he assume some responsibility? With a twist, the father's betrayal grants the daughter a second chance: to leave the village with her husband, to go their separate ways, or to marry him again on new terms.

This chapter connects the bust of stability—the Beethoven bust—to the many colloquial senses of busting and combustion that leave characters destabilized and disabled either *forever* or for a *brief time*. Being *busted* refers to those who are inebriated, where insobriety divides those who drink (Ryan) from those whose starry dreams intoxicate them with desire (Rosy). Busting brings Lean's film of three hours to its criticism as a "blockbuster," but also to its potentially rescuing analysis and critique. Marking a critical juncture in Lean's life as a filmmaker, *Ryan's Daughter* allows us to look backward and forward over the expanse of his oeuvre: to the string of films about fidelity and infidelity where the technology and transport map out the dynamics as well as the dynamite.

Focusing on the Beethoven bust is how I pursue different forms of fidelity with more attention paid to the marriage than to the affair. In general, critics focus on Lean's cinematic affairs; I focus more on the marriages. To prepare for the Beethoven in *Ryan's Daughter*, I look first at the Beethoven radio-moment in Coward and Lean's *This Happy Breed*. Focusing on the furniture-art, we come to see how little we can rely on what alone is scripted as speech. Looking and listening are indispensable to detecting Lean's direction of clues.

Regarding clues, the New York Public Library houses eight boxes of Stephen Silverman's materials for his book on Lean. Shorthand transcriptions report Lean's remarks on music: "general feeling–[music is there] from the beginning"; "never improvisation–script [like] Bible." And then no "ethnic association," which is odd given the Irish harp demanded for *Ryan's Daughter* and the balalaika for *Zhivago*, and for *Lawrence* and *A Passage* to have a musically inflected Arabic or Indian atmosphere. The remark on *Ryan's Daughter* stands out even more: "my fav. score" and "we tried to do things that [we] had never done before–not do'g Beethoven." If Lean was not doing Beethoven, what was he doing *with* Beethoven? And would this Beethoven be separated from "ethnic" association?

Lean's films are formally complete, yet hermeneutically replete with irresolution. They draw on the Romantic tension in the very idea of a work of art as fought out on battlefields of the ideal and the real, private and public. Through adaptation, they reveal a preoccupation with traditional norms and expectations that once brought social ensembles into family relations with musical ensembles. The idea extends back significantly to Johann Wolfgang von Goethe's *Elective Affinities*, to the "red thread" drawn from a stormy piracy or freebooting on the high seas into a home to address a quartet of emotions capable of re-patterning a married couple's divided loyalties. That the red thread long sustained the allegory between an affair of life and a work of art is all we need to know here to understand how the Beethoven bust brought so many modern stabilities and instabilities of meaning under the rubric of truth to a work (Goehr [1992] 2007: pt 2; 2008: ch. 1; 2021: ch. 17).

When, in 1945, Maurice Merleau-Ponty declared a new philosophy and psychology arriving in convergence with film, he invoked Goethe's dictum: "What is inside is also outside" (1964: 58–9). His argument overlapped with André Malraux's sketch regarding the technological invention of *découpage* as essential for generating film's shapes of image and sound (*Gestalten*) ([1939] 1958: 320). For both, the artistry, musicality, and mastery of cutting carried an existential doubt into the art-making. As trial and error, the camera's many retakes matched what painters did by putting and erasing lines and colors on a canvas or what musicians did when practicing to the point where land- and soundscapes emerged as right according not to rule but to touch. What was new about film, to adapt Goethe's dictum, was also old.

In broaching art's subjection to the modern condition of technological reproducibility, Walter Benjamin quoted Abel Gance from 1927: "Shakespeare, Rembrandt, Beethoven will make films. . . . All legends, all mythologies, and all myths, all the founders of religions, indeed, all religions, . . . await their celluloid resurrection, and the heroes are pressing at the gates" ([1939] 2003: 254–5). Abel

Gance described film's liquidation as a musicality of impermanence, when, with the fleeting quality of "radioactivity," words and images suspended their everyday meanings (Cuff 2016: xviii, 54, 73, 95). For Benjamin, the cultural heritage threatened an entire breakdown, when a bad liquidation replaced a desirable liquidation. From the new technology of the radio, gramophone, and television, an *imaginary museum without walls* was seeping under the public condition of unlimited dissemination into the most private of quarters to produce only a rigidity of the cultural conditions (Malraux 1947; Goehr [1992] 2007).

In 1941, George Orwell brought Goethe into conversation with Shakespeare. He offered a prescient description of "England Your England" in times of "supreme crisis." In "normal times," he wrote, the "snobbery and privilege" overwhelm alongside a "deep" dishonesty of class and press. In crisis, contrarily, behind all the restrictions on "free speech," something binds the nation: "an invisible chain" that "resembles a family" with "its private language and its common memories." England was neither the "jewelled" (or sceptred) isle of Shakespeare nor "the inferno depicted by Dr Goebbels." It was, rather, a perfectly imperfect family: "A family with [or despite] the wrong members in control—that, perhaps, is nearest as one can come to describing England in a phrase" (1971: 87–8).

Let us dial now into *This Happy Breed* to find a family fortress on a Shakespearean isle that, in a furniture arrangement beset by war, has Beethoven playing for a brief moment on the radio. The film's beginning and ending are marked by the opening and closing of a front door. In Coward's play of 1939, the set is a dining room. By month and year, the scenes follow the Gibbons family from the end of the First World War to the eve of the Second. The documentation of the political and cultural events, suggested on the stage, is then cut into the film through close-ups of magazine covers and newspaper front pages, billboards, banners, and ballots: the 1920 release of the Western *Desert Love* (dir. Jacques Jaccard), the 1924 British Empire Exhibition, the 1926 General Strike, the 1929 release of Harry Beaumont's *The Broadway Melody* in sound and technicolor (Figure 2), and then all the developing styles of dance, flight records across the Atlantic, and changes in Kodak cameras and wired

Figure 2 Broadway Melody 1929, *This Happy Breed*, directed by David Lean, Eagle-Lion Distributors/Two Cities Films, 1944.

radios. Clips of cinema and documentary photographs track the history. Royal events and large political quarrels regarding socialism and fascism, pacifism and warmongering, variously dissolve into the insularity of a home where imperfect family relations, dynamic and carefully timed, reveal a not-always-so-happy life for *this happy breed*.

The *Anna Karenina* moment in *Brief Encounter* at the train station is well documented. Less so, the same novel's first line as applied to *This Happy Breed*, where happy families all "alike" prove "unhappy," each "in its own way." We might compare this with the broken record for the radio's "The Happy Household Hour" in Fritz Lang's *Scarlet Street* of 1945 or Ludwig Wittgenstein's *Tractatus* of 1922, where "the world of the happy man" cannot be so cleanly severed from that of "the unhappy man" even as the difference is strongly propositioned. Reading proposition 6.43, Stanley Cavell broached unhappiness as a suspension of the security with which one tends to hold one's ways of knowing in one's hands. With suffering came doubt, and with this, a feminine erasure of the confidence of the male gaze. "In both skepticism and romance," he wrote, "knowledge, call it consciousness as a whole, must go out in order that better consciousness can come to light." Turning the tables on philosophical method, doubt was an advance on certainty. With doubt, happiness and unhappiness could exist with a perfect imperfection "within the same breast" ([1978] 2005: 7).

The cutting of the heart in *This Happy Breed* swirls around Celia Johnson's compounded role as Ethel: wife, mother, grandmother, daughter, and sister. Cutting and framing a family between the two wars, Coward and Lean begin and end with a panoramic shot over houses in London to arrive at the front door in Clapham. The home, with a piano, is rented for the film's duration. It is like no other home. Most of the conversation is a squabbling and nagging. A *To Let* sign marks the end. Comparable rent shots and luggage signs for entering and leaving homes are offered in *Blithe Spirit*, *Great Expectations*, *Oliver Twist*, *Madeleine*, and *Ryan's Daughter*. The first voice-over tells: *After four long years of war the men are coming home. . . . Hundreds and hundreds of houses are becoming homes once more.* The film cuts sustain a meaning and material condition for a furniture-art framed to challenge the magazine promise and popular print of the "ideal home" (Price 2021: 77–85). Women's magazines also become a staple in Lean's films. Beyond the weekly purchase of ideals, modern family breeding means renting furniture for a specific duration. To rent, to borrow: here is a deep analogy with an artist who rents material for a time with the purpose to give it a form.

So too, with the borrowing of popular songs. One image in *This Happy Breed* advertises an era given over to *jazz*, but what we hear are popular standards like "For He's a Jolly Good Fellow," "Take Me Back to Dear Old Blighty," "London Pride," and the forever song of Britannia to rule the waves. A terrible rendition of *The Kashmiri Song* is sung at the piano where, given the lyrics, the *pale hands crushing* the *throat* prove most apt (Figure 3). Then a rendition of *Birds of Night Divine* follows the father's (Robert Newton) escape from the piano room so that he can express the love of the English much more for their gardens.

Raised in the music hall tradition, Coward was self-taught at the piano and in everything else. Without learned capability, he wrote, apparently like Irving Berlin, simple songs mostly in the same key that were "easy to pick up and repeat" (Morley [1969] 1985: 47).

Figure 3 At the piano, *This Happy Breed,* directed by David Lean, Eagle-Lion Distributors/Two Cities Films, 1944.

But still, his songs appear in his films far less than familiar standards easily recognizable to an audience—including, in *Blithe Spirit*, a strategically chosen song by Berlin.

For the orchestral score of *This Happy Breed*, the credits say, "Music played by the London Symphony orchestra under the direction of Muir Mathieson." Company labels for the sound's production are below, but no composer is named. Today, partial credit is given to Clifton Parker, though Coward was clearly in charge. About the score, Andrew Higson notes the brief passages of harp music that, already following "Hollywood conventions," allowed fantasies or flashbacks to begin and end even when the unreality, as in this film, regards a very concrete string of political events (1995: 255–6). Higson's Hollywood reference finds a *Broadway melody* patterning a British film. But the radio introduced in Coward's play as a piece of furniture reveals yet more, as it joins the tea set, knitting needles, newspaper, and the dictionary needed for the crossword. *A brand-new shining radio stands on a little table above the fireplace. . . . It is playing softly* as the *tea-things* are brought *in and out*. Generally, the radio is dialed down when it gets on someone's nerves and dialed up to convey the rhythm of daily activities.

Beethoven was the favored composer of British choice for anti-German war documentaries in the 1940s, but also already for state-funeral processions. The play has no Beethoven, while the film has Beethoven entering the home via the radio following a close-up of wires coming through the roof. The family is shown sitting at the table. It is arranged almost to imitate the then dominant advertising image of a family sitting around the radio. A few measures from the seventh symphony's second movement, the Allegretto, prepare the bulletin announcing the (expected) death of George V (Figure 4). It is January 20, 1936. A cut shows the public (including the Gibbons family) passing in silence by the King's body lying in state at Westminster. A cutback brings the King's regalia to a wall calendar dated now December 11. A portrait of Edward VIII prepares for the broadcast of his abdication speech. The calendar is pulled down and thrown into the dustbin. The radio speaks and then falls silent: *Well, that's that*, says Frank, the father, as he rises from his chair to turn off the radio. (He repeats the phrase at the film's end.) Coward's play (Act III, Sc. I) specifies: *The remains of supper have been pushed aside to make way for the radio. . . . At the end of the*

Figure 4 Interruption on the radio, *This Happy Breed*, directed by David Lean, Eagle-Lion Distributors/Two Cities Films, 1944

broadcast the radio makes a few discordant wheezes and groans. Frank says: *Well—that's that. . . . There won't be anything more to listen to tonight, all the stations have closed down.* The scene ends: *better put the radio back where it belongs.*

An almost inaudible humming from Mozart's fortieth symphony in the film spurs the question as to whether spiritualism is preferable to medical science. An earlier episode has the radio playing from Mischa Spoliansky's incidental music from *Paradise for Two* (dir. Thornton Freeland, 1937). The light mood is interrupted when daughter Vi rushes in to tell of a fatal car accident. The local occurrence contrasts with the painful waiting for telegrams from battlefields far away. The quickstep rhythm continues to the scene's end, while the camera pans wide to the garden for the parents to be informed out of sight. The play reads: the *empty* room where *there is no sound except for the radio playing softly and the mowing machine next door. Presently FRANK and ETHEL come in alone. . . . He reaches out for her hand and they sit there in silence.* Many note the scene adapted to film as indicative of Lean's resolve to hide moments of extreme pain or brutality from view. But, in part, his decision was already prepared by the play.

Of a comparable moment from *In Which We Serve*, Richard Farmer admires the brilliant execution of a highly "controlled emotional manipulation" when, to report a death from a local air raid, Lean used "no close-ups of actors emoting" and "no non-diegetic music," but slowed the camera down to become "minimal and unobtrusive" (2016: 215). In *Oliver Twist*, Nancy's murder is staged behind a door that a dog scratches urgently trying to get entry. In *Ryan's Daughter*, Rosy's punishment—her hair shorn, her face slashed, and her clothes ripped away—is shown at its beginning and end. We see the result: Rosy shaking before a home hearth mantled by the Beethoven bust. Behind such scenes are the biblical and epic threads that Gotthold Ephraim Lessing pulled into modern aesthetic theory to describe the family statue of father and sons, the *Laocoön*. He wrote of the most extreme emotion or truth coming out as *intensified* when the just-before moment was seen, leaving the imagination to do the Shakespearean rest that was silence. In English, the silent rest is rendered the "pregnant moment," whereas in German, *der fruchtbarer Augenblick*, the fruitful moment or flash, has a near-inaudible identity with what is sometimes the most frightening (*furchtbarest*) moment. Against this background, Lean's camerawork may be seen as investigating the potential in the *limits* (*Grenzen*) of what each artistic medium, of sight, sound, and word, could bring to the new art of film ([1766] 1984; Goehr 2021: 251).

The radio is stressed again in *This Happy Breed* when the news comes on September 30, 1938 that Neville Chamberlain has returned from his meeting with Adolf Hitler. Frank walks home and away from the crowd: *It's exciting all right–if you like to see a lot of people . . . yelling their heads off without the faintest idea what they're yelling about*. And the retort: *Oh, how can you, Frank? They're cheering 'cause they've been saved from war*. Frank is chided for sentimentalizing the first Great War as a time when young men *enjoyed* themselves fighting for their country. He snaps back: *nobody but a bloody fool, without any imagination, would ever say that*. Returning from the Great War, Frank had found work offering *Tickler* tours of the battlefields. ("Tickler" was already a Dickensian term for the wax end of a cane. We will see lots of tickling in the words that keep track of things, including walking canes.) Tourism around the *glories of the Empire* was already a theme that Lean would pull to the extreme.

William Whitebait (May 27, 1944) found it "hard to overpraise" *This Happy Breed* for its "enhanced fidelity" to an English people coming to know themselves. Matthew Norgate (1944) saw in *This Happy Breed* a new and improved *Cavalcade* with less condescension toward the "Lower Middle Classes." (Some thought this improvement owed more to Lean.) Norgate stressed the fortitude and resilience of the common characters and how particularly their drabness came through with the film's striking use of technicolor. Between color and colorlessness, Coward's wit, it was often said, was in need of no "Hollywood" glamor (Hoare 1995: 337). Of course, Hollywood did not exhaust all that America had to offer. Barnaby Thompson's film of 2023, *Mad About the Boy,* tells how Coward brought the tempo of American theater back into his English wit to let certain lines, and sometimes the most important lines, become throwaway lines. Take the toast that ends Coward's *Cavalcade* of 1931, where a *drink* is offered to *couple the future* with England's *past*. Here, the hope is premised on how a *strange heaven* can emerge from an *unbelievable hell*. There is nothing to be thrown away here until we question what might make hell unbelievable, and the answer is fake news—to which then comes the brilliant response of a *Twentieth Century Blues. We've reached a headline—The Press headline—every sorrow, Blues values is News Value to-morrow* (1932: 136–7; Briggs 1981: 13f).

Focused on Coward's wit, commentators balk at the chastising he got from the press for his Mayfair affectations. Described as a "theatrical egoist" with a "smart equipage of bons and cutting mots," Peter Lennon (1983) proclaimed: "Nothing could be further from the truth." Coward, in fact, cultivated his public persona with the utmost care and determination to disguise his very poor background (and, more subtly, his homosexuality). Thompson's film describes him, as we will see Lawrence later, as his "own greatest invention." Coward's "conservative evolutionary philosophy" is generally explained in terms of his letting things develop (as in a garden) without too much foreign or unnatural interference or contrived reform. This meant that social class differences were to be neither overly hardened nor yet erased by any soft (read: American) democratization of human values (Aldgate and Richards 1986: 187ff.; MW: 30). Frances Gray stressed the jingoism that inspired Coward's presentation of the common sense of ordinary people who are supposed to know their place and stick to their station (1987: 76–7). In *This Happy Breed*, a daughter will strike out to have an affair; a son will consider Communism's promise of food and work for all; and a father will spend a lot of time hiding in the stairwell, reminiscing about old times to shots of whisky. In the end, they will all reconcile themselves to their common nature even as they close the door to their rented home.

From the many audience reactions reviewed by C. A. Lejeune (1947: 118), one stands out, of the film being not "just a photographic and microphonic record of suburban life" but a way, by use of its "art," to "conjure up," with the help of familiar symbols, things that are not perceptible to human eyes and ears. It must be a kind of second sight, what Baudelaire calls a "sorcellerie evocatoire." With heightened second sight, "an ordinary address" such as "17 Sycamore Road, Clapham," became "the symbol for a nation." While a Baudelairean sorcery soon became the very subject of

Blithe Spirit, a Baudelairean forest of color and sound later gave the famous open-air sex scene in *Ryan's Daughter* a musical feeling quite different from the drab wedding night at home. Moving on, let us note the critics' own family breeding, because what early critics found to praise in Coward and Lean's four films, critics, three decades later, were much more inclined to trash.

What did Lean have to *say* about Beethoven? Whether film counted as an art according to the tradition or altered the traditional conception of art depended on whether the technique of cutting could keep up with the technology: the aesthetic *medium* with the new *media*. One could not simply enter the cutting room assuming oneself still to be in the old ateliers of art—and Lean knew this. Yet, like so many others, Lean had few qualms about reaching back to old masters to insist that no detail of script, image, or sound be entered into a film without extreme deliberation. Focused on every detail, he insisted on the final form being entirely intentional even if something spontaneous or accidental occurred along the way. (The famous "match-cut" in *Lawrence* was one of those "accidents.")

To achieve the final form, Lean denied *improvisation*, though not the spontaneous musical and poetic idea associated with the Romantic *intuition*. Such an intuition came to the mind, he said, as a blueprint or as a photographic negative, or as a mental picture suspended in time. One produced the script as a carving and casting of a mold, after which came the massive team effort of its realization. "I don't believe in improvisation. . . . I don't think that a truly great artist, a great musician, like Beethoven, could improvise. It's meticulous work" (DL: 111). Elsewhere, when seeming to contradict himself by proclaiming Beethoven a great musician because he *could* improvise, he still only meant the dreaming up of perhaps an entirely detailed plan consistent with the subsequent craft of working it all out as a through-composed work. "None of the arts, at their best," he said, "are improvised. Consider a Beethoven composition, or a Hepplewhite chair" (DL: 53).

In a postwar culture declaring authoritarianism and, with this, the author dead, Lean emerged as a hands-on director of every detail. His craft, as he put it in Thomas Craven's documentary of

1971, a year after *Ryan's Daughter*, far outstripped his capability to make "great statements about life." "Outstripping" captures the sense of a filmstrip omitting "great statements" in favor of suspended possibilities emerging from reeling perspectives. Lean liked the handiwork: the labor of bringing an imagined world to its embodiment, but not to an embodiment where the conflicting drives of the imaginary were falsely resolved.

Corresponding with Robert Bolt on *Zhivago*, Lean had already found a Beethoven motif when describing a woman raised to the heights of passion not by a husband, but by an artist-poet capable of drawing her "up the scale." Like an entire orchestra, the woman would submit to the "doer," the "Beethoven," but only until the artist was ready to "hack away" at the marble. The artist would string his models along, displacing the sex act with a poetic sweep of passion, allowing "the full bouquet" to bring the *ideal feminine* muse into his work of art (KB: 501). Lean's description was almost a direct borrowing from the French discourse of *bohème*, while broad Wagnerian strains revealed a love and art reborn out of the unifying musical spirit of Goethe and Beethoven (Goehr 2021: 192–4).

On our way back now to *Ryan's Daughter*, consider Lothar Mendes's *Moonlight Sonata* of 1937, where Ignacy Jan Paderewski stars as himself (a musician serving the cause of Polish independence) to render Beethoven's sonata integral to the unfolding plot. The film opens with a striking twenty-minute recital of Chopin and Liszt in a concert hall at the Lindenborg estate. The modern staircase frames the guests in the house who, upstairs and down, listen with devotion. The pianist is there because of a plane's emergency landing. The same plane carries a con man who will try to woo a young heiress out of the family fortune. The *Moonlight Sonata* must save the young heiress from a bad choice. Then there is Francis Searle's 1946 *A Girl in a Million*, where a Beethoven bust is displayed in the private quarters of a butler who, in his free time, plays his cello and advises a young woman on marriage. Here, and there are many more such films (Slobin, ed. 2008: 337–65), threads and knots are reeled between alternating Beethovenian perspectives: political, personal, aesthetic, and musical.

In *Ryan's Daughter*, while Beethoven is placed on a record to authorize a tradition of art, its passion and pastorale of love are handed over to Jarre's score. This way, the film moves between the old and the new: the fine crafting of a bust (the marriage) and the explosive busting or bursting out of desire (the affair). Domesticated by the living room, the Beethoven *bust* will play to antiquated attitudes. But what then of the *luminous symphony*: Will it be released from the repetitive and rigidifying grooves of history's record?

Following *This Happy Breed*, *Ryan's Daughter* closes up on the telephone and then on the cutting of the wires as a way to parallel the many camera cuts to the Beethoven bust and gramophone in the home. Modern technology plays to the destabilization and disabling of public and private expectations. While the trio of husband, wife, and lover is foregrounded, the social landscape extends to the supporting cast, where the characters, like the bust, are attached to modes of disability, doubt, disorder, disillusion, and destruction. A wired telephone box communicates Ryan's information to the English army regarding the German weapons being delivered to the Irish rebels.

From its moment of making in 1970, the film looks back to early twentieth-century battles for Irish independence and women's rights, to the complex voice of a village people, and to the early films in which Coward and Lean pitted the Second World War against the First World War and its troubled aftermath. Its storm-and-stress of rebellion is made palpable by extreme patterns of weather. The idiom of "weathering a storm" draws a troubled sea into the political climate. The film, about a village, has a stone-hard insularity and tunnel vision made from a single street along which everything is seen (Pettitt 2000: 98–100). Around the village, for some critics, hidden oceanic surges of sublime femininity are released by small bodies of water and large oceans. For weather reasons alone, bits were shot in Cape Town, but that particular relocation has no stake. Some critics stress a historical thread of immigration and rupture when, as Lynne Truss noted in 1989, many, with dreams of leaving poverty behind, left a disabled Ireland for the promise of a better life in America. Others remark on the wounds cut from the "love-across-the-boundaries" characteristic of "Irish cinematic history and nationalist history" (Barton 2004: 132–4).

An out-of-datedness tallies with the Shakespearean out-of-jointness of a social edifice radically damaged by a world war that, first time around, and then again, broke the great promise to end war altogether. The shelving of the Beethoven bust affirms the stability of a past world, an England that, occupying the land, is refusing Ireland her independence—while Germany stands determined against England on the other side of the sea. Yet, Ireland, as damaged as England, plays to the postwar sense of empires crawling on their knees. Rosy's conflicted relations with men mirror conflicts of countries and of different sorts of music. An older music on record conflicts with the younger score by Jarre. Older modes of domination and devotion feel aged even if the husband's care comes across as sincere. That Rosy will marry an Irishman and take an English lover plays to the *perpetuum mobile*. Were the husband English and the lover Irish, the domestic alliances would be more transparent as political allegory. The alliances are twisted, however, to ask after a tired Ireland's attitude toward its independence from England's worn clutch and crutch. Fidelma Farley (2002) traces the end-of-empire theme as a broken thread: an impotence of masculinity and failure of fulfillment. She picks up the cinematic key that others, like Neil Sinyard (1998), turn to recall the weary Englishness in T. S. Eliot's line: "Home is where one starts from."

Kracauer described Hollywood as terrorizing audiences postwar not with images of destruction but, to the contrary, with shocking images of beauty. And *Ryan's Daughter*, from film to figure, is shockingly beautiful. With Adorno also, Kracauer associated the beauty with "infallible evidence" of "mental disintegration" in homes rendered out of joint by unfamiliar belongings and defamiliarizing longings (2012: 45; Adorno [1951] 1970 1:#18). The mental disintegration of disabled homes drew from Freud's *Unheimlich*, the condition where not feeling at home comes upon one with all the suddenness of an accident, an unintended encounter. In *Ryan's Daughter*, Rosy's passion, unfulfilled at home, drives her into the arms of a traumatized English soldier, and he into hers. The limbs of the body matter.

If Lean's films are about destabilization, then the dynamic that seeks restabilization brings the signpost in *Ryan's Daughter* back home to a Beethoven that must be separated from the nation-state that is a friend to the Irish rebels and an enemy to the English occupiers. How does Beethoven as figure and myth define the home and the countries of divided loyalties?

The home is cut through the camera's focus on Beethoven. The first reference comes, however, on the beach (at the Dingle Peninsula) when Charles Shaughnessy returns from Dublin and meets his former student Rosy according to her plan to meet him. Anticipating the film's end, hats that are blown away signal gestures of affection, a sense of order, and care against the threatening disorder. Some critics note a pantheism in how Lean's grand sweeps of nature allow different perspectives on life to swirl. Another detail, from *Brief Encounter*, puts something into Rosy's eye—a tear of desire that Charles won't satisfy.

On the beach, Mr. Shaughnessy (as she calls him) tells Rose (as he will always call her) that, in Dublin, *a party of us went to a couple of concerts* and that he'd saved the programs. Looking at them, Rosy remarks that the Royal Philharmonic was performing. Charles recalls works by *Berlioz and Tchaikovsky*. Rosy teasingly asks, *No Beethoven? No Beethoven*, he responds, and then: *Do you know that the British government has got a law now . . . forbidding the playing of German music*? When Rosy suggests that this is a foolishness of the British government, he counters with *all governments . . . more or less*. Charles's decision to ignore his country's ban on Beethoven to prove loyal to Beethoven in the privacy of his home distances him from both political and personal passions. Housing a universal ideal, the Beethoven bust sits on his mantelpiece for no country. But an antiquated attitude made alone from ideals, so Nietzsche warned, will keep a schoolmaster cut off from the real living of life (1997: 57–124).

Charles tells Rosy that he was accompanied to the concert by a most stimulating schoolteacher. Rosy is jealous until she learns that the school teacher was aged and had concentrated on her musical score. Rosy is glad that the academic behavior carried no *Bacchanalia*, a word Charles repeats more *precisely* as though still teaching his former student her best words. The intercourse has promise while hinting at the later Bacchanalian strain of the shrieking furies when the villagers tear Rosy to pieces. Charles's agedness, suggested by his having already lost his *pure* wife in 1913 when she was thirty-five, contrasts with Rosy's pupil-like youth as the *hanging matter* to be overcome. A cut to a gravestone suggests that no child was born to Charles and his first wife, Deborah.

Charles and Rosy's next meeting is in the schoolhouse that shares a thin wall with Charles's home. While Charles discusses politics in the local pub, Rosy enters the schoolroom to Jarre's mysterious pulses. She knocks on Charles's door. What *we* see on the other side, a room filled with pictures and busts predominantly of Beethoven, Rosy does not see. She only hears Charles's footsteps of return and (appropriately for 1916) the scratchy opening chords of Beethoven's Fifth. Charles enters the schoolroom carrying his books. Rosy reluctantly sits as though still a student. When she confesses her love, he apologizes for having misled her with tales of *Byron and Beethoven and Captain Blood. . . . I'm not one of them fellows myself.* Rosy quips that she is *not daft.* And he responds: *But you're terribly young.* When she asks if *that's a hanging matter,* he says *maybe*—but then maybe not. Both now standing, they kiss to the swelling music no longer of Beethoven but of Jarre. It's a misleading moment.

Charles's lineup of heroic figures, solid at home, becomes muddied in the schoolroom. Romanticism becomes romance for the brief moment of a kiss. The call of Byron draws from lines from *Don Juan*:

> the doubtless something in domestic doings
> Which forms, in fact, true love's antithesis;
> Romances paint at full length people's wooings,
> But only give a bust of marriages?

Run together with Captain Blood, one thinks of the swashbuckling pirate played by Errol Flynn in the Hollywood film of 1935. But how could a film about 1916 recall a figure from 1935, unless the figure had a prior life, say, from the 1922 adventure novel about a pirate in a rebellion fought in the Caribbean, itself distantly inspired by the 1685 trials, the Bloody Assizes, associated with England's Monmouth Rebellion? Lean would explain less the Captain Blood reference than Rosy's immediate attraction to Doryan as a disappointment with Charles when Charles failed to deliver what his heroic stories promised: the fireworks of "Brock's Benefit" (KB: 554). This was a benefit manufactured in the 1820s that, like so much else in the film, recalled a promise of intense passions from the age of Romanticism.

Backgrounding the wedding of Charles and Rosy and the very modest consummation of their marriage is a rowdy village party with an Irish reel heard first faintly and then with more volume. When, then, with suitcases, the newlyweds enter Charles's home, Charles gives Rosy a gift of white flowers. It is an ominous gift. Soon Charles will be seen pressing flowers into the pages of his heavy tomes that he bangs on the table in accord with a strong musical pulse. And soon thereafter, the white flowers will symbolize what England steals away: Rosy from Charles. What Rosy first admires as Charles's rarity—*you're a rare man*—she later resents as his preference always for Beethoven's pulse over hers. A music recorded, like a flower pressed, will never die if preserved and collected from the outset. And that is really the *hanging matter.*

As Rosy enters the bedroom, Charles remains at the door. He affectionately tells her that he cannot believe that she is his wife. Leaving her standing with open arms, he puts the needle to his record. That we hear not the start but the continuation of a Beethoven symphony (now the Third's first movement) makes for a home where the Beethoven needle is always tracing the groove. Returning to the bedroom door, Charles utters a single word: *Beethoven*, after which he turns toward the fireplace to light the fire as though also kneeling before the bust. With her open arms ignored, Rosy touches the dust covering the aged bed. (The touch of the hand is another Lean motif.)

Settled, Rosy embroiders and Charles presses flowers. The gramophone's horn looms large, splitting the couple, and facing in the direction of the oversized bust on the mantelpiece (Figure 5). Rosy expresses her preference for living flowers while the record label spins to show, in a close-up, the famous dog sitting before the gramophone horn: *His Master's Voice.* The satisfying needlework

Figure 5 Beethoven on the gramophone, *Ryan's Daughter*, Ryan's Daughter, directed by David Lean, Faraway Productions, 1970.

of the record contradicts the dissatisfaction that leads Rosy to suspend her needlework (like the wife in *Brief Encounter*) to seek a different music away from home.

The white plaster bust sits on a shelf with all the authority of tradition. It is but one of many busts and pictures of a scholarly and literary past. It stands out with a fossilized predication, as Walter Benjamin described this for his "concept of criticism." Symptomatic shifts allow subjects to see objects in their present moment while fossilized objects gaze back with the heavy, antiquated weight of history in their eyes ([1919] 1996: 145). To describe the currents of music's transmission by radio and phonograph, Adorno compared the small room of a home suffering from social forms of paralysis with the once-living largeness of the concert hall. He diagnosed an acoustic distortion and deception, a sense of closeness that, in truth, was really placing the work—and he named the Beethoven symphony as exemplary—at a great distance. Fidelity between work, performance, and recording, however much desired in the home, was impossible if closeness only increased the sense of alienation between its inhabitants (2006: 499ff). In Lean's film, the phonograph sits between the married couple as a dividing line between them. Lean gives the heavy shelving to Charles, to look at Rosy increasingly conscious of his inability to satisfy her. That he shelves her on the proverbial pedestal is inscribed into their marriage from the start. The musical grooves recall an ekphrastic technique in operas where unconditional devotion to an object of love was triggered by a picture or a song. For Charles, Rosy and Beethoven should hang together, but they don't. Again, the *hanging matter*.

Charles preserves the schoolmaster's lines as best he can. When teaching his pupils, he conducts their recitation of arithmetic tables to a precise rhythm. With rose-colored glasses, Rosy is prone more to fantasy. What is life without dreams of true love? The magazines she carries on the beach come with red flags of warning from Father Hugh. One magazine is an issue of *Olympia Novels*. A close-up shows Raoul du Barry's title, *The King's Mistress*. Rosy's desire to be swept off her feet is juxtaposed with political reports of battles shown in sweeping headlines from the tellingly titled newspaper: *The Irish Independent*. Father Hugh is on the beach in the first place to keep his ears and eyes open to the delivery of the weapons and explosives. From soldiers in the pub, words threaten *to capsize* the *whole cursed country* (Ireland)—and, then, that *Germans* (or at least the *clever lads* over in Germany) *are great talkers too*. Before the battles become the nightmares of the British soldier (Rosy's lover), they feed a local brutality when the Irish rebels shoot a policeman and throw his body down a shaft.

Rosy is shelved to become part of the furniture of marriage. If Charles tries to possess his wife, Rosy is possessed by romance. The plastered whiteness of the bust sitting above the fire generates no warmth for the woman who would like to live with the bright colors of inflamed desire. If Charles is transported by Beethoven at home, she is transported outside by Jarre's music. When, with Beethoven's *Eroica*, Charles imagines the lovers walking on the beach, he gives them an antiquated dress different from the reality and music of the nature walk he takes with his pupils in search of cuttlefish. The imagined scene then hits home with a reality when, back home with Beethoven, he finds a shell hidden in Rosy's drawer, a gift from Doryan. A dream image shows Doryan picking up a shell by a rock behind which Charles hides (Figure 6). The shell carries the beauty and roar of the sea. With no doubt left, Charles's world shatters. He runs from his home barefoot. Walking for hours in his nightshirt brings him to a realization of the part he has played in a marriage made on antiquated terms. While having sat shirtless at the dining table, not to Rosy's liking, he had not removed his nightshirt on their wedding night.

Figure 6 Dreamscape to Beethoven, *Ryan's Daughter*, directed by David Lean, Faraway Productions, 1970.

The seashell forefronts a core Lean motif: the husband who hears not and does not see. The explosive named in France the *grenade* drew from the blood-red seeds of bursting *pomegranates*. The idea of shell-shocked soldiers evokes a percussive rhythm made from the spray of bullets. The blood-red colors and tones seep into the lover's wound. For the husband, however, the rhythm of his listening, seemingly deaf to his wife, is directed to the strikingly large seashell horn of his gramophone. Benjamin described a technology of war as so betraying humanity with its mastery of nature that it transformed even the bridal bed into a sea of blood. Writing these words in his "The Planetarium," he wondered whether looking at the stars would bring nature back to its order ([1928] 2008: 58–9). Lean, too, pursued a listening that was already the oldest in the books: a siren song of the sea (Halliday 2013: 78; Kittler 1999: 51–2).

Lean's films fuse a psychoanalytic landscape for the suspecting eye with a soundscape for the suspecting ear. He would have known the many films that had worked through the traumatic events that left persons disabled: lost arms in *The Best Years of Our Lives* (dir. William Wyler, 1946), broken legs and damaged minds in Hitchcock's *Rear Window* (1954) and *Vertigo* (1958). Later, we will consider films about women pianists who, variously disabled, find themselves split between different lovers as an allegory of a choice to live a life with or without music. To love music is to love this or that man, or vice versa. Behind the music feeding the love was the technology that fed music as an electrical conductor or conduit in tandem with the emerging automation of a body that so often broke down (Abbate 2001).

The briefly stilled time when Rosy and Doryan make love is juxtaposed with the stilled time of a Beethoven recording. The juxtaposition recalls *Brief Encounter*'s living room, drawn first by Coward in the playlet he titled *Still Life*, as well as the famously stilled clock that marked a marriage that did not happen in *Great Expectations*. Time stilled briefly or forever is a theme also of *Blithe Spirit*, where one musical record is chosen over another. However, when Lean cut time and experience, he did this not to condemn only one figure outright. He rather reeled his figures between shifting subjectivities and alternating objectivities.

If Charles refuses or cannot achieve identification with any heroic figure made cheap, so Doryan's name alone forbids this soldier from forgetting all that Doric heroism once meant on the fields of war but which now, with his disability, he can't live up to. The bus that brings Charles home from Dublin and takes Rosy and Charles away at the end also brings Major Doryan to the village with a musical fanfare. Before the bus stop, he stands motionless, waiting for the military car to taxi him to his quarters. We immediately sense the limp of his gait and stride, as does mute Michael, who stares at the incoming enemy while holding Ireland's yellow flowers in his hands. There is no view of Doryan when he is not sad and not lighting a cigarette. With a scar beneath one eye, he is described by a fellow soldier as *a crippled bloody hero* while a villager jeeringly sings out *peg leg*. His limp is differently pronounced according to whether he is making love or making war. When he walks before his soldiers to stop the rebels from transporting their weapons, he strides almost with the cliched gait of an uptight German officer until, having shot the Irish rebel leader in a single long-distance shot, he lives up to the white as opposed to the black trench coat by collapsing from his memory of being shot himself. Throwing his weapon away, he offers the injured rebel leader a cigarette. Tim O'Leary accepts. Yet, asked by the major whether he wants anything else, O'Leary retorts: *Yes. Get out of my country*.

Doryan is not a shrewd seducer on the make. His immediate desire for Rosy is triggered by an almost crazed despair with his disability (Barton 2004: 133). An electricity generator beats out his terror. Having made love to Rosy, his mind returns to the traumatic *front line* of exploding bombs, which, in another passing moment, might account for an estrangement from a wife who has either left him or whom he has left behind in England. Doryan's first kiss with Rosy in the pub, following upon his memories of the battlefield, cannot but deliver sparks, while Michael bangs his foot nearby to the beat of a march. Everything explosive about Doryan is already inscribed into Rosy's fantasy. When she goes off one day to find her lover, no gramophone accompanies her into the forest. The forest is already replete with symbols: a Baudelairean orchestration of winds, waters, and mossy murmurs. A spider threads its web to bring out the heightened and stilled motion of the entwined bodies.

The staid movement between Charles's reality and unreality differs from the fluidity of the naked passion of lovers whom we see lying among trees, flowers, and butterflies. The white flower for England becomes Rosy's virginity to be re-broken. The whiteness is not the hard white stone of the Beethoven bust nor that which has kept England abled at Dover's shores. It attaches to Doryan in moments when his being disabled is disguised in favor of a suddenly heroic yet clichéd symbolism. Rosy's white mare, a present from her father, is said not to be *properly broke*, which is what Doryan, on his black horse, can do for Rosy: to wit, break her in properly. Moving through white lilies and lying in a forest of purple lilacs, her orange cardigan worn without an undergarment allows her breasts to be exposed and touched for the first time. When Rosy returns one day, she wears the brightest of reds, red sometimes being a most suspect color. Charles asks her whether she'd ever be *unfaithful* to him. He regrets the question. A musical intermission serves as a halfway mark in the film and promises a turning point.

In *The Reality Effect*, Joel Black quotes from Slavoj Žižek's *The Plague of Fantasies*, regarding the attempt in *Ryan's Daughter* "'to conceal (the) deadlocks' involved in representing physical intimacy 'by expressing sexual ecstasy through metaphors [and] musical accompaniment'" (2001: 241 n.27). Žižek describes the deadlocks as a perversion in the displacement that exposes the eroticism of the "illicit love" as a "pathetic" or "ridiculous bric-à-brac of clichés" precisely because the sight of the sex act is prohibited. Any Romantic sense of sublime pathos and ecstasy is deflated by the inflation of the vision into a Hollywood waterfall of sounds. Žižek also finds a deadlock not in *Brief Encounter* but in its "failed remake" about middle-class commuters taking a train between Connecticut and New York, Ulu Grosbard's *Falling in Love* of 1984 (1997: 182, 143), where the hypertext of an encounter collapses into mere boredom and banality.

For Hitchcock's *Vertigo*, Gregg Horowitz (2012) pursues an analysis where prohibition yields something more than a mere nothing. In Freud's terms, dreamwork offers a secondary editing of what a primary attempt covers over as the first imposition of sense. Awakening to morning's order and reason, night's memory is hidden, concealed, repressed. Horowitz draws from Laura Mulvey's classic essay (1975) on visual pleasure and narrative cinema to detect the gendered clues for a detective who, charged with detecting the strange behavior of a woman, behaves strangely himself. The disturbances, as Horowitz explains, invest every image—like a painting—with a "sudden opacity." The disablement of the central male protagonist spins (literally) around his being manipulated by a husband and former friend who, having murdered his wife, must deceive his hired detective with an impenetrable wall of sense. Made "to conspire with a form of intelligibility," the disabled detective becomes "a made-to-order witness." To witness is to see, but, for the analysis of a mind or of a film wherein the protagonist wants to comprehend a painted portrait, the seeing must be unraveled if another way of knowing, sidelined or concealed, is to emerge. The alternate order of knowing comes in this film not from the woman who doubles for the murdered wife but from a woman whose earlier love for the detective allows her to paint a different picture and thereby offer him a cure for his disability and a solution to his case.

The Lean team briefly considered titling their film *Michael's Day*, since, from the sidelines, Michael alone hears and sees with every strike of a match or clock. He is variously figured as a Caliban or Quasimodo. His disabled presence is always palpable. Having stolen some dynamite, Michael gives it to the major, who uses it to end his life. There is a sense of recognition among enemies. Similarly, when Rosy bids farewell to Michael with a kiss on the cheek, his having always inspired disgust in her, it corroborates the sense of their now sharing a wound. By the end, in fact, Doryan's facial scar brought to the village at the start has been graphed, through Michael's eyes and ears, onto the cheeks of Charles and Rosy, allowing for a wounded parting that no one, however near or far from the village, will ever forget.

In the film's public scenes, the villagers loaf around jeering at those whom they want to cast out as disabled in some way. They come off mostly as a nasty lot, with harsh tongues and too quick to blame—until, collecting the scattered booty from the raging sea, they align themselves with Ireland's rebellious cause. One girl steps out as caring for her schoolteacher. Leaving the village, Rosy stops along the road to see her father. Ryan praises Charles as a good man. Seeking forgiveness, he tells Rosy that he never hit his wife. Here is Ryan's wife: an absent figure of a mother whose own death or departure may have influenced the father's decision to betray his country and his daughter. Only a modicum of sympathy is extended to a father who, like the fathers in *This Happy Breed* and *Hobson's Choice*, mostly belches opinions with whisky breath in the *public house*.

The expulsion of Charles and Rosy from the village feels different from that of the mocked and disabled fool, Michael, who remains. Packing up their belongings, Charles leaves the Beethoven bust in one of the boxes left behind. Will the bust be sent on when, if ever again, he feels settled? Hanging a For Sale sign on the door and relinquishing his keys, he will unlikely return. He takes his gramophone, however, as still belonging to him alone: *Take all this, without the gramophone. . . . We'll split [the money] down the middle*. Walking through the village, he carries a bunch of flowers that he might or might not later press. Waiting for the bus to take Charles and Rosy away, Michael the fool blows through the gramophone's large horn that Charles has asked him to carry. Detached now from its body, the horn blows for a record that has momentarily reached its end. Father Hugh silences the horn to offer *the pair* an address in Dublin for a room at the decent price of six shillings. To Rosy, his *parting gift* is *supposed to be a fragment of St Patrick's staff*, though he adds, *I don't suppose it is*. To Charles, his equally questionable gift is the *doubt* not whether they should stay together but whether Charles should even *have it on [his] mind to part*. While Father Hugh suspects a separation, we (as the audience) have already been privy to the division of the belongings. In a final image reminiscent of *Casablanca* (dir. Michael Curtiz, 1942) but even more of *Kwai*'s final repeated invocation of madness, the mute fool and the muttering Father walk away: *I don't know, I don't know at all*. The disorder unfolded throughout supports an openness at the end: whether, despite the ghostly flames of passion (as in *Brief Encounter*), the marriage will be remade.

For Cavell, remarriage was always also the issue of doubt, a skepticism woven into his readings of films for the sake of philosophical investigation. To this weave, I have added the metaphorical and transportive musical terms that inscribe the movement between happiness and unhappiness into the Beethoven bust and into the recording of the Beethoven symphony that Charles plays on his gramophone. The Beethoven symphony has long been the exemplar for drawing out music's classical and romantic strains of fidelity. With loaded terms, it carries, like the record label, the connotations of being *long-playing* as long as *His Master's Voice* keeps the marital abode intact. Charles's devotion to Beethoven remains stable while he doubts that Rosy could be untrue to him. When, however, he finally grants that he'd somehow always known about her affair, he obscures the differences between suspecting, doubting, and knowing. His becoming less certain matters the most: *It's not all your doing, Rosy*.

Between 1970 and today, a cutting criticism has dominated, of extreme condemnation and extreme praise of Lean as filmmaker. After *Ryan's Daughter*, Lean withdrew from the public. Critics have assessed the political and personal, the political and poetic, the national and natural, and the masculine and feminine. From this, they have drawn out the competing strains between the epic and anti-epic. From the binaries, a critical thread ties the looking back to antique tragedy to the looking back to the biblical promise of *all things bright and beautiful* and of *all creatures great and small*. Working through Romanticism, the promise breaks when the big becomes too big, the long too long, and the small too slight of significance.

Constantine Santas reads *Ryan's Daughter* as growing to epic proportions out of what should have been a "little gem." How could so small an affair be so blown out of proportion? Or how did the great literature of Flaubert and James turn to the dime-a-dozen magazines of "damsels in distress" awaiting their savior? Taking a broad sweep of Lean's later films, Santas notes the small details: the hawk in *Kwai*, the eagle surveying the Marabar rocks (in *A Passage*), and the waves bursting against the Dingle beaches. Between the smallness and greatness of eternal symbols, the social disorder finally finds its calm in a natural order. As others report, so does Santas: Lean wanted a more poetic ending, a possible reconciliation for the married couple, whereas Robert Bolt imagined a great tragic flaw, a "complete breakdown of human relations," playing itself out from the very first note as a disabled trio symbolic of a world at war (2012: xxxvi, 89–96, 108). Lean and Bolt would battle out their sides in so many of their shared films, but, if each got his way, might not the result be an internally productive antagonism?

Weighing up the broad *dissent* among critics, Clive James (1970) saw the sides as coming "pretty close together." He seemed to want to know whether objectivity ever coincides with where extremes meet. Gavin Millar (1970) more easily blamed Bolt for the script and then the team for choosing a box office star like Robert Mitchum to play a part to which he was so ill-suited. But ill-suited was what Lean wanted: "Always cast against the part and it won't be boring" (DL: 53).

Assessing Lean's film as a visual transliteration of *Madame Bovary*, Franck Dalmas (2014) recalls from early film theory the plasticity through which a filmmaker produces a hypertext and counterpoint to an original and already multilayered text. The plasticity carries the potential for a *revision* of the entire social picture. André Bazin described a dissonance dissolving a false order to retrieve a cosmic order of harmony and humanity. In Chaplin's 1917 film, *The Adventurer*, a human figure becomes a tree with branches becoming his arms of resistance to the approach of "a file of German soldiers" ([1967] 1971: 146–53). Here, already, was the readiness of a character resisting a reality "made-to-order," a

Nietzschean resistance transferred to the camera when it allowed a detail to cut through an ideological frame that wanted to keep a threatening army of thoughts in place.

Mark Patrick Hederman looked back on *Ryan's Daughter* as "probably the most misunderstood of Lean's films." He saw its "essential energy" as "misconstrued." Focusing on the plot, one missed Lean's ways of promoting epic delusions of grandeur. Rosy's "romantic extravagance" was one such promotion, as she self-created a world in her imagination (1985: 338–40). But is extravagance entirely the same as epic grandeur? Inspired by Nietzsche, Simmel described the *adventure* of *youth* that, from Romanticism, "thrusts itself out of life" with an "overflow and exuberance" contra the historical mood of age that places too much coherence upon life ([1911] 2002: 230; Nietzsche 1999: 81). Along similar lines, Michael Tanner (2007) theorizes the film as a "troubled epic," while John Orr (2010) analyzes Rosy as a "troubled romantic." What makes for the "trouble"?

For Armida de la Garza, the geopolitical contours of sound and color sustain a traditional mirror of nature and natural rights, whereby Ireland as an island lies within the bosom and embrace of England qua motherland. A feminist cartography is then introduced to show how the unhappiness that leads to *private* transgressions can re-gender the *public* map, beginning with the *mappa mundi* shown on the schoolroom wall. More than retracing male steps in the sand (as we see more than once), the daughter is really resisting the occupier's or colonizer's path (2018: 645–5). Here, the infidelity has neither the barbarism of mob violence nor the mere immaturity of romantic desire. It is rather the longing at odds with the "epic" endings for Nicholson in *Kwai*, for Lawrence, and for Zhivago when and if their endings are construed as assertions of strength. But these figures are also "troubled" by the anti-epic stain that deflates Lawrence, breaks Zhivago, and defeats Nicholson when, by suicide or accident, he falls onto the trigger made to blow up the bridge.

Casting blame on Rosy plays to the potential bust of a marriage when, as in *Brief Encounter* and in *A Passage*, commentators like Melanie Williams find the woman being charged with making it all up (MW: 94). The charge places Rosy within a constellation of male standpoints: Charles, whose heroic tales are deflated by his grading of school books; Doryan, who silently lights his cigarettes and delivers sparks; Father Hugh, who warns Rosy that wanting more than she has will lead her only to unhappiness; Rosy's father, who spoiling his daughter also betrays her; and Michael, who silently seems to steer Rosy both toward and away from danger. But is there nothing, again, that subverts the traditional footsteps of masculinity and femininity—no capacity for the handiwork that, for example, Stanley Kubrick gave to Catlady in *A Clockwork Orange* (released almost at the same time): namely, a bust of Beethoven to strike down a man who invades her home assuming, like a rapist, that it is full of pussy—cats? *I'll teach you to break into real people's houses*! As she busts his body, he fights back with an oversized artwork, a solid white penis with testicles-cum-butt—and all to the accompaniment of Rossini's *La gazza ladra* overture. That this overture had already figured in Lean's *Summer Madness* is one point, while the broader point is that the staple opposition that pitted Beethoven against Rossini so ardently in music's history was clearly finding its twisted repetition in cinema.

Assessing the Beethoven motif in *Ryan's Daughter*, critics write differently from a film-theoretical or from a (film)-music-historical perspective. Michael Tanner notes Jarre's immersion in the filmmaking process from which came Rosy's romantic music, the fool's "jaunty, jerky, jangly tune," and "a brassy martial piece" (2007: 25). Roger Hillman notes, instead, Charles's Beethoven moment on the beach as arguably reiterating the first fear of film, that Lean put music into *service* only to *promote* the mind's internal production of images for the eye (1995: 182). Hillman referenced Christopher Palmer (1980: 553), who, in turn, was thinking back to Vaughan Williams's demand that were film ever to realize its "potentialities for the combination of all the arts," or if film were ever to "come into its own as one of the finest of the fine arts," it would have to prioritize the ear over the eye—far more than even Wagner ever dreamed of ([1945] 1986: 162–3).

Some bring their criticisms of the music as "high-pitched," "over-strident," or "self-indulgent" into broader irritations with the overall historical infidelities of the film, while others praise the subtle anachronisms alongside Lean's insistence never to have the stream of emotions be "sentimental." Those who hear a "very

Mediterranean quality" in the "bubble-and-squeak" soundtrack wish that there had been at least "one note of Irish music" (Rowan 2020: 311). The Mediterranean allusion comes with no compliment but, instead, with a condemnation of a picture-postcard tourism that turns *epic drama* merely into *epic excess*. Lynne Truss (1989) noted Lean's little steps into Ireland's history but much more admired his overwhelming vision of the Dingle Peninsula as "one of the most beautiful places on earth." She recalled Lean's film as "almost single-handedly" reviving the local economy, just as other of his films had variously generated an Oscar-winning global tourism by benefiting "large numbers of tour-operators, camel-handlers and makers of souvenir-Alec-Guinness-dolls." She quoted Alexander Walker: "instead of looking like the money it cost to make, [*Ryan's Daughter*] feels like the time it took to shoot."

Already for the *Harvard Crimson* in 1971, Mike Prokosch was condemning the waste of "thirteen million Super Panavision dollars" on "a million-dollar tinted postcard." A touristic parade of crass symbols of capitalism matched the endless parade of damaged characters. Anticipating Lean's decade-long break, he demanded that films like this be banned for "ten years" or "however long it takes for the American public to vomit up the last trace of the nonsensical sentimental myths Hollywood keeps pushing down its throat." He hoped a more intelligent public would later emerge, one capable of a "mass laughter" as "the only fit answer to such a retrograde monstrosity."

Twice in 1970 for the *New York Times*, Vincent Canby slammed the film. First, he compared Lean to a storyteller "who likes to play God," only then to dismiss Bolt as no Thomas Hardy. He thought the beauty salon was the right place for a film whose overblown "meteorological" pretensions matched the overblown hairdos of women belonging to easy-read book clubs. The second time around, he placed every moment of Lean's genius on par with the "approximately 276,480 works of pure and undiluted genius" from the great museums—"a rather staggering amount of Art to be contained by any single movie, but since [*Kwai*], all of David Lean's films have been statistically impressive." "Impressive" also meant "longer and longer." Lean's over-artistry, he concluded, had turned a true master's lesson into a tourist brochure.

Pauline Kael's review became almost iconic of film criticism at its worst—and best. Having reviewed nearly all of Lean's films with more or less favor, she found her disappointment with *Ryan's Daughter* overwhelming. Today, quoting Kael serves as often to advertise the film as to remind readers of how first it was received. Typically, one line is quoted: "Gush made respectable by millions of dollars tastefully wasted" (1982/1984: 507). Published as "Bolt and Lean" in the *New Yorker* (21 Nov. 1970: 116–18), her witty review ran fittingly over enough pages to show all that can go wrong in a film that lasts for so many hours. It began by referring to Virginia Woolf's extraordinary piece of 1926 "The Cinema" written out of the spirit of music: Woolf saw in cinema a savagery "beginning not with two bars of iron and working up to Mozart but with grand pianos and nothing to play." Taken to Ireland, the barbarism became the conceit of a film where, with so much to watch, nothing got played out. Kael found a self-defeating contradiction between Lean's British gentlemanly restraint and his embrace of the Hollywood colossus. While "humorlessly meticulous," the film had "no driving emotional energy, no passionate vision to conceal the heavy labor." Letting an Irish girl be aroused by a half-dead Englishman had nothing of Flaubert's irony. With a jibe at New York, Kael compared Lean's sets, built not to last, to the new Lincoln Center: as "Monumental Temporary." She saw Lean going "to the mountaintop," only "the mountains keep getting bigger." All that was large made the characters feel tediously diminished. Rosy was no Madame Bovary, Doryan no arriving savior, Michael no Quasimodo. And Charles— well, just another figure in a lifeless parade of stereotypes crawling along with their disabilities. In Michael's musical motif, she heard a "Felliniesque idiot-gambolling tune" used to no effect. She, too, found a cosmetic metaphor. The "face-lift of the world" had only produced a pointless fidelity to details. But her target, finally, was less the film and less Lean and far more the well-oiled "publicity machine" promoting "well-bred English epics" in America on all but artistic grounds.

Measuring Lean's films against an American gold standard, one learns a lot. But one also misses what makes Lean's films be about Britain with all its limbs and arms. This is Melanie Williams's warning—to be heeded in the next chapters. In this chapter, I have forefronted the Beethoven bust and the gramophone on display. I have addressed the furniture-art, first in *This Happy Breed*, that later inspired Lean to a busting and combustion in a film that, for so many critics, almost bust out of the seams. Yet, if the bust of Beethoven loomed a little too large in *Ryan's Daughter*, the Beethoven who was a master of his craft kept Lean's cutting over troubled waters going in ways that critics could also appreciate.

Behind the extremes of criticism, I hear early critical theorists describing the smooth grooves of the long-playing record as bringing the industry of high culture (with that German K for *Kultur* and *Kunst*) to Hollywood. Within the cultural colossus of great capital, democratized by a small "c," everything, they feared, was being reduced to kitschy slogans void of thought. Yet, when a given criticism gets repeated again and again across the decades, one needs to turn the record over to avoid turning a history of criticism into a string of headlines for a quick dismissal. This is what it means to turn criticism into critique.

Assessing the "mass ornament," Kracauer abstracted social patterns out of the movement of small things (1995: 77, 287). Where the ornamental suggested a superfluity of insignificance, he saw a crime of capital. Where, however, he saw witty cuts, it was because, like Chaplin in *The Adventurer*, each limb could still make a point. Benjamin comparably described the camera's ingenious ability to accentuate "hidden details in familiar objects," or to guide the experience of a commonplace milieu as its world is opened up to "a vast and unsuspected field of action" ([1939] 2003: 265–6). To open up a world was, as in an *encounter* or *adventure*, to *pull away* or *cut* something *out* from the stream of ordinary life, to offer a transport through and of time and space where the imagination could play on its own self-containing terms.

Following the Beethoven cues drawn from the record player into Jarre's soundtrack, John O'Flynn claims Jarre's score is a "major advance" for Irish filmmaking, "a radically different" approach to producing "correspondences between classical music forms and psychological strife" underscored by "ironic references" to Beethoven as part of the "end-of-empire subtext" (2022: 54–8). If this implies that Jarre's score releases the film from its worn classical bind, then the release means setting Beethoven apart also from any rigidifying record.

So consider again what "being true" comes to mean if its demand for subservience is remade into a discovery of freedom, beginning with Charles's releasing Beethoven from the government's prohibition. His infidelity becomes his fidelity to Beethoven—requiring no suicidal gesture at the end. In a productive dialectic between old and new, the old as released or rescued by the new means that no single standpoint of false totality or progress is reached. When it is asked whether film carries the concept of art forward under its technological condition or leaves it behind, the answer lies with keeping the question of art's possibility alive. It is the suspended terms for the claim and concept of art against which I am measuring Lean's films (Goehr 2021b).

With the reeling perspectivism, the oldest binary between fidelity and infidelity turns in Lean's films so that the most familiar things come over as just a little too large or as a little too small. Yet, at best, not too large and not too small. Drawn to the most passing of details, the micrological method clues us into the relations that come to the surface of interpretation or analysis when disabled and destabilized. Metaphors so often drawn from music capture the desirable expansion or enhancements of passing or fleeting words, or of little grace notes, ornaments, or accidentals, to produce signs of great and small significance.

We have seen the large and small at work in *Ryan's Daughter* and in the complex weave of *This Happy Breed*. It is time now to turn to the once Shakespearean wit of being brief that Coward and Lean invested in *Brief Encounter* and *Blithe Spirit*, not least to see an expansive musical matter and means being kept in check by every protective cover of English propriety. Brevity carries a gravity of wit and caricature, but not always in films made short. Asked once to cut a film that was not working, the young Lean cut the film to perfection by adding three minutes! (DL: xiii).

Rachmaninoff on Record

Blithe Spirit (1945), *Brief Encounter* (1945)

Chapter 3 works through Coward and Lean's *Brief Encounter* to connect a middle-class, suburban wife and mother to a train and to a concerto that takes her away to a lover and then brings her home. It forefronts the motif of *the accidental*, beginning with the fact that Rachmaninoff happens to be playing on the radio. The Rachmaninoff is Sergei Rachmaninoff's Second Piano Concerto in C Minor, opus 18 of 1900/1901. To prepare for *Brief Encounter*, the chapter attends first to a Rachmaninoff moment already in *Blithe Spirit*, as a music wittily refused. Might there be the same subtle refusal in *Brief Encounter*? After all, no character in this film listens to the concerto; nor does it come over as particularly liked. The next chapter brings the Rachmaninoff into a consideration of the circulation of love-affair films at home and abroad.

To speak of the Rachmaninoff on the radio is to ask after a particular performance and recording and then to seek its musical inscription in the film's cutting. Cutting comes with a dynamic flow whether or not music is present. When present, it matters. In *Brief Encounter*, there is no film score to be silenced. There is no spoken reference to a concerto or to Rachmaninoff. The script has only the radio being turned on—*Would some music throw you off your stride?—No, dear, I'd like it*. In 1946, Manny Farber reviewed the film as "a faithful record of an aborted infidelity occurring between two extremely proper persons." What does it mean for a record to be faithful? The Rachmaninoff Concerto was recorded and cut to give form and frame to the film's furniture as sight and sound. The furniture-art was premised on a modern technological condition (cf. Vanel 2013; Remes 2014). If the classical concerto was being altered by a new modern means of transmission and transport, how much modern marriage also?

Brief Encounter was supposed to follow *Blithe Spirit*, the latter, first a play then a film, having been a great success. With a drawing-room comedy set in a contemporary way, one could keep or seem to keep the war that was just ending out of sight. Yet wasn't the not so distant subject the total invasion of a foreign world spirit into every English home? Frances Gray recalled the strained parody in the program note handed out at the theater: "If an air raid warning be received during the performance the audience will be informed from the stage . . .[;] those desiring to leave the theatre may do so but the performance will continue" (1987: 177; MW: 34). What made *Blithe Spirit* so worthy of continuation?

Subtitled as an *improbable farce*, the film offers a spiritualism to string up dead wives as *indestructible*, a notion little lost on audiences bombarded by the *forever England* banner of war. The film is almost entirely set at home until the final speeding car draws the husband, a writer suitably named Charles Condomine (Rex Harrison), into a hell of two past wives that has become their seat of heavenly revenge. Shakespeare's "more things in heaven and earth" is *forever* present. A *condominium* marks the space of a contested dominion, usually between two but sometimes, as here, between three people. There are only a few outward glimpses of the home and the roads around it, mostly when cars or bicycles transport characters or spirits. The bridge over which the spiritualist Madame Arcati (Margaret Rutherford) speeds on her bicycle becomes the final crossing for Condomine: from life to death. The cycle of transport anticipates the cycle from life to death in *Lawrence*.

A warning sign surrounds a children's storybook imagery following the credits: *When we are young, we read and believe the most fantastic things.* The joke is whether anyone ever grows up: *When we grow older and wiser, we learn, with perhaps a little regret, that these things can never be.* A blank screen allows an upper-crust Rex Harrison to say: *We are quite, quite wrong.* The *once upon a time* now dissolves into a very *charming country house in which lived a very happily married couple.* The staircase leads to the bedroom where the second wife, Ruth, is instructing a maid to prepare the cocktails, after which Charles and Ruth (Constance Cummings) banter about the preparation for the evening séance. Under the influence (of spirits), nothing is ever as it seems.

The séance lets Elvira (Kay Hammond), Charles's first wife, return as an unwanted *ectoplasm.* Having died seven years prior, she is itching to tell Charles that she hasn't seen a movie for seven years. Charles, with Coward's wit, *congratulates* her. The second wife, Ruth, increasingly irritated by a ghost that only her husband (psychoanalytically) can see, later reports that Elvira died less *convalescing from pneumonia* than from a heart attack brought on by her laughing *helplessly at a musical programme* on the radio. Even later, we learn that the pneumonia came from when both Charles and Elvira were dallying with other partners. To dally is to flirt, as in this play of *ridiculous petty jealousies.*

Dissatisfied in death, Elvira wants most to complain of her dissatisfaction in life: *I wanted glamour and music and romance. What I got was potted palms, seven hours of every day on a damp golf course and a three-piece orchestra playing Merry England.* Charles quips: *Pity you didn't tell me so at the time.* She answers: *You wouldn't listen.* The farce's title draws from Shelley's first line *Hail to thee, blithe Spirit! Bird thou never wert. . . . Pourest thy full heart. In profuse strains of unpremeditated art.* Shelley's last line *The world should listen then, as I am listening now* carries then over to the husband whose ears and eyes will be newly opened to the words and worlds of his wives—the deader they are.

The murder-farce is no ordinary mystery. It parodies women less who complain constantly in life than who kill to guarantee that the marriage will last *always.* For Charles, the only *always* that interests him is to finish his book *To The Unseen,* about a *homocidal medium*. Mining from life material for a book becomes Charles's comeuppance, the more the medium strings up women—wives, maids, and a dead child—to interrupt his research. Discovering that she was invited to lead the séance *in a spirit of mockery*, Madame Arcati's perfectly affected confusion comes back to front, only, that is, after she has already exacted her revenge.

The more Charles flirts and spats with Elvira, the more Ruth desires death. Who can compete with a dead wife? While Charles quips that she isn't *the dying sort*, Elvira, hoping to kill Charles by fixing his car, takes Ruth first. With two dead wives now haunting his every thought, Charles bids them *goodbye, for the moment, my dears. We're bound to meet again one day, but, until we do, I'm going to enjoy myself as I've never enjoyed myself before*. The car, fixed again, drives itself. The tires screech and a whistling lands Charles between two happy wives *forever*. Here is the proverbial ending for all who desire to *live happily ever after*.

Full of ghostly vibrations and a craftily cut imagery, the film was declared by William Whitebait (April 14, 1945) "the wittiest, funniest creation of the English screen." He congratulated Coward for thinking "cinematically" and Lean for tiding over the "boring passages." The film won an Oscar for its "blushing" technicolor visual effects (Street 2010). Other critics appreciated the film as a redress to a British market flooded by films from across the Atlantic. Those less impressed found the play's "sparkling dialogue" insufficiently complemented by "pictorial inventiveness" (T. M. P. 1945). Pauline Kael found Coward's "flippant, ectoplasmic comedy" sagging "more than a little in this arch David Lean version" (1982: 62). Seeing Lean's first cut, Coward complained: "you've just fucked up the best thing I ever wrote." Lean apologized: "I did warn you I didn't know anything about high comedy" (KB: 190–1). What about a lower comedy: Did he know more?

Critics like Melanie Williams have certainly noted the music. But there is still more to be said. The conventional score by Richard Addinsell was performed by the London Symphony Orchestra, conducted by Muir Mathieson. But the true musical moment comes with the passing reference to Rachmaninoff. It clues us into the high-to-low wit of rearranging the furniture for the séance. Madame Arcati controls the transport of mind and mood as she glides toward

Figure 7 Rachmaninoff? Too florid. *Blithe Spirit*, directed by David Lean, Two Cities Films, 1945.

the record collection to say (in both play and film): *I presume that's the gramophone. . . . What have we here? Brahms. Oh, dear me—no. Rachmaninoff? Too florid. Where's the dance music?* (Figure 7). Instructed to look at the *loose* records (because classical music came in sets), she finds what she wants: Irving Berlin's song "Always," which (since 1925) has become the favorite of her medium, a child, Daphne, who died *February 6, 1884*. When the record comes on, it is a perfect rendition, to which Arcati responds by dancing in the shadows now cast by the dimmed lighting.

"Always" offers a perfect fit for the one (as the lyrics tell) who goes on loving whatever goes wrong. It will become Laura's word in *Brief Encounter*: *I want to remember every minute . . . always . . . always to the end of my days.* When "Always" is chosen, Charles is unnerved. Because he alone knows the song's significance, he alone sees Elvira. When, at Charles request, Madame Arcati performs every trick in her bag to get rid of two dead wives, nothing works until the maid is hypnotized to the subtle accompaniment of Berlin's song, only, this time, as in *This Happy Breed*, it is sung out of tune and with a shockingly bad voice. Suddenly, the *always* makes mincemeat of the *forever* of fidelity: when a song is not sung as it should be sung. The mincing equally impacts the marriage oath *Till death do us part*, since, for some, no parting is possible even in death. What then does *passing* over mean? For some, it means not listening as in closing off one's ears. For others, as for the husband in *This Happy Breed*, it means closing the door to any living room with a family piano.

In a play version for Live TV Theater in 1956, with Coward, Claudette Colbert, and Lauren Bacall, we get another twist. The song chosen was Coward's song from his 1929 operetta, *Bitter Sweet*, "I'll See You Again," with the invocation already of Berlin's repeated "always, always." In the play, Condomine comes off more the winner than the loser. Closing the front door, his dead wives remain forever in the house to throw his books from the shelves and smash his furniture! *Learning scales will never seem so sweet again*, the song says, *till our destiny shall let us meet again*.

The *always* for Madame Arcati plays wittily to the Victorian middle-class ring that, for Ruskin, in his 1865 essay on lilies, surpassed the brief relationship of lovers to capture what endured for a lifetime. "Do you not feel that marriage . . . is only the seal which marks the vowed transition of temporary into untiring service, and of fitful into eternal love?" Ruskin construed the sexes as completing each other through their differences. In completion, the "always" depended on the husband doing the "rough work" outside—guarding, defending, creating, discovering—while the wife inside commanded the "sweet ordering." Repeating a spat from *In Which We Serve*, Charles is described as having been subject not to a sweet ordering but to an *iron rod* from his mother *until* he *was twenty-three*, and then on. His (writing) project to liberate himself is his way of gaining the upper hand *from the altar to the grave*. In every middle-class farce, moreover, the cooking, cleaning, washing, and ironing are left to the lower classes, unless, anticipating *Brief Encounter*, a tea-lady in "untiring service" discovers that she has control over the ordering of the spirits. Many critics (including Graham Greene) complained about the film's weary taste (Hoare 1995: 321). But weariness was Coward's point—if only to retrieve a voice for working women at tea counters against a centuries-old woman-hating and man-baiting delivered, as it was said, to a Tittle or Tee.

When Madame Arcati quips that *Daphne's more attached to Irving Berlin than anyone else; she likes a tune she can hum*—she mocks those whose appreciation for a high classical music— Brahms and Rachmaninoff—produces no lasting whistle from their lips. Most songs come and go with fashion, but not a song by Irving Berlin. Recall Coward and Berlin being competitors for the best production of popular songs. What better way to pay homage? And then there's Ludwig Wittgenstein's front-row memory of "the days of silent films" when "all kinds of classical works were played as accompaniments, but not Brahms or Wagner. . . . Bruckner, contrarily, goes with a film" (1980: #25/25e).

Swapping a bad record of Rachmaninoff for words sung always to the same tune, wasn't Coward asking how seriously anyone could or should take the Rachmaninoff if, every time they switched on the radio or went to the cinema, the same concerto played? For the *New York Times* in 1946, Bosley Crowther responded to another film with the Rachmaninoff: "If there is any inveterate film- goer who has not yet got enough," then here's a film to give you a "stomach full" until it comes "dribbling" out of your ears.

In 1945, the radio would broadcast news and entertainment. Cut into *Brief Encounter*, it becomes the medium for a mind's transportation: for the doubling up of a woman's face in the marital abode and for a remembered displacement of her body for the duration of her affair. For the duration, the radio cannot be turned off; only its volume can be turned down. The radio belongs to the living room, a library with a fireplace, occupied not by a newly married couple but by one considered settled, approaching middle age. Putting their marriage on trial, transgression is tested beyond any strict thought of breaking a law. Yet, how high are the stakes if all the transgression means is letting a woman feel young again as she suddenly and accidentally falls in love? The answer draws the private world of another family into a world of great war and great peace.

Simmel described the "minutest externalities of life" streaming at just the moment "when the peculiar color, ardor, and rhythm of the life-process become decisive." In the streaming that is also a cutting, "mere experience" becomes an "adventure." While "life-links" become "interlocked" in a "continuous thread," "countercurrents" spin to make for troubled "knots" ([1911] 2002: 229 & 222). The knots recall the trial-knots (*Prozessknoten*) that Nietzsche found in a rebirth of tragedy drawn out of the spirit of music (1999). Kracauer later drew from this spirit to describe *Brief Encounter* as an exemplary contrivance of a "fictitious incident" emerging out of the "documentation of the real." In this way, the film entangles a world with the feeling that everything has suddenly been turned upside down and inside out: "topsy-turvy" (1960: 252).

Malraux found the birth of cinema in the radio program: "la composition radiophonique" ([1939] 1958). So, too, Merleau-Ponty: "Le véritable ancêtre du son cinématographique n'est pas le phonographe, mais le montage radiophonique" ([1945] 1964). Both addressed the existential and phenomenological paths for filmic form to reach beyond description or documentation to achieve the transfigured play of intensified expression. The word "play" was loaded by the wit and demands of an aesthetic theory articulated around 1800. But the term also corresponded to the play on the theater's stage. In the published translation of the French essays, "la composition radiophonique" is rendered "radio play" to stress the streaming of a live or now spoken performance coming into the home. But let's retranslate "la composition radiophonique" as "the radiophonic composition" more to bring out the "radioactive" potential to rearrange furniture in the working-through of film as the new art.

On this point, let's also consider Jean-Paul Sartre's 1931 remarks on the "motion picture art" where he compared "the solemn initiation to the rites of the theater" to the cinema that required no pomp and ceremony, no dressing up, no cessation of speech, and no demand for the music to stop or start with the entrance and exit of the audience. With so little separating cinema behavior from daily life, more analysis, he insisted, was needed, not less. To grasp how cinema was defamiliarizing modern selves and families in modern times, one had to work through the visible mirrors of easy familiarity and identification to reach the labyrinth where the drive of rhythm spun the concealed threads of meaning (1974: 53–9).

Produced by Coward and directed by Lean, *Brief Encounter* was an adaptation of Coward's one-act radio play, *Still Life* (1936), written for

"Tonight at 8:30." Coward would take the part of the lover opposite his great friend, Gertrude Lawrence. The film, set in 1938–9 on the verge of war, was made at the war's end in 1945. Scenes filmed in the dark and far from cities in ruin hid the troops still on the move. At the premiere at the still-standing New Gallery in Regent Street, London, on November 26, 1945, Coward thanked the Navy, much as, in character, he ended *In Which We Serve*. The New Gallery Cinema had opened in 1925 with an impressive screen and a Wurlitzer organ; in 1938, it had shown the first full-length animated cartoon. Coward and Lean knew this: the organ and cartoon, alongside the radio, figure as the wittiest furniture for the film.

Beginning as a radio play, the film gained its visual counterpoint to listening not only with the camera that is not seen but with the radio that is. The radio broadcast of music orchestrates Laura's recall of her affair and her (pre-war) dreams of a romantic travel far away. Cut across a great war, the furniture, style, and clothing come off as aged. Yet, by time's dislocation, a greater stilled life emerges as a Romantic fragment, an absolute triad of love, art, and death: the end of an aged form of life. But how, as in *Ryan's Daughter*, could a romantic ideal work with the reality of so troubled a country? Could anyone in 1945 remain blind to the rationing of food and daily provisions of, or prohibitions still on, cultural goods? Or did the ideal testify to the urgency of the times? Moving between the ordinary and the extraordinary, could the film let the real or the ideal remain intact with only the *quietism* of English restraint: *to be ordinarily contented, to be at peace*?

Discussing the film's title, Coward recalled the *brevity* of his "playlet," allowing us to appreciate that British pinch of Shakespearean salt that proverbially warns against the excess of too many limbs. That the play compares the lovers to Romeo and Juliet must equally be taken with salt, not least to bring their being so theatrically English into view. When Gladys Calthrop, Coward's faithful set designer, suggested *Brief Encounter*, the new title stuck. Why the play's title was not kept to keep the focus on what is *still life* or, indeed, *forever life*, despite the stilled cutout of the affair, remains a question in the background.

The real life preceding the *brief encounter* was *still* the *life* after its end. The play gave the affair months; the film only weeks. The film was cut to bring two strangers to their affair: Laura Jesson (Celia Johnson) and Alec Harvey (Trevor Howard). The film comes over as strategically plotless. A happily married wife has a brief affair that is made as a *love in the afternoon* (a long decade before Billy Wilder's 1957 musical film with this title). The lovers take time out from their ordinary work and domestic duties to *play truant*, as Alec says in the film: to go to lunch or the movies or to take a country drive. Laura quips: *Not a very exciting routine, but it makes a change*—but what a change it made when, at the station, the *first awful feeling of danger swept over* her. Commentators are reminded also of *Love Affair* (dir. Leo McCarey, 1939) and *Casablanca* (dir. Michael Curtiz, 1942). Described as "the British *Casablanca*," *Brief Encounter*'s qualification as "British" suggests perhaps a too-comfortable domestication of a great political danger. However, domestication is not equal to domestic comfort, especially when a Russian musical transport gives Laura *Anna Karenina*-like thoughts of suicide in a world where *war and peace* are at stake in every home.

The film opens in silence with the double-faced sign next to the words announcing the company maker: Janus Films. The censor's certificate determines that the film is for *Public Exhibition to Adult Audiences*, after which church bells sound first alone and then as orchestrated to accompany the information regarding the film's distribution by *G.C.F.* and *Eagle-Lion*. The economic information is grounded by an iconographic image of London's St. Paul's Cathedral and New York's skyscrapers. Still, the film is to serve the British film industry. "Anyone," writes Brian McFarlane in his *Twenty British Films*, "who has ever written about British cinema has had to come to terms with *Brief Encounter.*" His book cover, with an image from the film, affirms the film not as his favorite but as the most British—meaning also the most English. Crediting its "cinematic fluency" to Lean, he notes how the early reviewers mostly directed their praise toward Coward (2015: 47–60).

During the credits, when the church bells chime for a secular world, some are reminded of Edward Ward's "Lullaby of the Bells" from Arthur Lubin's 1943 *Phantom of the Opera*. Most, however, hear the Russian bells that inspired Rachmaninoff to his piano concerto's ever-loudening opening chords. The chords dissolve out of the roar of the express boat train that, not coming toward the audience, is moving away to show an empty platform at night at a railway station named Milford Junction (filmed at Carnforth Station). With locomotive steam, the credits roll up against the night sky to show something we come to know only later, that this is the end of the affair and not its beginning, that the story at the station is its remembrance. A sharp cut reverses the train's direction. The story begins, and the Rachmaninoff temporarily ends. That the music is by Rachmaninoff seems to *matter* from the first moment, suggesting that the film will have no other music other than the Rachmaninoff. But this is false: popular songs will allow the affair outside the home to further unsettle the settled marriage at home. Even in the home, the radio plays, but the music as composed by Rachmaninoff does not matter for the marriage. Does it even matter for the affair?

The credits tell that the Rachmaninoff Concerto is *played by Eileen Joyce with The National Symphony Orchestra, conducted by Muir Mathieson*. There is no first name of the composer and no note to tell us that this will be the recording broadcast on the radio. Nor do we know whether the recording corresponds to one made independently. Why wasn't Rachmaninoff's 1929 recording with Leopold Stokowski and The Philadelphia Orchestra used to invest an authenticity straight from the master's hand? In *The Piano on Film*, David Huckvale notes other period recordings, a 1946 Decca recording, for example, included in "Incidental Music from British Films" (2022: 46). This is relevant insofar as later recordings would increasingly advertise themselves by reference to the film, as though the film had made it impossible for the concerto to have a life any longer of its own.

Heralded as a work of "classical" music, the "classic status" of *the Rachmaninoff* in film around 1945 owed much to its popularizing use for a popularizing art. Regarding *Brief Encounter*, Mathieson insisted on its being played straight in the correct sequence without any popularizing interference, arrangement, or recomposition. Even if cuts were made, preserving its order would sustain the impression of its being played continuously straight through (Hetherington & Brownrigg 2006: 96). For *Films in Review* in 1956, Edward Connor noted the newness of using Mendelssohn's score for *A Midsummer Night's Dream, the Rachmaninoff* for *Brief Encounter,* and concertos by Vivaldi and Bach for *Les enfants terribles*—all as "classics . . . played straight." Insisting on an "intelligent" use of the "classics," he feared a mashing. Fair enough. His newness more tellingly referred to a premeditated composition different from the old improvising "expressly for silent pictures." Making this difference paramount, as that also between a live and a live-transmitted music, *Brief Encounter* would put on show conceptual issues pertaining as much to music's history as to cinema's.

Coward set his play entirely in a busy waiting room. The film takes place at home. Only in Laura's memory is space expanded to make the waiting room different from the refreshment room and then different from the marital abode, a borrowed flat, a cinema, a lunch cafe, and a boatyard. Likewise, for the transport by foot, car, boat, and train. Street scenes in the fictional rural town of Milford capture the changing mood of the day that, for the lovers, is always a Thursday: *Do you come here every Thursday?—Next Thursday, the same time—Next Thursday?* Coward named Thursday in several of his plays, perhaps as the workday just prior to the weekend or because Thursday's child has far to go. Simmel wrote: "The more 'adventurous' an adventure . . . the more fully it realizes its idea, the more 'dreamlike' it becomes in our memory" ([1911] 2002: 222). In the film, the radio captures a live performance that under the condition of a recording is "live" no longer. In reliving the affair, Laura sets Thursday's colors of the day against the *darkness* of the evening partings.

Turning time, or mixing up the tenses of historical time, sustains the film's cyclical, elliptical, and episodic form. Antonia Caroline Lant would perfectly detail the sequencing of the six meetings of the love affair—6,1,2,3,4,6,4,5,6—and much else besides (1991: 174 (153–96)). My key turns more with the eight chords that warn us that, far from being an external film track or independent work, the Rachmaninoff will structure the plot. Here, we are clued into the thought of Mathieson recording the concerto precisely to cut it according to the episodic sequencing. Through the cutting, the film in one sense begins and ends at home while the "brief encounter" is remade through the concerto to begin and end at the station.

Whereas Jarre's soundtrack for *Ryan's Daughter* picks up bits of Beethoven to produce something diegetically distinct from what Charles plays on his gramophone, the Rachmaninoff in *Brief Encounter* plays for the marriage *and* for the affair. In *Ryan's Daughter*, Beethoven serves the husband in mutual devotion; in *Brief Encounter*, the Rachmaninoff serves the wife, but not because she loves the work. Is either spouse clued into the record on the gramophone or the recording on the radio? However "straight" its reproduction, as suggested by the radio transmission of a recording perhaps of a live performance, the Rachmaninoff is not listened to by anyone in the film straightforwardly. If neither the Rachmaninoff Concerto nor a Beethoven symphony could be played "straight" (without cuts), then maybe Coward and Lean were changing the tracks for how film was using music. From the radio play to the film: the radio broadcast of the concerto, *incidental* for those at home who hear the radio in the background, cuts out the *accidental* affair with its fantasy and frame. If the film bears on musical listening, it is as an education for an audience in 1945 being shown all that film as a total and multimedia art could newly mean.

Trains pass the station in the film as express trains without stopping, or they stop very decisively for the lovers to arrive and depart at the proper times. The idea of passengers preoccupied by a brief encounter places British propriety under acute observation. The transport by train cannot do without the mind's transport. Roger Manvell regarded the train-work exemplary: "a visual cliché" remade into "an inspired symbol" ([1944] 1950: 64). (When did it become a visual cliché?) Laura's weekly journeys by train give her time to reflect, to gaze at herself in a window that becomes a mirror of her fantasies: *I stared out of that railway carriage window into the dark . . . I saw us in Paris, in a box at the opera. The orchestra was tuning up. Then we were in Venice, drifting along the Grand Canal in a gondola . . . with the sound of mandolins coming to us over the water*. Noting how the audience watches Laura on the train watching herself, Kent Puckett quotes Charles Barr's view of Laura "summoning up her own story on a cinema screen" (2017: 139). Barr had described the "subjective logic" shaping "Laura's world of trains and shadows" as turning the "documentary surface" into a "projection of psychic states" (1986: 16–17).

Anderegg found the music and sound used "self-consciously and with great subtlety." Laura holds on to a memoryscape constantly interrupted by train noises and station stops with chilling names: "Ketchworth, Churley, Longdean, Perford" (MA: 30–3). The Rachmaninoff duly punctuated tracks her crossed lines of joy and misery. Whereas one feels Tolstoy's first and last train stations designed for crossed lives, the British climate preserves a moderation of moods. Whenever passions rise, so, too, does the volume of the Rachmaninoff. Then the wings get clipped: *I got out at Ketchworth and gave up my ticket . . . and walked home as usual, quite soberly and without wings . . . without any wings at all.*

Before *Brief Encounter*, the Rachmaninoff was used in Ben Hecht and Charles MacArthur's *The Scoundrel* (1935). Made in New York, the film's Oscar-winning script offers a searing drama about a literary agent with an acid tongue. It was Coward's first *starring* role in a film. While a piano is part of the furniture of an educated home, no Rachmaninoff emerges from its keys. Still, the credits roll by to an orchestral mash-up of the concerto by musical director Frank Tours, and, toward the end, the piano-less version conveys a tearful love that, beyond any marriage or affair, has become a matter of life and death. A score by George Antheil was apparently commissioned but rejected. Despite Coward's overall dissatisfaction with the film (Morley [1969] 1985: 184–5), he had few qualms about borrowing from it for *Brief Encounter*. This has received almost no comment by critics, excepting Philip K. Scheuer, who, reviewing the film for the *Los Angeles Times* (October 19, 1946: A5), began, "Coward obviously has a soft spot for Rachmaninoff's . . . Concerto. . . . He used it as the music behind the first film . . . 'Scoundrel'. He uses it again—and in a similarly telling fashion—in 'Brief Encounter.'" Scheuer was exaggerating: *The Scoundrel* was not Coward's film even if he might have had a say about the music. But would he have used the Rachmaninoff in this highly adapted way? More interesting is the motivic influence of *The Scoundrel*'s plot on *Brief Encounter*: when, in the former, a pianist composes a concerto as a *waltz for the night express*; when life's quest is construed as a train journey with no destination; when the conversation that finds no agreement on the subject of love lets the man constantly interrupt the woman with crossword clues; and, last but not least, when the Rachmaninoff gets silenced on the street by a popular brass band playing "The Blue Danube."

In his well-titled monograph *Reeled In*, Jonathan Godsall offers another useful contrast. In *Brief Encounter*, the concerto heard with the credits matches the credit's attribution of the film score, whereas, in *Trading Places* (dir. John Landis, 1983), the credit "Music by Elmer Bernstein" is accompanied by the overture from Mozart's *Marriage of Figaro* (2018: 54). But consider that if *Trading Places* cannot do without its Mozartian comedy, so *Brief Encounter* is carried by the contradiction sustained by the Rachmaninoff that allows Laura to trade places every time, from her armchair, she moves into the remembered spaces of her affair.

Addressing "mute music" in Roman Polanski's *The Pianist* (2002) and Jane Campion's *The Piano* (1993), Michel Chion asks whether a music cut from a prior existing music ought always to be called "music." "When a bit of what we call music occurs in a film, this does not mean that *music* and all it normally entails is involved." Chion's alert, not to import music's traditional terms into cinema blindly, is well taken. His essay, published in the excellent collection *Beyond the Soundtrack*, focuses, like the other essays, on how cinema's way of putting music on view as performance or as technology encourages audiences not to turn every sound into an experience for the ears alone. The promise of a sensory totality, with all the tensions played out, frees music from any *mere* accompanying or soundtrack associations. Chion describes cinema's space as like an ecosystem wherein the ordinary becomes enigmatic. Within the closed milieu, "everything interacts with everything else": "a texture or a shadow, a car passing, a camera movement." Out of the interaction of the smallest things emerges the enormous "gulf-effect," a revitalization of the "forgotten dimension" of Romantic music, or a "feminine" estrangement that rearranges orders of knowledge to make the playing of a piano no longer an ordinary fact of life. Chion considers films where pianos are transported into estranged places to be played under extraordinary conditions. The instrument's body and its strings suggest to him a feminine and maternal threading back to *Genesis* as the first act of creation, thereafter reproduced in and for every generation (2007: 87, 91–5). I am reminded more of *Exodus*, of persons assessing their naming as a people. In this regard, I have written elsewhere about the transport, trading, and portability of the most unportable instruments—the piano, harp, and double bass—in early musical-film comedies of exile and immigration and about the telephone transport in early opera and film (2016, 2021a, 2022). In *Brief Encounter*, while no piano is present in the living room at home, its trade-in for a radio allows for the imaginary to emerge by the mere touch of the dial. And in more of Lean's films, gramophones, harmonicas, and penny whistles are carried with the wit of a popular song when wanting to see someone *again* brings them to all *the old familiar places*.

Estrangement and liberation are at stake in a home where Rachmaninoff has become a (Dickensian) *household name*, as Beethoven has earlier. This matter comes with another, equally pressing, in 1945, regarding prohibitions on broadcasting a "foreign" music. In Britain, broadcasting Russian music was less problematic than broadcasting German or Italian music, unless a composer's name or a canonic work of any nation could, as in *Ryan's Daughter*, be divested of its national origin to serve the cause of freedom *wherever* claimed. Once divested, a work could then be domesticated in the hope of protecting a home from any outside threat. We already know that *being true to a work* runs along security lines parallel to *loyalty* to a nation and to *fidelity* within a marriage. Wartime breaks of convention were seen as interruptions or as signs of great change. The more a woman left home to join the wartime labor force, the more credit she got so long as she returned home. Other reasons for leaving home, like having an affair, placed such credit into question.

Many in 1945 feared that radio broadcasts would equalize, rationalize, or democratize music given the uniform constraints of a machine. The less human or anthropomorphic the means, the more boxed-in the products. No more speakers looking, as in *Ryan's Daughter*, like large ears or giant seashells communicating *His Master's Voice*, but modern music boxes disembodied by straight lines and cold wires. From this came complaints against the *soundbite streaming* and *streamlining* of programming: "Next tonight, music by Beethoven, Berlioz, Wagner, Puccini"—a potpourri of bits and pieces sold as *the greatest hits* whenever and wherever worldwide. Against the complaints, *Brief Encounter* offered a comeback. With music's broadcast on view, its technology and artistry would be *shown* as working together to expand lifeworlds in ways never before experienced. Offering music, noise, and striking moments of silence, the film would give new meaning to what it meant to turn a live performance into a record *of* a home and *for* the home.

Criticism of the music's use in *Brief Encounter* played into the film's general criticism. When the film was deemed overly sentimental, so too was the concerto. The more the condemnation of an art turning into "disposable kitsch," or into "a heart-throbbing little valentine made with great skill . . . and low-budget details," the more critics worried that the reputations of both the filmmaker and composer would be permanently damaged (Huckvale 2022: 62). In 1976, Geoffrey Norris wrote of the concerto as "notable for its conciseness and for its lyrical themes, which are just sufficiently contrasted to ensure that they are not spoilt either by overabundance or overexposure" (1976: 115). Being about the composition, this observation didn't touch the concerto's remarkable overexposure in a whole slew of films made before and after the film with which it became *most* identified: *Brief Encounter*. When, in 1958, C. A. Lejeune used "Brief Encounter" to title her *Observer* review of Ingmar Bergman's *Summer with Monika* (1953), she affirmed a new phrase in the *lingua franca* of film in Britain and abroad.

By 1993, Richard Dyer could write that "Celia Johnson is probably what most people remember of the film, along with trains and Rachmaninov," and that "no film could be more a case of a drama unfolded to music, the literal definition of melodrama—*Brief Encounter* without Rachmaninov is unimaginable" (49). In 2022, David Huckvale reiterates the point: the film makes Rachmaninoff and the locomotives appear "almost synonymous" (35). The "almost" is key.

Commentators observe that Laura's memory-construction of her affair is spoken in silence as though a confession. Yet, the confession is never spoken out loud: *Fred, dear Fred. . . . If only it were somebody else's story and not mine. As it is, you are the only one in the world . . . I can never tell.* Her *never, never* is the counterpoint to *the always always*. In the radio play, the husband is an absent presence; he is referred to by name twice. The play forefronts the affair; the film expands the frame to include the marriage. When, at the film's end, Fred approaches Laura in her armchair, he says: *Whatever your dream was, it wasn't a very happy one, was it? . . . Is there anything I can do to help*? She replies: *Yes, Fred. You always help*. He thanks her for returning: *You've been a long way away. . . . Thank you for coming back to me*. Does he know where she's been? When earlier Laura had told him: *I had lunch with a strange man today, and he took me to the movies*, Fred had responded: *Good for you*! We know that what distracts a husband from seeing and hearing is a repeated Lean motif.

In *Brief Encounter*, one confession lets Laura admit that something is awry; another would admit to the affair. If there were nothing strictly to confess, would we think the affair only ever a dream? The family life shows laughter and wit far more than any marital storm or stress. It is a place of safety. Laura recalls: *This is my home. . . . I am a happily married woman . . . or, rather, I was until a few weeks ago*. Only in safety can Laura, in her armchair, recall the violence and shock of the brief encounter as it becomes a confrontation face-to-face: her face with her own, with her husband's face, and with her lover's face—as each looks back at her. When Laura recalls her being an ordinary woman to whom violent things don't ordinarily happen, she remembers the first ordinary day in the most ordinary place when first a man came in from the platform with an *ordinary mack*. With his hat turned down, she didn't even see his face. With his face closing in on hers, he removed a little piece of grit from her eye. Gertrud Koch wrote in "Why Women Go to the Movies" that the emotional push and pull is between the gazes of women in the film and the audience (1982: 51–3). But what more emerges where the return gaze within the film is of husbands or lovers blinkered in some way, or of women who drown out all communication in idle talk?

A key train journey has Laura's voice-over smothering the ceaseless chatter of her friend, Dolly Messiter, where "Messiter" suggests a "mashing" and "stirring." *I wish you were a wise, kind friend, instead of a gossiping acquaintance. . . . I wish. I wish*. The repetitive wishing reminds commentators again of a confessional prayer. Laura's wish quickly turns her irritation at Dolly back to her own misery. The Rachmaninoff carries the changing mood. *Nothing lasts, really . . . neither happiness nor despair. . . . There'll come a time in the future when I shan't mind about this anymore. . . . No, no, . . . I want to remember every minute . . . always . . . always.* The "always" counterpoints the "brevity" of the weekly meetings. Back home, Laura tells her husband that Dolly *talked and talked . . . until I wanted to strangle her*, but attributes her despair to her being *a little rundown*. When Fred questions her *fainting spell*, she recalls having had another once at her son's school concert (she'd just told Dolly the same). And again, when Fred once *insisted on taking [her] to that symphony concert at the town hall*, she'd said: *I suppose I must be that type of woman.* What sort of woman and why this reaction so often at musical events?

At home, Fred seeks a seven-letter word for the crossword clue given by Keats's poem *When I Have Fears That I May Cease to Be*. The poem's title cues the line: *When I behold, upon the night's starr'd face, Huge cloudy symbols of a high -------.* Fred reads the line to intensify the significance of Laura knowing the answer: ROMANCE. His satisfaction depends solely on the fit of the word with the words he's already found: DELIRIUM and BALUCHISTAN (a former territory of *British India*). She stands (fourteen minutes in) to turn the radio dial to the concerto that has already started (as the Beethoven symphony had already started in *Ryan's Daughter*) (Figure 8). She selects a music that will require her neither to listen nor to clue Fred into the despair she feels at the affair's having ended just hours earlier. In a later cut, when the volume overwhelms because Laura is recalling the first declaration of love between her and Alec, Fred stands to turn the dial down. Shouldn't the volume have given something away?

Robert Murphy described Laura as "she listens to Rachmaninov's Piano Concerto in her over-comfortable home" (1989: 95). Richard Dyer noted that Laura "chooses Rachmaninov over dance music or French speech," and because the music is associated with her, it is "positively dissociated from anyone else" (1993: 17). Catherine Moraitis stresses the "irony" and "emphatic counterpoints" between Laura's choosing Rachmaninov and becoming emotionally absorbed by it and Fred saying "that he rather enjoys music," so that, apart from his concern with the volume, the music impacts him only "on a

Figure 8 Rachmaninoff on the radio. *Brief Encounter*, directed by David Lean (Eagle-Lion Distributors/Cineguild, 1945).

diegetic level" (2001: 100, 116). What Fred actually says is, *I'd like it*, when Laura asks him whether *some music* would *throw* him *off his stride*. Even if the radio music means something different to each, this doesn't mean that she chooses the Rachmaninoff for musical reasons. She will tell Alec that her husband *isn't musical at all*. It doesn't follow that she is.

Critics assess the Rachmaninoff and the voice-over as parallel tracks for Laura's transport. Yet, viewing the cutting of the frames of time and place, they find a genre (silent or noir), with once clear lines, becoming now blurred. The sound production, by 1945, made, they said, the voice-over technique "redundant." C. A. Lejeune (May and November 1945) pronounced Coward's first really "mature work" exemplary of a British cinema that had survived "six years of struggle." Even if appreciating the film's honesty, she doubted it would become "generally popular." Thinking the "off-screen commentary" a "technical trick," she quipped: Isn't "Miss Johnson's face" enough? "Good wine needs no bush. Good acting needs no explanation." While silent about the radio, she noted how Chopin "after a tough competition with swing had become" (likely in Charles Vidor's 1945 *A Song to Remember*) "the symbol of music for the millions." When would Rachmaninoff take Chopin's place?

In 1948, Clifford Leech praised the film as perfectly illustrating Eisenstein's proposal for a Joycean "internal monologue" to serve the vehicular needs without falling back into "theatrical soliloquy." But even he warned that, with overuse, a technique can become "threadbare." Jerry Vermilye simply dismissed the voice-over as coming over as little more than a tedious sort of *I feel dreadful* complaint (1978: 93). But were the voice-over erased, would the radio music have to be erased too? The voice-over worked along with the black-and-white cinematography and the visit to the *picture house* where the lovers see a film trailer already suggestive of Technicolor and a Donald Duck "silly symphony" dependent on the overlay of music and voice. An early advertising poster for Coward and Lean's film—in red—both made and missed the point to show just how much of cinema's history with music and sound was inscribed into *Brief Encounter* to make the film be also *about* film. The monochrome technique produced a perfect contrast for the two sides of Laura's experience: the reality of everyday life and the unreality of her dream states. Yet, despite traces of film-noir melodrama, no single side is taken, good or bad, right or wrong, black or white.

When Manny Farber (1946) branded the film a "Middle-Aged Fling," he turned the entire lack of excitement into the very reason for its success. Something "haunting" emerged in the exactness of its naturalistic and realistic detail. It could, he remarked, have become a "soap opera" apropos the *Ladies Home Journal*. But no, precisely its high "intelligence" made it a "faithful record." By letting the lovers act out "the most exciting event of their lives" as though disabled by a "limp," or by "aborting" the lovers' sexual infidelity, or by subtly showing a lack of choices on a cafe menu, the film expressed its fidelity to a world of war, disability, and prohibition that audiences knew so well but wanted (at least briefly) to forget. If Farber had a criticism, it bore on the "stereotyped and grotesque" portrayal of the working class and on how Fred came off as extraneous, as though his passion alone was for "all-day lollypops."

Most early critics liked the film's absence of "Hollywood," meaning its refusal of glamor in favor of a middlebrow ordinariness set at a crossroads somewhere in the middle of England. Laura's ordinary look (with ordinary crooked teeth) rendered her no diva, nor, as Kent Puckett notes, the sort of saint that Coward and Lean would have seen in Carl Theodor Dreyer's 1928 *La Passion de Jeanne d'Arc* (2017: 170–1). In 1945, for BFI, one R.M. praised the film's unity and poetry as made "harsh, cruel and lovely" less by the plot than by the film noir "trains, corridors and platforms, the rush and roar of passion, the loneliness of half-lit stretches, the illicit secrecy of damp stone passages." He thought there had "been few better British films than *Brief Encounter* even at a time when our studios are taking their place in the vanguard of this great contemporary art." Writing for Baltimore's *The Sun*, Donald Kirkley (1946) found the demand for a "high IQ and [a] degree of taste" to reside in a "serene and laudable disregard for movie conventions."

Recent commentators have remarked on Laura's lowbrow taste for romances as weekly she borrows them from Boots (Lant 1991: 180; McFarlane 2015: 56). The books are, suggestively, Kate O'Brien's romances: *The Ante-Room* (1934) and *Prayer for the Wanderer* (1938). The second romance addresses home's security and the freedom to wander; the first, from its Afterword, tells of "how monstrous . . . little sins can be" (317). Passing by the bookshop, Laura sees new releases in the window. At least two books, *Something in My Heart* (1944) by Walter Greenwood and *Winter's Tales* (1942) by Karen Blixen, carry no sense of a cheap romance. Greenwood's novel was a sequel to the successful 1933 *Love on the Dole* (adapted for cinema) that had dramatized the General Strike and mass unemployment in the North of England.

Borrowing books signals Laura's desire to *borrow* the word ROMANCE to construct the affair as an accidental crossing of words and paths. The accidental renders the affair less cheap than a way for her to live within her moderate means. In the play, Alec says: *An accidental meeting—then another accidental meeting . . . what could be more ordinary?*

"Accidental" captures a married woman, a wife and mother of the middle class, unexpectedly confronting the broad social upheaval of war when staying at home was not possible. That the marriage was happy *until a few weeks ago* stands allegorically for a world that was at peace *until a few years ago*. We go on in a form of life until suddenly we find ourselves spiraling down into a world that makes no sense. The fear of falling is matched by the rise of passions that feel out of our control. Tony Williams has discussed Leslie Arliss's *Love Story* of 1944, where a concert pianist threatened by heart failure is persuaded by a lover who is losing his sight that *Happiness such as we can have is worth grasping, even if it is for just a day, an hour. . . . [W]e're all living dangerously, there isn't any more certainty. Just today and the possibility of tomorrow* (2000: 39).

"Living dangerously" is part of humanity's preparation for a future life that Nietzsche described as joyous: "Send your ships into uncharted seas!" (2001: Bk 4, #283: 160–1). Brought into the arts, however, the danger of a sea storm risks being overly tempered by the unreality that assumes too safe a distance. One of C. G. Jung's most famous quotations was used by Roger Manvell in 1944 for his book *Film*: "The cinema, like the detective story, makes it possible to experience without danger all the excitement, passion and desirousness which must be repressed in a humanitarian ordering of life" (1944: 10). Jung described a body for dancing and sport endangered in 1933 by humanitarian claims being made and abused by the League of Nations. He saw cinema remodeling "self-estimation" as a "re-estimation" of "human nature," to re-empower a poetic revenge as in the German poet, Friedrich Hölderlin's "Danger itself / Fosters the rescuing power" (1933: 253–4). For Coward, the danger in the stilled life had to be less exposed. Theatrical temptations of body and mind had to be choreographed with a more tempered or closeted meter, with an English propriety that made it seem as though no very large license or transgression had occurred.

In the film, borrowing books matches the borrowed flat where Laura and Alec might have had sex had their moment of living dangerously not been interrupted. Leaving her scarf behind, Laura runs away through the back door. Alec remains but doesn't give her identity away. When, at a lunch, Laura fears she has been seen by a friend, she concocts a lie again so she won't be caught out. Borrowing is like renting a space: one has neither to own it nor own up to it.

"Accidental" means an affair that, not of one's making, had nothing to do with the deliberation of married persons who, wanting a divorce, needed by law to be caught out in an act of adultery. By the 1960s, the Matrimonial Causes Act had offered reforms to allow a marriage "irretrievably broken down" as no longer having to prove *fault* by the indubitable evidence of a private detective's photograph. (Photographs can't lie!) In the new peacetime society under the Labour government, changes in the law toward adultery, divorce, bigamy, cohabitation, contraception, and illegitimate birth brought a desirable uncertainty of new possibilities for some and, for others, a dread that the old world was entirely gone. An impressive literature today addresses the war's *unintended* casualties and its *unforeseen* potential. Here, again, *Brief Encounter* is called up as exemplary, but of what? Not divorce, not marital stress, not adultery for fun, but only an *accidental encounter* that, by the end, *necessitates* the return to a marriage in accord with the unbreakable spine of a nation declaring itself undefeatable: "Forever England" (Light 1991: 209–10; Rattigan 2001; Langhamer 2006).

"On the whole, good films get a good press and bad films get panned!" So wrote Catherine de la Roche in 1949, in part to bring the reader's attention to a wartime cinema that had not only produced masks of unreality to conceal the realities of the violence but also the "feminine angle" so strategically erased and effaced from women's *ideal home* magazines. "You would not have guessed . . . that this was the century of women's emancipation."

Changes in conditions of labor moved in tandem with postwar class mobility. With change came anxiety. Laura tells Alec: *Self-respect matters, and decency. I can't go on any longer.* In the play, the misery motivates Alec's declaration of innocence. From innocence comes a little lunch or an afternoon movie. Laura says *firmly*: *I'm a respectable married woman.* But then Alec responds with a let's not be *too respectable.* When, in the play and film, Laura asks him about his wife, Madeleine, and he about her husband, we mostly learn that Madeleine is *small, dark, rather delicate*. Mentioning them little interrupts the *tremendous* intensity the lovers feel in sudden moments, the *desperately difficult* feelings immeasurable by *the values of our ordinary lives*. Such moments feel then degraded by the secrecy and guilt, so that Alec can say: *all the circumstances of our lives—those have got to go on unaltered. We're nice people . . . and we've got to go on being nice*. What difference will the affair then make, not to Alec's marriage about which we know so little, but to Laura's marriage about which we know just a little more?

"Accidental" plays to the *little piece of grit* that Laura gets in her eye when an express train passes by. The grit in the term "integrity" preserves the decorum. Alec's specialty is preventative medicine: he works on grit. Laura recalls: *That's how it all began*. Lant noted how Alec uses Latin medical words to turn the grit into a twinkle in her eyes: a little pain turned suddenly to joy (1991: 182). In the play, Dolly responds to Laura: *My dear—how very romantic! I'm always getting things in my eye and nobody the least bit attractive has ever paid the faintest attention—which reminds me*. And she goes on to gossip about an adulterous couple caught out at the Tate museum in London. That the woman in trouble is named Lucy Jenner echoes Laura's married name: Laura Jesson. The film fades out Dolly's gossip to let Laura drift into a dream world of European locations. Her romantic dream is then counteracted by Alec's sober decision to end their affair "naturally," to take his research and his family far away to Africa. All that will remain is their love—*always, always*.

Time and tide wait for no man. When Alec tells Dolly in the refreshment room that he'll soon be leaving England, he leaves quickly for the train. She says: *He'll have to run, or he'll miss it*. His wanting to wait longer is his not wanting to bid Laura a final farewell. Dolly's gossip about shopping marks the end of the affair, as does her purchase of chocolate bars (strikingly unavailable in 1945). With Alec gone, Laura runs to the platform in her Anna Karenina moment. The first scene does not show her on the platform, unlike the repeated scene at the end.

J. E. Smyth observes: Laura is no Anna and Celia Johnson is no Garbo: "she's British and has the good sense not to jump" (2016:

53–4). James Agee ([1946] 2005) thought that the "vanity-sized *Anna Karenina*," even if "relatively dinky and sentimental," should be "thoroughly respected." Respect played to English morals while the dream played to a Russian drama supported by a Russian concerto taken briefly out of the home. Yet, because the Russian concerto found its domestication in a British radio broadcast, its threat as foreign and its status as classical became as contained as the "brief encounter." A woman's suicide in the nineteenth-century novel—Anna Karenina's jump or Madame Bovary's poison—could not happen in *Brief Encounter* or later in *The Passionate Friends*.

"Accidental" attaches to the idea of *saving face*. Melanie Bell (2009) finds a "femininity in the frame" into which Melanie Williams sets a triad of three Rs: "respectability, rain, and Rachmaninoff" (MW: 102). Even if the fourth R of romance steals away with the Rachmaninoff briefly to suspend the respect and the rain, the English climate proves stable. Going to the botanical gardens one Thursday afternoon, Laura surmises that *if we lived in a warm, sunny climate all the time, we shouldn't be so withdrawn*. Blaming the weather is part of a broader commentary on country and class. One feels the anticipation here of Nancy Mitford's 1949 novel *Love in a Cold Climate* sitting on a bookshelf, having drawn its title from George Orwell's *Keep the Aspidistra Flying* of 1936, the year also of Coward's play. Orwell had concluded Chapter 6: "There are so many pairs of lovers in London with 'nowhere to go'; only the streets and the parks, where there is no privacy and it is always cold. It is not easy to make love in a cold climate when you have no money. The 'never the time and place' motif is not made enough of in words." In *Brief Encounter*, as later in *The Passionate Friends*, making love in streets and parks signifies no shortage of money, only public prohibitions and then private ones whenever dangerous passions threaten to break out.

Investigating the fractures in the film's modern moral picture, commentators address the conflicted, double morality with all the transgression, panic, return, and affirmation implied therein. All the contrasts of the prohibitions and allowances of the home, the refreshment room, the stranger's flat, or the public square are accentuated. Every temptation is then moderated by a film that was so deliberately striking out against the Gainsborough melodramas, which, in 1945, were apparently running away with the box office. The old aristocratic wickedness in *The Wicked Lady* (dir. Leslie Arliss, 1945) was not an option for a drama that was allowing only the smallest misdemeanor to become momentous for but a brief and accidental moment.

The Rachmaninoff on the radio registers a certain class status. Laura and Fred are suburban. Cosmopolitan London is hardly mentioned. Did suburban life correspond to the demographic of a growing postwar audience for film and radio (before television) to broadcast the news close to and away from home? How, as Coward had already asked in *This Happy Breed* and *Blithe Spirit*, was a technology at home erasing distinctions of class in the name of a democratizing art? How would a choice of classical music on the radio be dissolved into a choice for something more popular?

Rearranging the furniture in *Blithe Spirit* prefigures the same dynamic in *Brief Encounter*. While the middle-class lovers take time out of ordinary life with a little refreshment, the working couple in the refreshment room allows Coward a lightness of touch in the very first lines—reminiscent of Hitchcock's opening train scene of *Suspicion* (1941). Coward also made a cameo appearance. The *dust-up* between the station master and the passenger who wants to travel first class with a third class ticket contrasts with the grit in the wit that makes for the middle-class story. So too, the flirting between the station master and the tea-lady. Would the War's end erase the weary class warfare? When Lean later thought back to the "Cockney" interludes, he, like the critics, regretted the caricature (KB: 201). But wasn't the out-there caricature of the working class how Coward better targeted his unease with a middle-class seriousness and secrecy, an unease also quite different from his unease with upper-class snobberies and pretensions?

Coward set his play as an *expression of the fanciful side of MYRTLE's imagination*, with *rows of tea-cups and glasses symmetrically arranged . . . Schweppes' bottles of soda and Tonic water . . . placed in circles and squares. Even the rock cakes mount each other on the glass stands in a disciplined pattern*. From this order, and not from the living room, Coward cut out the lovers' encounter. No radio and no Rachmaninoff: only a recommendation to go see the pre-code *The Broadway Melody* (as in *This Happy Breed*). The recommendation is made by the station master Mr. Godby (Stanley Holloway), a name laden with connotations of goading, to his sparring partner, Myrtle Bagot (Joyce Carey), a name laden with exasperation. She rejects the recommendation as unfitting in such difficult times. She'd much rather see the latest *Claudette Colbert*, so long as Mr. Godby doesn't spend the entire movie, as she says, *hissing in me ear*. In 1936, Coward likely had the adventure romance, *Under Two Flags* (dir. Frank Lloyd), in mind so that the "flags" could suggestively mean "sheets." Dreaming without interference is also what this working class woman wants at the cinema.

Adapting the play, Lean pressed Coward to include a visit to the cinema. Coward agreed: "Only if they go to a bad film" (KB: 195). The film would show just how bad a weekly film at the picture house could be. At the cinema, Laura and Alec hear the music of the Wurlitzer before the trailer for the *stupendous, colossal*, and *epoch-making* film *Flames of Passion.* An advertisement for a baby pram follows. The trailer comes with its soundtrack: bombastic, "Hollywood" style, and unattributed. The lovers laugh at the musician who rises with the Wurlitzer because they've already seen her playing the cello not very well in the ladies' orchestra during their lunch in the Kardomah Cafe (Figure 9). *Will you just look at the cellist? . . . There should be a society for the prevention of cruelty to musical instruments*. (My favorite line!) Leaving the cafe, the trio, suddenly playing better, goes unnoticed. Next time around, Laura is not so happy: *The ladies' orchestra was playing away, as usual. I looked at the cellist. She seemed to be so funny last week, but today, she didn't seem funny anymore. . . . I hadn't enjoyed the pictures much. It was one of those noisy musical things, and I'm so sick of them.* Again, Laura seems not overly to like music. The Kardomah Cafe was a chain enterprise in England noted for its musical offerings. In many early films, as in Buster Keaton's 1921 *The Playhouse*, a musician or a song moved between instruments as fast as daily laborers changed jobs. In *Brief Encounter*, one woman could run from the cafe at lunch to the cinema in the afternoon, from cello to organ, to make ends meet.

Figure 9 The Ladies Orchestra, *Brief Encounter*, directed by David Lean (Eagle-Lion Distributors/Cineguild, 1945).

First time around, the lovers choose *Love in a Mist* at the Palladium over *The Loves of Cardinal Richelieu* at the Palace because, as Alec quips: *I was once very sick on a channel steamer called Cardinal Richelieu*. *Cardinal Richelieu* (dir. Rowland V. Lee, 1935) was a Hollywood movie about a Frenchman consumed between two fidelities: to God and to Country. The fictionalized title suggested something more illicit. At the cinema again, when the lovers watch a Disney cartoon, Alec quips that even if *the universe go[es] up in flames, and the world crash[es] around us, . . . there'll always be Donald Duck*. Another *always* for a popular offering. As the main event, *Flames of Passion,* begins, Alec says against a moment of unattributed background music: *no more laughter. Prepare for tears*. The lovers quickly flee. Laura recalls: *It was a terribly bad picture. We crept out before the end, rather furtively, as though we were committing a crime.* The word "crime" appears once more, when, having bought a *terribly expensive* present for her husband, she describes *having committed the crime, I suddenly felt reckless and gay*. When the Rachmaninoff returns, the pleasure of their *little* crime at the cinema dissolves into a guilt writ *large*. "A fragmentary incident," Simmel wrote, is "like a dream, as it gathers all passions into itself . . . ; like gaming, it contrasts with seriousness, . . . [to move] between the highest gain and [the highest] destruction" ([1911] 2002: 225).

With its steamy *flames*, the trailer the lovers watch wittily suggests more the wild passions of King Kong than the *Gentle Summer* indicated as the source novel on the screen, by one Alice Porter Stoughey, a pseudonym apparently derived from three women scriptwriters of the period. That the film had to be bad was how Coward and Lean took potshots at Alexander Korda's films with their overeagerness to bring Hollywood into British cinema (Smyth 2016: 53–4). Writing generally about trailers and coming attractions, Adorno found a "trade-in" of the culture industry, where films, treated like "popular hits," were advertised through reductions to a single slogan or image. He described the film wearing its "commodity character" like a "mark of Cain," likely from *The Mark of Cain* of 1947 (dir. Brian Desmond Hurst) (1981: 205; Street 2009). Gestures and slogans packaged for the sake of a good sale promised a delivery of something that, because reduced, necessarily failed to satisfy.

Flames of Passion was not the commercially successful silent British movie of 1922 (dir. Graham Cutts) whose title for US distribution was more modestly *A Woman's Secret*. That film staged the affair between a barrister's wife and a chauffeur who accidentally ran down a child born out of wedlock. His trial revealed him as the father, but the marriage survived. Coward might have been inspired to use its title in *Brief Encounter* given that the 1922 movie had been playing next door when, in 1926, his *Easy Virtue* opened in Manchester. As Philip Hoare reported, the local council had demanded that Coward change the immoral title of his play. Sweet revenge, then, for Coward later to flash the far worse title on the screen as a reminder of the once-attempted censoring of his work on the stage (1995: 360n).

Nor, of course, was *Flames of Passion* the highly praised black-and-white movie made in 1989 as a "gay homage" to *Brief Encounter*. Shot at a literally steamy railway station, a man carrying a newspaper is distracted by photos of another man left in the photo booth. With AIDS, many began to read *Brief Encounter* as being about the love "that dares not speak its name," the line concluding Lord Alfred Douglas's 1892 poem "Two Loves," revised by Oscar Wilde into a silencing homosexual act, later mocked as the "No Sex Please, We're British" atmosphere that Coward knew so well (Halligan 2022: 24f.; Gray 1987: 64–7).

While the Rachmaninoff plays seemingly without pause, it is sidetracked every time Laura turns to a different music. Choosing popular songs for *Brief Encounter*, Coward did not use his own songs even if, as often in his film scripts, he used already famous lines from his songs minus the tunes. (Lean would later use Coward's lines similarly.) Coward was famous for songs like "Mad Dogs and Englishmen" and "Don't Let's be Beastly to the Germans." Given a country that hardly ever saw the midday sun, the *British*, we hear accordingly in *Brief Encounter*, *have always been nice to mad people*. In preparatory notes, moreover, Coward declared Laura "bored" by George Bernard Shaw, and "not particularly musical," yet she would love "gangster" movies, Walt Disney's "Silly Symphonies," and "Travelogues" (Day 2004: 102). (What made a symphony "silly" would prove a deep question for early film comedy and animation.) When Laura hears the vaudeville classic of the first "Great War" *Let the Great Big World Keep Turning*—it is less the song then its source that grabs her attention: *you know how I love barrel organs*.

Setting *Brief Encounter* on the verge of war allows the war an invisibility on par with the affair's invisibility in the marital abode. Invisibility and absence play to a bracketing of fear, when, in *Brief Encounter* (and later in *The Sound Barrier*), the cinema offers a respite for a brief while. Critics, like Puckett (2017: 143–6), see the "great hiatus" as a middle term for what Benjamin described as a dialectical image (1999: 492, #N2a,3). Moving through tenses of time, the image brings time to a standstill. With a war or an affair over, will the ordinary flow of life continue? Or will the extraordinary bring something back to the home that is more than a souvenir to be placed on the mantlepiece? When Laura tells Alec that her love for him has made her *a stranger in my own house*, she describes her estrangement from her surroundings of *familiar things, ordinary things . . . the dining-room curtains, and the wooden tub with a silver top that holds biscuits and a watercolour of San Remo that my mother painted*. Still, she is safe: her mother's painting carries the familial tie that can't be cut whatever her rearranging of the furniture.

Markers of war enter obliquely: in Alec's reference to a world in flames, or when, one evening, Laura sits near an old war memorial. Set before the recent war, there are no bombed buildings. Before *Ryan's Daughter* allows too many words to be spoken in the pub, Coward allows soldiers on the homefront to chide Mrs. Bagot for not serving alcohol: are we in *a free country or a bloody* (in the play) *and blooming* (in the film) *Sunday school*? Licensing hours or the call of *Time gentlemen, please*, introduced to keep the industry going in the First World War, remained as strict in the Second World War—as strict as Mrs. Bagot's ordering of her tea counter.

In his *A Mirror for England*, Raymond Durgnat described *Brief Encounter* less according to its witty counterpoint than to its refusal to offer a happy fireside settlement at the end. He found in Laura's face a trauma and wreckage, "a nadir of abjectness" to extinguish every last flame of passion. Watching the film "twenty years on," he recalled the first audiences who'd laughed at the British prohibition more on sex than alcohol: "Make tea not love." Surveying Lean's "love stories," he saw the director negotiating cinema's ways of cutting and casting women with a frozen whiteness as though to deny them agency ([1970] 2011: 214–15, 223, 250). He saw Lean trying to give some agency back to women.

Adding to the agency, Williams finds warmth in the intermingling of Rachmaninoff's "soft and delicate" melody with the train's rhythm. When Alec asks Laura if they can meet again next Thursday, and the screen "fades to black," "seldom" has "[r]omantic renunciation . . . looked—or sounded—so bewitchingly beautiful." Williams feels a (Shakespearean) "sweet sorrow" as the lovers part with only the most discreet touch on the shoulder. But still, she asks: Was the affair of Laura's making, a dream accompanied by a needlework, even induced by a Viennese hysteria? (MW: 94, 98–9). To be sure, Laura could be seen as controlling everything (barring the volume) from her armchair, even moments when she isn't there: in the refreshment room or in the flat after she has run away. But is this hysteria or a quite ordinary dreaming where one's presence intervenes to render any situation suddenly not like the ordinariness of waking life? (Heather Wiebe's just-released study of British music and war films (2024) significantly develops the theme of cinematic hysteria and mental illness.)

In the 1970s, Molly Haskell looked back to "the woman's film" to compare its capability on both sides of the Atlantic to stress and stretch sexual and social priorities and prohibitions to their breaking points. In *Brief Encounter* and *The Seventh Veil* (dir. Compton Bennett, 1945), she found "soap opera elements" rendering women mostly casualties of the double standards implicit in middle-class morality (1974: ch. 4). The sense of disablement or diminishment was premised on a wife's adultery remaining unacknowledged or unconfessed, so that, returning home, the affair could be reconstructed as but a small misdemeanor. The smallness rendered the transgression safe, and, with this, the film itself safe in a highly censorious society. Little stretched to the extreme actually snapped.

In *Blackout* (1991), Antonia Caroline Lant tied the monochrome technique to film noir to address the self-effacement, the concealed prejudicial or conventional structures in wartime cinema, and the cosmetics of the face that had so often to hide the distress. She highlighted the episodic form in *Brief Encounter* that sustained an urgency in the ending of the affair, a desperation on Laura's part that in fact she could not bring everything back to memory. The lapses and breakages were akin to the condition of the wartime blitz, when blackouts, demanded to keep houses and homes safe, made "radio contact" matter the most. This is a brilliant insight, corresponding to all the early films where Coward and Lean drew the radio into the home to protect something and someone, and most especially because some members of the household had gone away if not to love, then to fight. From the protection of something past came a promise of a protected future. Lant's chapter on *Brief Encounter* has one epigraph from Haskell and another from a July 1945 editorial review in *Britain Today*:

> We have all made up our minds . . . that we are not simply going back to the so-called peace and civilization of 1939. If it really is the case that wars are turning points between epochs, then we are standing on the threshold of a new epoch whose character we have yet to discover—or, better still, create.

For many, all the ready-made stuff out of which Shakespearean dreams had been made had melted into air. There was no return to pre-war England. Lant described the paradigmatic turn that followed from women working during the war, when tonics from cheap magazines no longer pacified them in their roles as wives, mothers, daughters, or sisters. (When, really, had women been so pacified?) Yet, for all the promise, a backlash came with another sort of blackout, when husbands, watching women return to the home, swept any transgression under the carpet (1991: 175, 153). Not asking, not seeing, not listening—another "whereof one cannot speak"—accorded with the English reserve, with the gratitude that at least some of the women had come home.

Sue Harper comparably focused on a cinematic representation of women to which, through Cineguild, so many of the Coward and then Lean team contributed. If women were agents of change in a world of conservative constraint, then their agency was effected through an ambiguity and non-predictability of motive and morality. Rendering them "unfathomable" enhanced the mystery of the romance while yet keeping them safe. While men were made to bear the weight of tradition, women turned the keys of change without fully being seen (1992: 226–7; 2010: 135–6). Later, we see figures like Lawrence emerging as unfathomable to both inflate and deflate the myth of a hero.

We are not yet finished with *Brief Encounter* or with keys opening and closing doors. But one thing we know is that by focusing on the blithe spirit of wit, we are rewarded not only with a display of middle-class sentiments but also with the jibes of working women in homes, cafes, shops, cinemas, and refreshment rooms that can carry the woman's complaint. *You can't expect me to be a cook, housekeeper and char during the day,* quips Mrs. Bagot, *and a loving wife in the evening—And I packed me boxes then and there and left him*. Not listening to the wit across classes, however weary it feels, we risk taking the seriousness of *Brief Encounter,* and then more of Lean's films, *too* seriously.

The Rachmaninoff was chosen for *Brief Encounter* because it was apparently Coward's favorite. Little, however, did this prevent Lean from cutting the record with a careful hand. To fear that the concerto, if not played straight, would lose its integrity played to the romantic untouchability of classical works: no tampering. When Mathieson expressed this worry, it was because he wanted a music, and, as we will see, a British music, to be composed specifically for the film. Didn't *Brief Encounter* deserve its own score? The quarrel is well documented: Wouldn't the famous concerto, independently known, only distract audiences from looking at the film? Coward retorted: "No, no, no. (Laura) listens to Rachmaninoff on the radio, she borrows her books from the Boots Library and she eats at the Kardomah" (KB: 202). Rendered intrinsic to the plot, the concerto would have to come in through the radio, assuming the radio, like the record player in *Blithe Spirit*, to be a trustworthy medium. When the concerto came in, Mathieson conceded that no other music could have been quite so effective. Mathieson's concession was as suspect as Coward's wit. To assume that the Rachmaninoff was recorded as a score for the film overlooks its status as a piece of furniture, a radio piece to make a furniture-art par excellence for a new art of film. And within the film, wasn't Laura the first and the last not to respect the concerto as something to be listened to? If *not listening* to the Rachmaninoff on the radio recorded new ways of listening to film, so, too, new ways of *not looking*. Redirecting ears and eyes was one way to unsettle the heavy minds and morals of a nation so recently at war. Remember Shelley: "The world should listen then, as I am listening now."

Chapter 4

Concerto for All Hands

In Which We Serve (1942), Brief Encounter (1945)

In 1947, ninety-year-old George Bernard Shaw surveyed the "the world in England" to recall pre-radio days when acquaintance with music came through public concerts or piano arrangements for the home. Today, however, he continued, "radio sets" are "as common as kitchen clocks, the Eroica, the seventh, the ninth, are as familiar to every Tom, Dick, and Harriet" (to replace Harry). "Highbrow music is everywhere, as audible in the slums as in the squares. And it is all due to radio." Shaw marveled at radio's limitless possibilities while also targeting the BBC's "propaganda of musical obscenity." How could music be passed off with only "passable intonation"? More precision in performance was needed, better microphones for discriminating voices, and more accommodation for radio to do justice to music, serious or popular, no matter its scale, size, or type. He minded not the cutting up of symphonies, concerti, or operas to one intelligent act or movement, only the cutting "to ribbons" where no sense of the original whole remained. Whatever the type of music, there was no reason to wreck it.

Shaw influenced Coward and Lean. Lean had worked on Shaw's *Pygmalion* in 1938 (about the comeuppance of class pretensions) and *Major Barbara* in 1941 (about the hypocrisy of Christian charity organizations). From his play, *Man and Superman*, Shaw had been inspired to Nietzschean "maxims for revolutionists"—as this one: "A moderately honest man with a moderately faithful wife, moderate drinkers both, in a moderately healthy house: that is the true middle class unit" (1903: 238). Lean recalled Shaw's visits to the film studio, how he'd sat "in a huge chair" from the property department—"a throne, really" (SS: 33). From Shaw, Lean learned how to establish a good angle, how to approach English moderation, and how to sit on a throne.

In 1949, R. K. Neilson Baxter mocked the new film director, who, with more the anxiety than the confidence of a king, hovered like an "agonised seagull" over his team. Encouraging a more democratic collaboration, he recalled *Brief Encounter* to ask who was deserving credit and for what. In the same year, A. L. Vargas praised *In Which We Serve* and *Brief Encounter* for their maturity in having produced a cinema arising "healthily and naturally out of the people." While appreciating the impact of British film on the international stage, he warned filmmakers not to rest on their laurels: "British films are at the crossroads" between an "unending stream of . . . novel and play adaptations" and a new art bearing on "life as it is in Britain today." He described *Brief Encounter* as "one of the finest British films ever made": no Technicolor, no stars, no subplot—none of the "usual safe box-office clichés." A film with a realistic meaning for everyone, from "the director down to the clapper boy." Forty years on, Anderegg quoted a historian describing postwar British cinema as rising "to an apogee," after which it fell "to an apology." Lean was named for the rise (MA: 37). Many more critics turned the tables to question the national character of postwar cinema the more they saw it pitting itself against the pursuit of an international *flag-free* intellectualism, experimentalism, or avant-gardism (Manvell 1947; Andrew Higson 1989, 1995; Marcia Landy 2000).

Chapter 4 starts with *In Which We Serve* and continues with *Brief Encounter* to reach the question again: Why the Rachmaninoff? The question is motivated by a jibe from a radio version of *Brief Encounter*: *Would you like some music on the phonograph? There is a favorite of yours—it's some concerto or other*. Did it matter which concerto it was? On the way, the chapter investigates what was said about Lean (and Coward) at home and abroad. The wit of the criticism is always revealing.

Lean's first film as co-director with Coward was *In Which We Serve* (1942). The photographer Ronald Neame recalled the negotiation that led to the three of them sharing a single screen of credit (2003: 58). Another credit specifying "Noël Coward's musical score" suggests that Coward determined the musical offerings even if Muir Mathieson oversaw the general musical production (Hetherington and Brownrigg 2006: 168). Three more contributing composers are named today: Clifton Parker (who also apparently worked on *This Happy Breed*), Ray Douglas, and William Alwyn (Donnelly 2007: 132). Cambridge University's archive safeguards two Alwyn sketches, of which one, for the title sequence, names Lord Mountbatten's ship the "Kelly," torpedoed in 1940. *In Which We Serve* fictionalizes the story of this ship, renamed the *HMS Torrin*, where the new name connotes the guardianship of a mound or small isle. Archivist Margaret Jones told me that Alwyn (oddly) never mentioned his work on this film. Ian Johnson further documents the similarity between Alwyn's sketch and the march in *Desert Victory*, a 1943 documentary made by the British Ministry of Information (2005: 55). The lack of archival documentation for these early films is striking.

In Which We Serve has a conventional score but, again, it internalizes popular songs to feed the love and courage of four families. Separated by class, the families are tracked in tandem with the fathers, brothers, and sons whose navy rank defines their public service to a ship that, for most of the film, is sinking to the bottom of the sea. For the British in 1942, a sinking ship signaled a victory that was not guaranteed, while, as propaganda, it documented the resilience of Britain whatever the cost. The *story of a ship*, the film shows Luftwaffe planes striking ships or blitzing cities of the "sceptred Isle." Radios and newspapers, at home and aboard ship, announce, as in *This Happy Breed*, landmark events: notably Churchill's declaration of war. Aldgate and Richards note the sad contradiction of this declaration with the *Daily Express*'s headline shown floating in the water months prior: "No war this year" (1986: 197). Landmark events dissolve into personal and class-ridden opinions. Being prepared dominates families awaiting *another* war, having experienced one great war already: *We're living in strange times, darling. It's as well to be prepared*. Or, from the lower class:

*Do you really think we'll have another war? . . . What would [Hitler]
expect to gain by having a war? World domination. . . . They haven't
got enough to eat in Germany as it is.*

The film about a ship is about a nation preserving its cables
and strings of belonging as intact. It opens with a striking
newsreel-documentary-montage of the ship's construction. With
the ship having been sunk quickly by the enemy, the survivors
await their rescue. They hold onto a life raft, suddenly equalized
in rank, from which, through flashbacks, each thinks back to their
very different lives at home. The *Good old white cliffs of Dover*
symbolize the *forever* of *such a little island*, only *20 miles* from
France. The ship's sinking suggests less a breakage than an
almost biblical fall, so that, in all things great and small, another
ship will rise. Cyclical and episodic flashbacks record the ship's
greatest naval feats, say at Dunkirk. Great feats are measured by
the handling of the smallest links. Termed a *casualty*, the smallest
link becomes, in a just war, just one of so many intended and
unintended deaths.

On and off the ship, the captain (Coward) demands family loyalty
and a natural order of all servers of the sea. *A very happy and a
very efficient ship*. He knows his men: he speaks their names at the
beginning and at the end to both personalize and theologize the
belief, as in *This Happy Breed* and later in *Zhivago*, that every person
counts in sustaining a nation's happiness. Drawn from the *Book of
Common Prayer*—"Be pleased to receive into thy Almighty . . . the
Fleet in which we serve"—the film's title offers a liberation narrative for
a life of service. One thread pulls the narrative back to a Christmas
once spent at *the Red Sea*, where, with wit about the climate, the
heat let a shipman fry *an egg on the deck*. Christmas is celebrated by
the families around dining tables so that each can toast the ship with
a pride of place over the daily vicissitudes of life. The captain's wife
(Celia Johnson) delivers her family's toast with a little envy: *Whether
it be a battleship or a sloop*, her *husband's ship . . . holds first place
in his heart. It comes before wife, home, children, everything*. The
ship enters every home to ally everyone and everything in public
loyalty. Little and large unhappinesses may define a family each in its
own way, but not, in a time of war, to threaten the nation's collective
happiness. Everyday details of home are conveyed in private letters

and telegrams coming in and going out in parallel to the public distribution of news.

Marching bands play, hymns of celebration are sung with vigor, and familiar music hall songs find their way into popular instruments. "Run, Rabbit Run" is played with the hope of rescue on a harmonica at sea (Figure 10). When a "young stoker" (Richard Attenborough) is chided for leaving his post, he runs to a bar with a pianola that runs its tune out without words. In the staged address about disloyalty, the captain, as father, insists on taking responsibility this time for the young stoker, but not next time. What destroys a family destroys a ship; what rescues the one rescues the other: *There'll always be an England, eh*? The Captain's final farewell to his surviving crew is affirmed in the narrator's voice-over: *Through all our centuries, the sea has ruled our destiny. . . . [In] spite of changing values in a changing world, [the ships] give, to us . . . eternal and indomitable pride*. Other songs, like the German Beer Barrel Polka, wittily warn the Germans to keep on their toes—to *run, run, run*.

Howard Maxford likes the barrel organ that accompanies the moment when a mother and wife await news of the sailor, Shorty (John Mills), after which an "East End cliché" is twisted when good

Figure 10 Harmonica at sea, *In Which We Serve*, directed by Noël Coward and David Lean, British Lion Films/Two Cities Films, 1942.

news arrives to the tune of "If you were the Only Boy in the World!" He says, "The film is full of clever details like this" (2000: 40–1). But if Shorty is the "only boy" who matters to this mother and wife, the song is actually about the "only girl," as sung earlier by passengers on a train when Shorty and his wife-to-be, Freda (Kay Walsh), first meet.

Composed a century prior, in 1842, for Shakespeare's *A Midsummer Night's Dream*, Mendelssohn's Wedding March plays to the film's intergenerational quarrels of old and new attitudes toward war and marriage. If the (Ruskinian) home affirms the man serving in public, then, on the homefront, the woman *weeps* as a sign of her caring. Yet, with a wit spiced and spliced into the film, the protective veneer is not cracked but strengthened. Just prior to eating a *delicious piece of railway fish* in the dining car of the Great Western, the captain claims (as later in *Blithe Spirit*) that his wife rules him "with a rod of iron." They recall then the first quarrel of their honeymoon when "The Blue Danube" played in the background. Music in the background matters for the *always, always*.

Frances Gray recorded the lavish praise from Soviet filmmakers of the "documentary realism," the widespread international appreciation of the circular life raft as a "profoundly democratic symbol," and then the response in Germany when Coward was placed on the most wanted list of "persons to be shot" the moment the Nazis reached Britain (1987: 78–80). The list was long. Also listed, besides Winston Churchill, were the likes of J. B. Priestley, Rebecca West, and Alexander Korda, this way testifying to a strong conviction in the power of art and film. Critics who found Coward's wit a little suspect were irritated, while others were calmed by Coward's purpose to play a completely *ordinary* captain without staging the glory of his model, Lord Mountbatten (Aldgate and Richards 1986: 193, 197). Being a "superman," in Shaw's prior vision, would not keep Britain afloat. But was moderation in all things, as Nietzsche would ask too, the right or best (Aristotelian) answer?

Attitudes toward postwar British cinema mirrored changing attitudes toward Lean's films. Repetition in the critics' choices of examples to illustrate this or that quality, good or bad, often revealed prejudices regarding national character, still more or less in evidence today.

Regularly surveying "the World's Studios" for *Penguin Film Review*, H. H. Wollenberg declared that, since 1940, the "British studios are second to none as regards the rise of fresh directing talent, led by Laurence Olivier, Carol Reed, and David Lean" (PFR6: 41). He liked the films that were testing national against international impulses and individual against collective drives. *Brief Encounter* was an "outstanding instance of individualistic film style," he said, given how Laura was made to stand out from the (albeit excellent) cast. Listing literally *out-standing* directors, he named the likes of Clair, Clouzot, Lang, Capra, and Cocteau, after which he noted Lean particularly for his "discreet romanticism" (PFR7: 95). In "Dialogue for Stage and Screen," also from 1948, Clifford Leech urged directors to take the "high road" of individuality above the collective "panacea" and "prejudice" of propaganda (PFR6: 102).

In her *Cross-Channel Perspectives*, Leila Wimmer covers the reception of British film in France after the liberation from German occupation into the Cold War. She reads the *Cinémonde*, of which the 1946 issue was dedicated to proving how British cinema was "set to conquer the world." *This Happy Breed* and *Brief Encounter* were already in 1946, she writes, hailed as flagships for a new self-confidence, premised on peace and a freedom from Hollywood's clutches (2009: 34). Pursuing her sources further is worthwhile to draw out the stakes of a French realism by which to measure the English reel. When, in 1974, Gerald Pratley recorded the early praise of *Brief Encounter* as being "more like a French film," he told that such praise had once counted as the "highest commendation" of the day (55).

Asking what cinema *is*, André Bazin recalled the rebirth of English film out of a realism made from the documentary's social and technical resources. Articulating its independence from Hollywood, he described the "highly refined aestheticism"—*plus construit et plus concerté*—that had brought *Brief Encounter* to its "portrait *plus réaliste* of English manners and psychology." He followed with a backhanded compliment: "Certainly David Lean has gained nothing by making over, this year [of 1949], a kind of second *Brève rencontre*" [*Les Amis passionnés/The Passionate Friends*] presented at the Cannes festival. One can reasonably protest against the "repetition" of the subject matter, he explained, but not the "techniques" that could be used "indefinitely." Later modifying his "unguarded" praise of the first *Brève rencontre* as "the glory of English Cinema," he highlighted (as others before and after him) its "self-effacement" of reality. If *Brief Encounter* once impressed him as on par with *Roma, Citta Aperta* (dir. Roberto Rossellini, 1945), time had told him "which of the two had a real cinematic future" (1967/1971: 48–9; 1949: 820–32). A real future, he was saying, of cinematic realism.

In 1946, Georges Sadoul named *Brief Encounter*, with its discretion and light touches, as contradicting the fashionable "Vedding cakes" of which Britain's *Caesar and Cleopatra* (dir. Gabriel Pascal, 1945) was the "catastrophic" prototype. The close-ups on Laura's face had none of Hollywood's "degenerate and plastic femininity." Sadoul compared Coward and Lean's highly crafted studio work with Italy's more open-air improvisation, of which Rossellini's *Roma* and *Paisà* (1946) again were the examples (Wimmer 2009: 66–7). René Clair likewise, in 1950, named *Brief Encounter* and *Paisà* to state the (polemically obvious) lesson coming from Europeans in and out of the studio: that films made, as in Hollywood, would never be either "original," meaning also "real," if made to the order of premade cinematic conventions (1972: 75).

Jean Quéval described France's acknowledgment that "the British" were making the "best films in colour." But then he named Lean's black-and-white Dickens adaptations as "unrivalled 'period' works" and *Brief Encounter*, in black and white, as exemplary given its "narrative value." He saw British and French critics divided by preferences: for the conventional *or* experimental, for the aesthetic *or* technical. "The French go by ideological fashions," he quipped, "the British decidedly do not" (1950: 198–200). Following the later release of *The Sound Barrier* (*Le Mur du son*), he described Lean as one of "the most consecrated directors" (le *mieux consacré'*) who had chosen an "exceptional subject matter" to flatter (*flattent*) "the super-technician." That the film was both made from and about supersonic effects was not lost on this critic who had already praised *Brief Encounter*'s sound innovations. In a piece titled "Néo-cinéma," he had described an absolute gain (*un gain absolu*) in the "eloquent use of stereophony" when a "sound relief" was "obtained by the arrangement of the speakers." He liked how the "emancipated" train sound produced a sense of a train passing out of sight, yet how there was somehow an exact knowingness of the train's location. He saw a soundscape liberated from mere imitation and a narrative serving the tethering of effects to the real in the new "cinema of interiority" (*cinéma d'intériorité*) (1954: 105, 17). Realism was clearly moving inside to the mind.

Critics who assessed British film from a French perspective often also pitted the French perspective against the standard bearer: the best and worst of Hollywood. Were *Brief Encounter*'s innovations of episodic cycling and foreground-background perspectivism not already there in Orson Welles's *Citizen Kane* of 1941? (Wimmer 2009: 45; Bordwell 2017: 26). Writing from New York in 1949, Kracauer saw *Brief Encounter* as "nothing to get excited about," while yet, as a *European* film, it exposed the wrongs of Hollywood. He liked how, from the "commonplace incident," it drew "a maximum of suspense." It showed without being "showy." He noted the punctuated patterns of circulating persons and trains. Titling his piece for *Penguin Film Review* after Shakespeare, "The Mirror up to Nature," he reprimanded Hollywood for disappointing audiences who wanted the realism of seeing their own lives on the screen. No one, he said, recognizes the "rush of gay parties" in George Sidney's 1947 *Cass Timberlane* or the "glamour" in William Wyler's 1942 *Mrs. Miniver*. He compared the intensification of *Brief Encounter*'s "seemingly banal affair" to *Paisà*: "You can almost touch and taste the horror, the suffering and the generosity they depict." With an *exactness* of *exaggeration*, cinema's realism was borne from improvising around the "incredible difficulties" in the war's aftermath: "Wrung from life," the films bore life's "ineffaceable stamp." He looked across the *big pond* to find the stamp of life effaced by a tumor made from Hollywood's studios of administered conventions, specialisms, codings, and formulae. He asked Hollywood to put itself on trial not as a McCarthyite attack but as a Shakespearean mirroring of conscience. If some Hollywood films were already doing this, he conceded, the number was too small (2012: 105, 223–4).

Praise for *Brief Encounter* never subsided: the "most perfect" of all films *for all time, without qualification*, or, with one qualification, the most perfect because the *most characteristic* of British film. The high praise was matched by a national and international condemnation of the film as pompous, false, sentimental, impersonal, out of date, overly stylized, too ordinary, too slight—overall, in every sense, "a sorry affair." If, as Wimmer tells, intellectuals in Paris were throwing all the prizes at the film for its realism, ordinariness, and discretion, "provincial French spectators" were laughing with frustration at the characteristically English inability ever to get into bed! (2009: 65, 71) But then, many in England were laughing at this too—including, quietly, Coward and Lean.

How, now, did *Brief Encounter* become a test case for the capabilities of cinema as a modern art with its use particularly of *the* Rachmaninoff? When John Huntley published his *British Film Music* in 1947, Muir Mathieson wrote the foreword. Mathieson, according to John Thornley (1989), was "one of the towering figures of the British musical scene, . . . an energetic, salty-tongued Scot who arranged and conducted the music for most of the serious films of the Forties and early Fifties." John Huntley became *the* source for how *the* Rachmaninoff got into *Brief Encounter.* About the "famous concert pianist Eileen Joyce," he noted how "in the last two years," she had "become a film star of the soundtrack"—with her many on- and off-screen contributions (1947: 82). Joyce's life tells a story of the piano in cinema (Davis 2001; Tunley and Meher-Homji 2017). She played for the "docu-drama" *Battle for Music*, about the trials and tribulations of the London Philharmonic Orchestra on the eve of the Second World War (dir. Charles Latour et al. 1943). Lean told Silverman later that he'd been asked to "do" this (or a very similar) film, but that he'd opted for Coward's "naval thing" instead (SS: 43).

Joyce also played for W. Somerset Maugham's *Quartet* with four directors, made in 1948, with a score by John Greenwood. One of its stories concludes with the suicide of George, a would-be concert pianist, following a sad test of his talent. The unanimous court verdict of his death as "accidental" is rationalized by the story's almost cockney last line: as to the *business* of his music, we attach no importance to it because a *gentleman* of George's *standing would never go an' shoot himself just because he couldn't play the piano good.* More of Joyce's contributions will be mentioned in due course.

Although Huntley declared *Brief Encounter* "a very fine British film," he deemed it a "mistake" to have used "the Rachmaninoff .

. . in this particular case." Liking the concerto "too well," he found no true connection of the concerto to the film. If the film was a "feast" of wit, acting, and camerawork, why produce "indigestion" with a world-famous concerto? Either, he answered, you listen to Rachmaninoff or to Coward—but you can't do both at the same time. So he went to the cinema twice: "once to see Noël Coward's film and once to listen to the Rachmaninoff concerto" (1947: 82). Walking and chewing gum aside, his judgment makes sense only if one listens to the music without also looking at how it comes from the radio in the living room. Listening without looking, he would have heard the concerto in its sequential order, although as meaninglessly cut. Approaching the music as a detachable "film score" made the problem explicit: whether any music, serious or popular, would distract within a film because prior and independently known. But then, if too well adapted or cut for the film, wouldn't the original be corrupted? Mathieson, to recall, had urged Coward not to use the Rachmaninoff, but if he used it, then to use it with integrity. Even better, he thought, would be to compose original music *for* the film.

William Whitebait praised "the talkies" for their adaptations of literary works while finding "no corresponding development of the soundtrack." René Clair's *Sous toits de Paris* (1930) was his lone exception. In *Brief Encounter*, he appreciated the "weaving in and out" of the Rachmaninoff less for its contribution as music than for the link it forged to Tolstoy's *The Kreutzer Sonata* (1946: 100). The thought here was of how British and Russian films together were resisting a market pressure originating in America to produce meaningless *quota quickies*. Across the Atlantic, when Horkheimer and Adorno felt the "hot air" or "windy excuses" blowing around Hollywood, it was because adaptations of a "Beethoven symphony" or a "Tolstoy novel" were "touching" audiences regardless of their (social) needs ([1944] 1981: 130; 2002: 96). These were adaptations made to be full of effects, as the idiom puts it, without due cause.

Addressing adaptations of Shakespeare to film, Charles Livermore Hurtgen reiterated the general anxiety: "if Music draws attention to itself, it will, as pictures that do so, distract a spectator from the words" (1962: 82). Yet, to repeat, wasn't the new problem of film music already the oldest problem in the books, hence less a problem than a productive tension? Music had always been set to words, pictures, and vice versa in singular and multiple media works of art. Hadn't the Beethoven paradigm already set up the modern anxieties when a purely instrumental musical work was promoted precisely to stand above any and all instrumental or occasional use? (Goehr [1992] 2007). Wasn't the "problem" for film music reemerging with a little of the farce of a *second-time-around* repetition of history? If *Brief Encounter* was to solve "the problem," why not take Coward seriously and bring Rachmaninoff into the film as a piece of its furniture? This way, no one would think to listen without also looking. It is striking how few critics ever got Coward's point, so that endless misconstrued complaints about the misuse of the concerto could rain down over the film's reception.

Most press announcements for the upcoming attraction noted the Rachmaninoff as a "background music" offered by "Eileen Joyce and the National Symphony Orchestra" (Figure 11). Almost no early review mentions that the concerto was broadcast on the radio, allowing the diminishing sense of its being merely a background music to stick. Between 1946 and 1948, reviewers praised the Rachmaninoff variously and often simply because "it recalls the film." An announcement in the *Los Angeles Times* said that the Rachmaninoff would be used for a picture and that the "late composer" had written it "with no bows in the direction of Tin-Pan Alley" (September 29, 1946). In *Popular Photography*,

Figure 11 Detroit Free Press announcement for *Brief Encounter*, directed by David Lean (Eagle-Lion Distributors/Cineguild, 1945).

it was mentioned as providing "stirring theme music" (April 1948: 128). From *Theatre Arts*, we read: "Prestige Pictures has chosen an auspicious time for the arrival of Noël Coward's *Brief Encounter*. [The concerto] rumbles in the background providing a remarkably fecund accompaniment to a full range of human emotions" (1946, v.30: 604). From *Music Clubs Magazine*, we get: the "entire score consisted of the second Piano Concerto" (1946, v.28: 11). In *Commonweal*, Lean was highly praised (a rarity when Coward was still receiving most of the credit), but the Rachmaninoff was misidentified: Lean's "direction is exceedingly skillful throughout the picture . . . (mainly Rachmaninoff's Concerto No. 3 [*sic*] . . .) is excellent" (1946, v.44: 527).

Another misidentification comes later in an otherwise interesting chapter on the new audience for film. John Ellis compares *Brief Encounter* with the satirical musical revue (with an anti-Nazi pastiche) *Radio Parade* of 1935 (dir. Arthur B. Woods, 1934/5) after *Radio Parade* (dir. Archie de Baer, 1933). He describes Lean's film as "an almost hysterical attempt to control its meanings, from the heavy use of Rachmaninov's Piano Concerto No. 1 [*sic*] (101), through the burlesque of the main theme . . . which enables a double closure of the narrative." He then selects *Brief Encounter* as a "limit-case" for cinema's "performance habits," based on the construction of a self-contained text with a demand then for its negotiation with an audience. He sees the filmmaker's control impacting a better class of audience made to sit in concentration before a movie screen (2000: 95–109). His argument about "film exhibition" recalls how concert hall audiences once sat in accord with the work-concept according to the Beethoven paradigm. But what of the less "better" or different "class" of "patron"? Consider all the early freedoms to smoke, talk, eat, or make out in the dark, or, as in *Brief Encounter*, to run out before the film's end. Wasn't cinema remolding all sorts of audiences? And what then happened when cinema, like music, became a furniture-art for the living room, when families, as in *This Happy Breed*, sat with every mood and emotion around "the box"? In 1989, Thornley reported a composer working with Alexander Korda saying that "Korda may have got the Beethoven Symphonies a bit mixed up, but at least he knew them!"

Mixing, matching, and mashing made for a slew of films related to *Brief Encounter* in musical and other ways. *A Girl in a Million* (dir. Francis Searle, 1946, Benjamin Frankel score) has the Beethoven bust but also a staged performance of César Franck's *Symphonic Variations* with Eileen Joyce and Mathieson, where the finger flight across the keyboard matches the women's chatter in a plot about a woman who has lost her voice. The men are directed to enjoy her disability more than her cure. *Millions Like Us* (dir. Frank Launder and Sidney Gilliat, 1943) is filled with many sorts of music, from Beethoven's *Fifth* over the credits to "Colonel Bogey's March" (before Lean's *Kwai*) to inspire the "millions" to their war work. André De Toth's *The Other Love* (1947) treats the unspecified disability of a concert pianist as a contest between lovers and between ways of living. With music, from Beethoven to Liszt, its disability theme connects to the many films that chose rather to use the Rachmaninoff.

The *always* and *forever* of *Forget Me Not* (dir. Zoltan Korda 1936) stars Beniamino Gigli with music by Mischa Spoliansky and Mathieson. *Song of Freedom* (dir. J. Elder Wills 1936) has Paul Robeson playing a dockworker who, discovered by one Gabriel Donozetti, returns to Africa. *Men of Two Worlds* (dir. Thorold Dickinson, 1946, score by Arthur Bliss, with Joyce and Mathieson) is similarly about Kisenga, who, educated in London, produces a concerto, after which he returns to his preferred world of music and medicine in Tanganyika. Then there is *The Glass Mountain* (dir. Henry Cass, 1949) about which Huckvale remarks maybe too quickly that while it shares the train and much else with *Brief Encounter*, "[a]dmittedly, Nino Rota was no Rachmaninoff, and Henry Cass no David Lean" (2022: 51). And *Dangerous Moonlight* (dir. Brian Desmond Hurst, 1941) in which Richard Addinsell (also of *Blithe Spirit*) is behind the Polish pianist who, in love, composes his Warsaw Concerto Rachmaninoff-style while bombs fall all around, after which he flees to England to serve. One more example is a Hollywood film noir, Joseph L. Mankiewicz's 1949 *House of Strangers* (score by Daniele Amfitheatrof), about a son who recounts, by use of his father's gramophone and love of Italian opera, how his once poor and honest family from Palermo was destroyed by the *everything new* branding of what it meant to be rich in America.

Robert Murphy described *The Common Touch* (dir. John Baxter, 1941) as "considerably more sentimental than George Orwell's explorations of the lower depths in *Down and Out in Paris and London* and *The Road to Wigan Pier* [as] people lean out of windows and listen in silent wonder to itinerant pianists playing Rachmaninoff" (1989: 20). But it's actually Tchaikovsky's First Piano Concerto that carries the honest touch of a "common" house for the homeless in London. The opening scored music by Kennedy Russell imitates Tchaikovsky before the pounding chords of the first movement are played for commoners by a down-and-out pianist, an exile from Hitler's Germany, nicknamed "Chopin" and pronounced "Choppin(g)." On perfectly sticky keys of an upright piano in the street, the pianist earns his keep while, in a dream sequence, he remembers his once great performances in the concert halls of Europe and New York. The film is calling for America to join the war.

When, in 1945, Grace Widney Mabee praised film's capability to educate new audiences about "music of these great masters!," she noted the slew of films dramatizing the lives of Chopin, Clara and Robert Schumann, Tchaikovsky, Liszt, and Jerome Kern. Soon, she added, the Republic corporation will "feature the music of Rachmaninoff" (1945: 31). Egon Larsen affirmed the educational opportunity, but then, with *The Common Touch* and *Brief Encounter* in mind, expressed boredom with all the masculine stocktaking in cinematic love affairs. Must a young composer always have a "great concerto up his sleeve" or an old master-teacher always die listening to "a concerto over the radio" with the proverbial fifty-violin "accompaniment of an angelic choir" (1950: 122–4). Increasingly, accusations of a "mindless" use of serious music were met with contrary declarations, as when David Wilson in California sent a letter to *Hi Fi/Stereo Review* to pronounce "truly ridiculous" the thought that the "characteristically British attitude to Rachmaninoff" was now one of "mindless adoration." Perhaps, he added, those saying this were watching *Brief Encounter* "too often on the telly" (1966: 12).

In 1945, when James Agate reviewed *Brief Encounter*, he found a film that was not yet cinematic enough. There was too much residue of the theater and psychological novel that had once offered, in Robert

Louis Stevenson's words, a world "of the hesitating conscience." Even if he thought that, without the music, the whole "would just collapse," he balked at the "very nearly full-length performance of the Rachmaninoff" with all its "pound[ing] and dron[ing] and rattl[ing] in the background." He chided Coward for setting a "frightful example." Wouldn't *Tristan* with Thomas Beecham conducting the London Philharmonic Orchestra better have suited a film titled "Chance Meeting"? Not long after, he praised the French for their "genius for making beautiful small films" to urge the English to do likewise, but not as was done in *Brief Encounter*, where, again, the director too nervously hid "behind the skirts" of the concerto (1948: 70).

Herman G. Weinberg asked in 1959: "What is the difference between the silent era when actors emoted to music and today when most films rely so much for their emotional effects on the musical soundtrack? What would *Brief Encounter* be without [the] Rachmaninoff?" The silent *Nju* (dir. Paul Czinner, of 1924) hadn't needed such a "musical crutch" (88). *Nju–eine unverstandene Frau* had opened with captions announcing its cast and subject matter in Spanish and English: Emil Jannings *en Amante o Marido*. Set in Varsovia in 1920, it was captioned as *A drama of yesterday—tomorrow—of any and all times and places so long as there will be—love and marriage*. Straightaway, the cold English "and" of love and marriage turned to a warm Spanish "or" to encourage the wife to seek a lover.

In 1983, N. Roy Clifton repeated the lasting impression that *Brief Encounter* had been "composed as incidental" to the obviously overbearing concerto! (249). A decade later, Richard Dyer repeated the sense of a turbulence that allowed the Rachmaninoff to seize and cut Laura out as an "individual." With more insight, he saw a concerto soloist standing apart from the orchestra as comparable to a woman breaking free from a controlling cast who, in a test of fidelity, claimed to know her better than she knew herself. Dyer noted Alec's response to Laura as being *too sane and uncomplicated* when she said that she might have had *a tremendous, burning talent* for music (1993: 17, 59). How could he have known that so fast? A prior line gives us a clue: *You don't play the piano, I hope?* Alec had said, and she'd quipped back: *I was forced to as a child.*

In early criticism, Lean figured less than Coward and less than Rachmaninoff. When, however, the film became Lean's, more attention was paid to the almost equation of an already *classic* and *domesticated* classical musical work with a now *classic* British film. The more that *Brief Encounter* supplanted the original play, the more it became a Lean original to which all future film referred. The transfer happened fast, meaning that even in the first post-film adaptations of Coward's play, references were made to Lean's film and often by reference to the music, as though Lean had been responsible for that too.

Brian McFarlane 2019 study of *Brief Encounter* as a "never ending" possibility and film of influence focuses in part on the many radio adaptations following the film. Here are my own favorite examples. An adaptation from April 6, 1947, for Theater Guild on the Air, is set in Long Island. It begins on a Thursday evening with Laura (Ingrid Bergman) returning home late, pale, and tired. With the children calmed, she bursts into tears. Fred (no longer absent as in the original play) asks: *Would you like some music on the phonograph? There is a favorite of yours—it's some concerto or other*. The orchestral schmalz that follows soon becomes overblown. *Some concerto*: does it matter which one? And then there is Coward's own 1956 radio reproduction that allows a snippet of the Rachmaninoff to introduce the first conversation at the station over cups of tea. One could have heard the concerto in 1936 in Coward's play, 1936 being also the year of *The Scoundrel*, but I've found no evidence of Coward demanding already this music on his stage.

Different piano compositions by Rachmaninoff could have become *the Rachmaninoff*, given Mickey Mouse's performance of the C-sharp Minor *Prelude* in *The Opry House* of 1929 or Harpo's "Wreckmaninoff" in the Marx Brothers' *A Day at the Races* of 1937—where, by dismantling the piano, Harpo extracts a perfectly stringed harp to play in its place. More "serious" examples include a young Albert Ferber playing from the First Concerto in Hurst's 1947 *The Mark of Cain*.

Addressing Rachmaninoff's legacy in 1966, John Culshaw began with the composer's death in 1943 making no difference to his popularity for a mass audience. Yet, while so many thought Rachmaninoff's music simply "old-fashioned," Culshaw heard in it a genuine nostalgia for Russia, for Tchaikovsky, Borodin, and Mussorgsky. This was a nostalgia, he added, far preferable to *Brief Encounter*'s self-pitying nostalgia, not least because it sustained in the music an indestructible "fresh as ever" quality (328).

The genesis of Rachmaninoff's Second concerto is well documented, as following from the successful therapy of the depressed composer by the neurologist Nikolai Dahl, to whom the concerto was then dedicated. Depression stuck to Rachmaninoff when, in Alex Ross's words as quoted by Kent Puckett, the composer still in 1939 was "like a ghost wandering in a world grown alien," unable to "cast out the old way of writing . . . [to] acquire the new" (2017: 164). Ross would compare Rachmaninoff's mood with the moods of Puccini, Stravinsky, and Sibelius better to understand the full scope of modernist anxieties (2007: 174). Along similar lines, Huckvale recalls George Roy Hill's 1964 film *The World of Henry Orient*, which (unlike the Faustian struggle of Thomas Mann's Adrian Leverkühn) shows a concert pianist (an Oscar Levant) promoting a "New Music" from which then the Rachmaninoff must be rescued (2022: 60–1).

In 1943, his name was fast becoming a household staple in Britain and abroad, and the concerto a "Tabloid" concerto, in John Huntley's more generally used description of 1948 (PFR6: 94–5). Composer Miklós Rózsa described the emerging "Broadway-cum-Rachmaninoff idiom" of film-music-making, where Rachmaninoff clearly was beating out other candidate composers: Beethoven, Chopin, Wagner, Puccini. Music critic and orchestrator Lawrence Morton addressed the "antimusical forces" for which the film-composer-arranger-orchestrator stood. Writing in 1951, he saw a factory line on par with a threefold "musico-sociologico-economical" analysis that, instead of relating each part of a work to the whole, produced only shreds, as "the shredding" of the Rachmaninoff in *Brief Encounter*. So "unmusicianly" was the result, no real musician on the team, he surmised, could have been involved. He decided to "leave it to Mr. Keller to departmentalize the blame and put it where it belongs" (2010: 331).

Mr. Keller was Hans Keller, who, as an exiled Viennese critic living in England, took on the documentary and newsreels from which came the great media problem of propaganda.

> What would we say if one day the BBC announcer started delivering himself of the daily atomic news to the accompaniment of the funeral march from Beethoven's Third? We should say that the news and the muse won't go together, and that the poetic leading articles we often encounter are bad enough. If we mix up fact and fancy, we easily end up by fancying facts.

And then, with words as relevant today as in his own time:

> Newsreel music misuses the music as well as the news. Every newsreel should be an intentional document of our time, not an unintentional document of our immaturity. If we cannot face unadorned facts in a comfortable cinema seat, what hope is there that we shall face up to the outside? . . . What is wrong with civilization is its pretence of having grown up. (2006: 28)

The Rachmaninoff was used liberally in *Tunisian Victory* (dir. Frank Capra et al. 1944) as a follow-up to a military march. No screen credit was given to Rachmaninoff nor to any other composer for the film score, although, off-screen, Dmitri Tiomkin and William Alwyn are named today. The film failed, apparently, for not accommodating the escapism audiences desired, despite its being about a war far from home. Escapism is a fascinating subject in its own right (Farmer 2016: ch. 6). Ian Johnson wonders whether Lean (and presumably Coward) knew the film when making *Brief Encounter*, whereas, equally, if not more pertinently, the question is whether Coward and Lean noticed the similarity of its opening scene of construction to their own opening of *In Which We Serve*. Turning to *Brief Encounter*, Johnson condemns the "soundtrack" in worn terms: so "inflexibly lush," the music disabled Lean of any "subtlety" (2005: 80, 191).

In *The Seventh Veil* of 1945, Ann Todd plays a pianist, Francesca Cunningham, whose opening suicide attempt leads to a hypnosis therapy to produce flashbacks to her past relationships: first with an unreliable school friend who becomes a wealthy, gossipy woman, and then with a cruel and disabled "uncle," Nicholas (James Mason). Her problem lies with her hands. She can no longer play. Close-ups (I think) show Todd's and sometimes Eileen Joyce's larger hands at the keyboard. Taking care of hands is Nicholas's obsession. (Lean liked hands also.) Studying Rachmaninoff's Rhapsody (we see the score), Francesca meets Peter, an eventually successful bandleader of *swing*. Invited by Peter to the cinema, because film takes you out of yourself, she claims that she'd do better to practice. Peter scripts a love affair for them, and it works. Back home, Nicholas chides her for playing *suburban shopgirl trash*. She then scripts a proposal to Peter, which Nicholas violently destroys so that he can take her away to become a world-famous pianist. Traveling worldwide (in a mixture of fact and fiction), she performs *the* Rachmaninoff at London's Albert Hall with Mathieson and the London Symphony Orchestra. Having lost Peter, she falls for a painter. Her heart is broken again. When her hands stop playing, her analyst devises a test: to play sample records on the gramophone as a measure of the three loves. Choosing Nicholas, she chooses music (the true first love) as the victory over the monstrous beast (from *Salome*), the driving male force. Music brings down the seventh veil. Ann Todd went on to make three films with Lean: *The Passionate Friends*, *Madeleine*, and *The Sound Barrier*. She also married him.

George Sidney's *Holiday in Mexico* (1946) opens with a cartoon display of the credits (comparable to Lean's later *Hobson's Choice* and *Summer Madness*). A young woman sings to an orchestral accompaniment played as a (music-minus-one) record on the large gramophone box. She invites a pianist, José Iturbi, to play the Rachmaninoff at a party. The pianist declares it too long but says that he'll try his best. The concerto's opening chords follow with a potpourri of its parts interrupted by chatter and distracting shots. The camera juxtaposes close-ups of his fingers pressing the keys with the internal pads inside the piano pressing the strings.

The Rachmaninoff begins with the credits in Frank Borzage's *I've Always Loved You* (1946). The film opens with auditions in a room overblown by statuary and busts. A world-famous pianist with a Russian name, Leopold Goronoff, has a taste for whiskey and women. He dismisses marriage in favor of *hands* that can play Beethoven's *Appassionata* before Rachmaninoff. A stagehand at Carnegie

Hall affirms the preference for Beethoven. The Rachmaninoff, nevertheless, will track the conflict between the *forever* of a woman's fidelity to her abusive master and the *always* of her consummated marriage (issuing in a daughter) to her once childhood sweetheart and now unwaveringly faithful farmhand. Named Myra Hassman, the woman reminds Huckvale of Myra Hess with her wartime concerts in London (2022: 51–3). The film credits list the composers played in the film as from *Piano Recordings by Artur Rubinstein, World's Greatest Pianist*. Debussy is not included, however, because when a young pianist (André Previn) tries to audition with a French music with which he feels *more in tune*, Goronoff asks instead for *Bach*. The master takes no further interest in this pianist of *pure genius*. In 2009, Previn composed an opera, *Brief Encounter*, based mostly on Coward's play. He avoided making it sound too much like the Rachmaninoff (Döhl 2013: 311–32).

In William Dieterle's *September Affair* (1950), Kurt Weill and Maxwell Anderson's "September Song" defines the affair that lasts the season: May to September. This is true even if the lovers eventually get together for *always*. The song is played in a Naples restaurant for the lovers following a background accompaniment of Donizetti's "Una furtiva lagrima." A gramophone is there for their use, and an upright piano for the playing of the popular song. The woman is a great pianist who subsequently practices the Rachmaninoff with her (female) friend and teacher in Italy in preparation for a final concert in Carnegie Hall. The "solo piano recordings" are credited to Leonard Pennario. 1950 was the year Weill died and when, as Stephen Hinton notes, "September Song" from the 1938 Broadway musical *Knickerbocker Holiday* was re-recorded to smooth over the original New Deal's "missing tooth" and "lame gait." Hinton acknowledges the influence of *Brief Encounter* but praises more Victor Young's orchestration for making it seem in *September Affair* as though Weill had cowritten the Rachmaninoff into which the song seamlessly dissolves (2012: 284). This way, the popular song becomes a classic while the classical work becomes a popular hit.

A Rachmaninoff performance proves decisive in a woman's decision to choose a faithful pianist, now her husband, over an unfaithful violinist, once her lover, in Charles Vidor's glamorous

Rhapsody (1954). The Rachmaninoff supports the opening credits before it is performed in a public concert just before the final credits tell that Claudio Arrau and Michael Rabin are playing behind different scenes. The first movement is played straight with close-ups of the pianist, who must prove that he can play without the crutch of his wife, while the wife (Elizabeth Taylor), hiding in the concert hall, is choosing between her two men. Proving his independence through music, the pianist, always faithful to her, wins her fidelity to him—as now a man.

Billy Wilder's *The Seven Year Itch* of 1955 has a pianist (Tom Ewell) demonstrating that the Rachmaninoff *never misses* when seduction is the name of the game. Most critics read Wilder as spoofing the concerto as an overused music for film. Pounding out the concerto sends the young woman (Marilyn Monroe), who appears like a blithe spirit, into an erotic frenzy of Laura-like doubt without the English restraint: *It shakes me. It quakes me! . . . I don't know where I am, or who I am, or what I'm doing! . . . Don't ever stop*. Her loss of identity approximates the imagined heights of a Wagnerian *Liebestod* mocked in every cinematic fidelity *bis zum Tod*. In 1956, François Truffaut described Wilder's "vengeful slap" as affirming Lean's film as "the least sensual and most sentimental film ever wept over—inexhaustible tears from English crocodiles for whom the 'Rachmaninoff' never loses its effect." He sensed "a kind of worn-down regret, good humor, and kindness" parodied by Wilder the more the film with its smutty title was weaponized to demystify English cinema (1978: 160).

Surprisingly few critics go to Wilder's source play of 1952, *The Seven Year Itch*, written by George Axelrod to be a *Romantic Comedy in Three Acts*. Here, Rachmaninoff is parodied with worn words explicitly borrowed from *Blithe·Spirit* and *Brief Encounter*, beginning with Richard claiming: *I'm a happily married man, for Pete's sake!* He comes over *very suave. Very Noël Coward*, to say: *Maybe we ought to have a little soft music, just for atmosphere! He goes over to phonograph, looks at record on player. . . . How about the 2nd Piano Concerto? Maybe Rachmaninoff would be overdoing it a little. This kid is probably more for old show tunes.* A bit of "Just One of Those Things" plays (by Cole Porter, 1935). *That's more like it. The old nostalgia. Never misses.* When then he sits at the piano, he leaves the lid down—to fake it. A bit of Rachmaninoff's Prelude in C# Minor is heard offstage. To the piano bench comes the girl, with her champagne glass in hand: *Oh! I was afraid you could really play. I can play that too*! And what do they play—*chopsticks*! The wit of their *Rachmaninoff Dream sequence* quickly turns the piano bench into an analyst's couch. Richard recalls his criminal *assault on a piano bench* to broach the theme of marriage. The rest is silence. Behind Axelrod's scene, I hear not only Coward but also George Bernard Shaw with his plotless playlet *The Music Cure*, written on the eve of the First World War. Parodying a scandal about wireless radio, it offers an *analysis* of a depressed man through a four-handed developing affair on a piano bench. From early analysis to a later séance, the itch of a war construed as a seven-year hiatus between periods of peace runs deep.

And finally—Feliks Mironer and Marlen Khutsiev's 1956 Soviet era *Spring on Zarechnaya Street* has a talented girl, Sasha, agreeing to help an admiring boy with his studies only if he waits while she listens to the radio broadcast she has requested of the Rachmaninoff. While she listens, he fidgets, smokes, and soon departs. Julian Graffy contrasts the youthful "inexperience and fear of emotion" of these lovers with "the genuine and mature feeling" of the lovers in *Brief Encounter* (2011: 236). Is maturity really the issue—or the fact that whereas this girl is transported forward into a musical world that might one day include her, Laura is transported only backward into her now finished affair?

Barring a wonderfully passing Rachmaninoff moment in *Zhivago*, the Rachmaninoff was not used by Lean again. Nor was it used by Carlo Ponti when he produced in 1974 a remake of *Brief Encounter* with Richard Burton as Alec and Sophia Loren renamed Anna—to make her what—more Russian? The key moment finds Alec's wife, reading at home, asking Alec *to turn that thing down . . . I can't concentrate*. Alec stands to turn the volume down. *That thing* is a record, any old record playing indiscernible guitar chords. Apparently, Lean was surprised when he heard that Ponti was remaking his film, a surprise then matched when he learned that *Great Expectations* was being made into a musical (KB: 596; McFarlane 2014: 97). The idea was inspired by the earlier success of Lionel Bart's musical *Oliver!* of 1968, but was soon dropped in favor of a conventional film, directed by Joseph Hardy, for which Maurice Jarre composed the score, while Sarah Miles (from *Ryan's Daughter*) played Estella. The critics panned the film mostly by comparison to Lean's "classic."

One more remake of *Brief Encounter* was well-titled *Staying On* (dir. Silvio Narizzano, 1980). Trevor Howard and Celia Johnson come together again to act out the last days of their marriage in the last days of England's rule of India. Little details from *Brief Encounter* are carried over: the wife's enjoyment of going to the cinema as a release from her husband's homespun *til death-do us part* fidelity. Had Laura gone to Africa with Alec, would endless lollypops have been the outcome?

Through repetition and parody, the Rachmaninoff spread into every nook and cranny of every globally distributed art, with the ghostly hands of a piano player pulling strings in every public and private space of entertainment. It became a highly successful popular song by Buddy Kaye and Ted Mossman, "Full Moon and Empty Arms" (1945), and again as Eric Carmen's hit of 1975, "All by Myself." The latter opens *Bridget Jones's Diary* (dir. Sharon Maguire, 2001). As a reduced piano version, the Rachmaninoff accompanies the closing credits for Clint Eastwood's *Hereafter* (2010). The farewells and the ending of *Brief Encounter* figure in Melvin Frank's *A Touch of Class* (1973), in David Jones's *84 Charing Cross Road* (1987), in Anthony Minghella's *Truly Madly Deeply* (1989), and then in many more films and TV series worldwide. The number of adaptations or musical quotations of the Rachmaninoff approximates the number of films that note or quote *Brief Encounter* in passing.

In 1947, E. Arnot Robertson named *Brief Encounter* a glorious exception to films demanding that women be cute while also aproned in the kitchen. (One Coward line has Fred telling Laura: *Hurry up with all this beautifying. I want my dinner.*) The "most moving film ever made," Arnot Robertson declared. She turned then to the "lampshade lady," Dolly, who, blinded by her endless chatter, wastes the "precious time" of the parting lovers. With the Dickensian wit of *household words*, she warned audiences not to waste the time of others with a private and domesticated home furnishing. A marvelous "Brief Encounter" parody by Victoria Wood (ca. 2007) twists the same thread when Laura, finally rejecting Alec at the station, and then men in general, runs off with Dolly.

For *This Happy Breed*, Coward drew from Shakespeare's "moat defensive to a house," the body of water protecting "this England." The England of Richard II prepared the England of Richard III so that, in *Brief Encounter*, when Fred recites the king's utterance in his crossword, *My kingdom for a horse*, he can add: *Well, I wish to goodness he hadn't, cause it spoils everything*.

Spoiling everything for England impacted Lean's detailed assessment, written in 1947, of *Brief Encounter*'s reception (PFR4: 27–35). Tracking box office sales and fan letters, he described the pressure of a film industry dominated by the US market: the dominating profit motive in an industry advertising "a liberal diet of saccharin and silver linings" for a Hollywood escapism played by those "fifty violins and a heavenly choir." He quoted reviews that stressed the emerging rivalry between America's glamor and Britain's "next door neighbour" realism with its English austerity. But he was not going to be defeated. He noted how Hollywood's "big-gun" directors were becoming envious of the British films sweeping America "by storm." Had, he asked, British film not recently achieved its independence?—knowing full well his answer. Pre-war, the distributor was in charge of most things, but, with *In Which We Serve*, the situation changed. The filmmaker, and he named Coward, assumed "complete control over story, casting, and production." With authority came a "freedom" rivaled worldwide.

> Let the facts speak for themselves. . . . We of Independent Pictures can make any subject we wish. . . . We can cast whatever actors we choose, and we have no interference at all in the way the film is made. No one sees the films until they are finished, and no cuts are made without the consent of the Director or Producer. . . . Such is the enviable position of British filmmakers today, and such are the conditions which have at last given our films a style and nationality of their own. (ibid.35)

Poor Hollywood—so constantly attacked—but without it, impossible! This and the previous chapter have shown *brief encounter* becoming a generic description for affairs lasting a season and *the Rachmaninoff* becoming a stock concerto for anyone making choices of love, life, and art. All this happened, as we will see ever more urgently, in a postwar context of a nationalized filmmaking that was still pitting a cinema at home against imports of the foreign. Export was a different matter, though equally urgent, not least when filmmakers, like Lean, seemed to export themselves and their entire teams abroad.

In their shared films, Coward and Lean made a filmic furniture-art with instructions that music, dialed up and down to its most extreme extensions, should be as much seen as heard. Seeing music put the taste for music, classical and popular, on trial, especially when the sight was of a music box on a sideboard or, as later, a bust on a mantelpiece. With all the wit, the films safeguarded happy and efficient families in a world shipwrecked by war. The next chapter investigates Lean's place in building a cinema of literary and musical heritage and adaptation in a cutting room more now of his own.

Chapter 5

Of Craft and Craftiness

Great Expectations (1946), *Oliver Twist* (1948), *Hobson's Choice* (1954)

"No wonder British films are so good these days. Look at the screenwriters they've got: William Shakespeare and Charles Dickens." So Guy Morgan quoted from an anonymous critic writing in an American newspaper. The year was 1948.

Chapter 5 begins with Lean's two Dickens adaptations: *Great Expectations* and *Oliver Twist*. The films are read for their complex soundscapes, for their themes of home, identity, and belonging, and for a raw politics bearing on anti-Semitism. Twists of great expectations sustain the overall method of analysis, while specific difficulties arise regarding the employment in Britain of foreign composers or the introduction of Jewish figures into films made in the shadow of the Second World War. Mastering a craft and making a home are juxtaposed with the craftiness of hand and step, of suspect reasons, justifications, and opinions. We see this then further in the comic-tragedy *Hobson's Choice*, where the marriage of three rebellious daughters is construed as a betrayal of the Lear-like father, until the father is given no choice other than to concur with his daughters' choices. Hobson's choice was the "no choice but this one" given by the poet John Milton to a livery stable manager, Thomas Hobson.

Roger Manvell admired the revolution of sound beyond color for the expansion of a sensory consciousness, for a temporality of anticipation, and for a dynamics of attention and mood. He praised *Brief Encounter*, *Great Expectations*, *The Sound Barrier*, and *Hobson's Choice* for their striking subtlety and idiosyncrasy of sound production. He appreciated Lean's grammar of "punctuation" as far surpassing the library of stockpile clichés first compiled as a "Kinothek" for silent film by Giuseppe Becce with so characteristic an "Italian musical ingenuity." Borrowing from Maurice Joubert, Manvell found a musical grammar that neither explained nor simply added to the "visual impressions." He liked very much Joubert's subtle comparison of film music to a wallpaper that one both notices and does not notice. But few, in Manvell's view, were getting the point: if style took "time, money and imagination," then "the Russians had the time, the Americans the money, and the French the imagination."

And the British? Manvell noted the striking design of Arthur Bliss's music for William Cameron Menzies's 1936 *Things to Come*, H. G. Wells's space odyssey to places far from this world's plague and anarchy. Wells's work would inspire Lean later to make his *The Passionate Friends*, where traveling to the Swiss Alps was already a place far enough to go. Praising the art of film, Manvell remained wary of the technology. He had opened his book *Film* with a provocation: "God made the fine arts but man made the film." This was one suspect claim, while the second was his assertion that (silent) cinema, "being mute," had had "to make its appeal visually"—as though film as a visual art had arisen as a compensation for an art without sound. He then described the "cheap press, gramophone and radio" as debasing "the arts," where the debasement owed significantly to the foreign importation from America of technology and models into British film. He concluded: If British film is to prove itself a true art (on par with the great poets of the Great War), its "maturity" means evermore refusing Hollywood as its model (1944: 3, 14, 18–9, 62–3).

Arguments pro and contra film music in Britain threw their punches at the emerging entertainment industry, so often construed as a foreign import. Commitments to *being British* meant strong words against foreign sponsorship and foreign employees. In a period of exile and displacement, the quarrels of war and peace turned less on the mere fact of someone's or something being foreign per se than on the equation of the foreign with the enemy. Whereas Rachmaninoff, as a Russian (especially a Russian in exile), proved less worrisome in Britain, being German, Austrian, or Italian caused great consternation—unless, as we have already seen, the offerings could be shown either to have transcended national identity altogether or to have a national identity, say, German or Italian, distinct from what counted as, say, Nazi in Germany or Fascist in Italy. Classical music offered an exemplary case, as reports revealed the twisted reasoning that went into rescuing, say, Beethoven and Puccini from the broad sweep of Britain's own censorious policies.

We read of *official* policies prohibiting the broadcast of an enemy art but of an unofficial inclusion nonetheless. Maintaining policies as vague allowed for a wiggle space for a national audience that wanted to hear the world's "best" music—where the best, apparently, wasn't always British. The arguments were neither subtle nor always made explicit, although they were often met with the obvious reminder that associations of ethnicity or exile or emigration couldn't be read easily out of, or directly into, the notes. Such reminders had, however, to be strategically tentative, even banal, lest it be thought that no music thereby had national characteristics—and if not music, then maybe not film. What, then, of producing a national cinema? Surely a composer born abroad could compose in the *style* of the English, just as so many composers *born and bred* in Britain composed after Beethoven, Wagner, or Brahms. Here, one unofficial policy for the BBC allowed that if British composers composed symphonies as good as Beethoven's or operas on par with Puccini's, then and only then would censoring Beethoven or Puccini in favor of the British equal be justified (Gough-Yates 1991; Bergfelder and Cargnelli 2008).

Lean's two Dickens films may be approached via two war and postwar prongs of anti-Semitism: the more obvious negative display of a Jewish figure in *Oliver Twist*, the second of Lean's Dickens films, and the less obvious assumption about *Great Expectations*: that, as a British film, it would be tainted were its score composed by a German-born Jew. In a "musico-sociologico-economical" blur:

being a Jew and being German got all mixed up with a musical modernism associated with degeneracy and/or dissonance. With a less heavy hand, some simply declared a certain development of "modern" music as out of sync with the best developments of music in Britain. Nor should we forget that the Dickens films were obviously much more than their music or their engagement with Judaism.

Read as a *classic* of British cinema, *Great Expectations* raised the matter of adaptation. Lean had seen and liked a theater adaptation staged in 1939 in the Rudolf Steiner Hall. There had also been several radio versions (Hammond 2015: 85, 103f., 117). Lean's film was nominated and won several prizes. "For some time now I've been troubled by an uncomfortable urge to overpraise British films," admitted Richard Winnington in 1947:

> I ask you to note a definite break from discreet miniature and delicate water-color into full canvas. I ask you to pay attention to the first *big* British film to have been made, a film that confidently sweeps our cloistered virtues into the open. The film is *Great Expectations*. . . . It is a landmark in the history of British films: not only because it is taken from the most shapely, mature, and filmable of all Dickens' novels, not because it has the best photography I've seen for years or because the casting is nearly perfect or because of its knife edge cutting or its furious pace, but because it casts a complete spell derived from some inner power.

Winnington named Lean as supplying the inner power: "Some time ago I wrote to the effect that when this outfit should break away from Noël Coward, we should recognise in David Lean Britain's leading film director. I was right" (PFR2: 16–17). However, not everything learned from Coward was erased: not least a wit that was once also Dickens's wit.

The film contributed to the cinematic *Bildungsroman* with its subject matter of inheritance: birthright, parenting, childhood, marriage, and the education of a young woman, Estella (Jean Simmons/Valerie Hobson), to reject the attentions of a young man,

Pip (Anthony Wager/John Mills), who attends to her with undying fidelity. *Forever stilled*, because jilted by her fiancé, Miss Havisham (Martita Hunt) twists her relationship with her adopted ward through mirrors that play to class divisions and social mobility. Unbeknownst to her until the end, Estella is the daughter of Magwitch (Finlay Currie), a common criminal who, with great kindness, guides Pip's life—beginning, however, with a brief and most fearful encounter. Against a background of crime, prejudice, and expectation, the film drives toward the union of a young couple of shared common origins.

Nearly everyone reports on *Great Expectations* as opening with an ominous orchestration of nature's sounds: stormy winds and creaking trees. There are lots of creaking sounds in Lean's films. The natural objects, almost with human faces, anticipate a rising danger for an orphaned child. Without music or sound, nature's silence becomes deafening in monochrome and as metaphor. Yet, the film actually opens prior, with a musical score accompanying the credits, after which, with the music fading, a man with a young and rather upper-crust British accent (despite his common origin) reads from Dickens's novel, of which Chapter 1, page 1 is shown as not quite legible. The page becomes a visual credit to Dickens and an explicit acknowledgment of the film as an adaptation. The voice-over names the boy as Pip, this being the only name that the boy can work out as right for him. *My father's family name being Pirrip . . . I called myself Pip*. The pages flip forward to show the young boy running over a coastal landscape, past ominous poles (of punishment?), toward the graveyard where his parents are buried in a shared grave. As the natural sounds intensify to a point of terror, Pip is grabbed by an escaped convict in chains.

Naming is a driving motif. Given the opportunity to become a gentleman, Pip is told that he must never ask for his benefactor's identity or change his name. To become a gentleman is to learn to manage one's affairs of finance and passion, but it is also to accept one's identity as inextricable from one's social origin or birthright. The last scene inscribes the words of the film's title over the image of Pip and Estella running away from a repressive house, Satis House, that was never a home. A large For Sale sign hangs on the wall—a prior life and history without warmth put up for sale.

A psychoanalytic reading stresses the continuities and discontinuities of sound, music, voice, word, and image to capture the contradictions of drives, the wants and needs, the splits of consciousness when one's identity remains opaque as a self-knowing. The music cannot be separated from the rest. The approach also takes the analytical symptoms in Dickens's novel to assess Lean's film as an adaptation. Adaptation becomes, by association and dissociation, a *working-through* of a heritage, a trial and error of revelation and rescue. Pip is driven obsessively to rescue Estella from Miss Havisham : the more distant Estella, the greater his determination. For several commentators, *agency* emerges as the main matter—who is active and who is passive in a life where fate, mobility, and change structure what is and isn't possible. Knowing and not knowing brings Pip constantly to respond to the situations in which he finds himself. Only in the last act of bringing down the curtains and letting the light in does he show this action as the *first* taken by him. If, for all the *great* expectations, *small* expectations are promoted as more suitable for those of lower or lesser origin, what expectations suit the one who, despite his class, becomes a gentleman, a man of kindness and gentility? Errors of estimation cause Pip to take a hard look at himself in a mirror. For the *analysis*, Lean's cuts are said to correspond well to the *ellipses* in Dickens's sentences, when spaces of expression leave thoughts unspoken. In the end, gentility and class don't quite match up, to leave a reeling loom of tangled social and aesthetic mobilities (Glavin ed. 2003: 1–26; McFarlane 1992: 69; Silver 1974; Zambrano 1974).

Pip's passage marks a complicated transport: journeys by foot over the rural landscape, by carriage to and from London, by boat in a rescue mission, and in the final exit from Satis House—*forever*. Then there are the homes: Pip's childhood home, at first brutal then loving; Miss Havisham's house that, stilled in time, cannot become a home for living or loving. On first entering the home, Pip notices the stilled clock. Before *Ryan's Daughter*, the dust on the aged furniture is waiting to combust—into a terrible fire. Pip and Pocket (Alec Guinness) also make a home, with a piano, for would-be gentlemen of *great expectations*. Molière-style, Pip learns from a violin teacher to dance as a bourgeois gentleman with a chair (Figure 12). One might seek hints here of Handel's "harmonious

Figure 12 Dance lesson for a gentleman, *Great Expectations*, directed by David Lean, Cineguild, 1946.

blacksmith" music, given Pocket's desire to rename Pip "Handel" (in the novel) when feeling the gentle beat of the blacksmith who first gave Pip a home. Having arrived in London, with St Paul's Cathedral so often looming in the background of Lean's films, Pip finds a city of dreams and of crime. A public trial is staged while a private trial is existentially presented for lives overseen by a lawyer, Mr. Jaggers, who, weighing the social and moral coins and costs, protects the central characters in their known and concealed family relations.

Regarded, by some, as the first of Lean's really postwar films, *Great Expectations* still ends, for others, with a wartime image of rubble. The rubble recalls Lant's "blackout" analysis of London during the Blitz when curtains were tightly drawn. The light that comes with Pip's ripping the curtains down suggests a new cinema emerging, but not one that resolves the tension between a peace or harmony achieved at home and a continuation of the fear of invasion by dissonant forces from abroad. Shadowing the Reign of Terror in France, and anticipating what Lean will show in *Zhivago*, we see a public execution entirely through the shocked eyes of Pip, as he looks through a window from above. While Lean acknowledged the influence of techniques from "foreign" filmmakers and theorists, he did not easily, or without trouble from his team or backers, embrace the *new waves* or *modernist keys* that were being claimed in Britain most to jeopardize the national identity of its cultural products.

A film about naming and identity brings pathos to the controversy over who composed the music for *Great Expectations*. The musical score was credited on screen to Walter Goehr. Today, two other names are noted, Kenneth Pakeman and G. Linley, mostly without investigation and sometimes silently to sideline Goehr's contribution. There is an oddity, however: G. Linley, if it was George Linley, was a composer and songwriter of the nineteenth century (1797–1865). I have found no other Linley on record. Perhaps Kenneth Pakeman (1911–65) borrowed from Linley. Dickens would use a line from a Linley song, though not in *Great Expectations*.

The naming and the name of the composer received, from the start, rather more comment than the music produced. The music is conventionally leitmotivic, with dissonant moments for expressions of fear and disappointment and melodic moments of happiness and hope. There is a lot of music in the film, but little that is separable from the broader sound and landscape. Anticipating *Hobson's Choice*, there is an almost comic nightmare sequence of sounds where animals assume cartoon voices to accuse Pip of what will turn out to be the most generous act of theft he ever committed: of food and tools to aid a convict. A music of expectation and danger accompanies the many arrivals and departures of Pip, as when he first enters Satis House or when Magwitch is taken from a boat of escape to prison. But no music is used for the trial scene when Magwitch, sitting incapacitated, receives his death sentence in a long row of *common* criminals.

Why did the music give Lean trouble? If Lean was as hands-on as he claimed always to be, wasn't he working closely with Goehr? Manvell noted Lean's direction, for "forty seconds here, a minute and ten seconds there, and so on, measured with a stop watch against script and screen. Bring it up here; take it out there; hold it behind the dialogue!" Manvell stressed the "intricate affair of coordination" between all the team members (1955: 65). Why did this collaboration prove so fraught? How much did the problem have to do with Lean? I think it had more to do with the Lean team.

Muir Mathieson wrote in 1947: "We must ensure that every British film sound-track is an ambassador of the great revival of interest in the musical compositions of this century, which are to-day beginning to have their effect upon the music of the world" (PFR4: 46). Recalling Arnold Bax and Malcolm Arnold's contributions to Lean's films, Ronald Neame, a long-time Lean collaborator, recalled Mathieson's old-fashioned alarm clock as opposed to the "click track" approach that replaced a rigid "exact timing" with a better sense of the musical flow. And he continued: "As a matter of principle, he refused to conduct unless a British composer had written the score. . . . Many of us feel Muir was overlooked and should have been knighted as a champion of British music" (2003: 113).

Conductor and overseer of British film music, Mathieson was apparently resentful of Goehr's rising reputation: "Goehr's arrangements," we read elsewhere, have "become a by-word in the light music world." The confused case against Goehr usually begins by recording Lean's bitter disappointment with the score. Lean had no qualms working with recent arrivals in England. The film industry was full of the foreign-born, of emigres and exiles. Kevin Gough-Yates listed the countless "foreign-born" designers, screenwriters, photographers, composers, and so on. We know that Lean employed those being blacklisted on political grounds postwar, even if screen credit was sometimes omitted. Even Lean had to prove his credentials in matters of membership and unionization of this or that group (Gough-Yates 1991: v, 116f., 198, 257).

Gough-Yates noted a "Secret memorandum from the Ministry of Information to the BBC entitled 'Fifth Column Tricks'," where Goehr was described as a person of suspicion, after which it was noted (with a misspelling): "Gore and his compositions are obviously not essential (for I can name at least two arrangers who are probably quite as good as he, and happen to be British—and out of work)." Defenders stepped forward: Goehr was already "naturalized" British; he was a political exile "first and foremost" before being a "racial exile." Not all, however, were persuaded that the naturalization of citizenship translated into a natural British style. Sometimes with sarcasm, defenders asked that Goehr's name be spelled correctly and that his identity be sorted out, given that he was also working under a protective, non-German-sounding pseudonym, George Walter.

Gough-Yates detailed the case to highlight a "characteristic BBC muddle": The war situation intensified the muddle between having to exclude foreign intrusions, wanting to exclude them, and working out how secretly to subvert public censorship. Gough-Yates thought xenophobia less the problem than a musical conservatism rationalized ideologically by hortative judgment. Being less of a problem didn't, however, make xenophobia not a problem. Gough-Yates focused on the intentionally vague space emerging for situations to be gotten around, as when ad hoc or temporary contracts sidelined official policies prohibiting permanent employment. The Goehr case also got involved in the muddled matter of "English broadcast music" from another prong: when he was more criticized than congratulated for eroding "the traditional division between popular and concert music." Again, a slew of opinions expressed official and private anxieties: "We British should be grateful that so many non-British compositions are poured into our ears, but somehow we are not amused." Or: since "Walter Goehr is paid by British money subscribed by British listeners, it would be an act of courtesy if he featured more British works." Or: "We have saved the English film industry from American competition only to surrender it to a far more alien control" (Gough-Yates 1991: xiii; 264–5; 259; Mackay 2000; 2000a; 2006; 2006a; Goody 2018; Hajkowski 2002).

A scholar today of William Alwyn, Adrian Wright writes: "Alwyn's way with drama and sentiment would have come up trumps with Dickens, but this was another category that was denied him, as other composers won the day: Walter Goehr, an unfortunate choice for David Lean's *Great Expectations* (1946), because Lean couldn't stand the man or his score" (2008: 134–5). Gene Phillips adds more:

> Since Noël Coward was no longer around to take charge of the musical score, Lean obtained the services of the German composer Walter Goehr. . . . Goehr was used to symphonic scoring especially for pictures like the Douglas Fairbanks Jr.

adventure film *The Amateur Gentleman* [dir. Thornton Freeland, 1936] and Lean thought this the right kind of music for *Great Expectations*. Nevertheless, he ultimately found Goehr's score too heavy and turgid.

Because, as the story continues, it was too late to have the score entirely recomposed, Lean hired *Pakeman and Linley* "to modify some of the more fulsome passages." When the question of credit then arose, "their work was uncredited . . . since Goehr was very protective of his screen credit as sole author of the score" (2006: 107–8). Little is documented regarding the reworking of the score, though some suggest that there were major revisions. It is hard to know what's what, but little in the score feels particularly heavy or unsuited to the overall land- and soundscape.

The "corrected" credit, to include Pakeman and Linley, was mentioned already in the 1970s, but the story, repeated almost verbatim, is sourced mostly to Kevin Brownlow's phone interview with John Huntley on October 14, 1992, when Huntley, born in 1921, was recalling something that had happened a half-century earlier. (Note also the misspelling of Pakeman's name.)

> Composer Walter Goehr had been recommended to David, though when he heard the music, he was bitterly disappointed. He decided the only alternative was to cut back Goehr's score—there was no time to redo everything—and make way for the work of another composer. Kenneth Paxman [*sic*] and G. Linley were also credited alongside Goehr. Goehr was a pet hate of Muir Mathieson, the studio's resident composer and orchestrator. "Muir was very possessive," said his assistant, John Huntley, "and wanted to conduct everything himself. Goehr evidently agreed and then ratted on him and took the conducting—and the credit—out of his hands." (KB: 222–3)

Huntley's *British Film Music* included informative lists of the 1947 BBC and British broadcasts, lectures, recordings, and film uses of a "serious" music. And then a biographical index where Pakeman got a brief entry, Linley no entry, and Goehr a detailed entry. One detail, that he came to England "from Austria in 1933," is a mistake, owing perhaps to Goehr's having studied with Arnold Schoenberg. These lessons were taken in Berlin. The entry generously recorded Goehr's work for HMV and Columbia, his radio war-work, his "light" work with the Orchestre Raymonde, and his film-music in Britain and "on the Continent," including Julien Duvivier's *David Golder* (1931) (1947: 205–6). A year later, in a revised biographical index for *British Music*, Russell Palmer mentioned neither Pakeman nor Linley but added to Goehr's biography that his father was "a prosperous Berlin merchant" (he wasn't that prosperous!) who wanted "his son to enter the business!" but that, from his mother, Walter learned to read music before even a book (1948: 103–4). Even if true, it's also a cliché.

S. J. Hetherington and Mark Brownrigg repeat Huntley's story still in 2006, turning the "pet hate" to a "cordial dislike." (Both phrases are compounded by their contradictory terms!) The authors then note the anti-Semitic complaint regarding *Oliver Twist*, as though the two cases were connected. But really, they just want to congratulate *Great Expectations* as the "marginally" more "sparkling" film (118–19).

In the decisive year of 1971, Page Cook took issue with the claim that "David Lean is probably the greatest living director now that Carl Dreyer is dead." Integrity or finesse was less the issue for Cook than the striking musical "lapses of intelligence and taste" in a director of such stature. Cook ran through Lean's "finest films" to note a blandness, indecision, and repetitive ineffectuality in the scores by Richard Addinsell for *Blithe Spirit*, William Alwyn for *Madeleine*, Arnold Bax for *Oliver Twist*, and Malcolm Arnold for *The Sound Barrier, Hobson's Choice*, and *Kwai*. Even, he wrote, Alessandro Icini's (short for Cicognini) melody for *Summer Madness* "helped make that film a success, but it was repetitive, and one pleasant theme does not a good score make." He thought the Rachmaninoff didn't work either. Less targeting composers, Cook was out to get Lean mostly for a musical deafness in having allowed the "musical flotsam" of *Ryan's Daughter* to come to the screen. Cook concluded: "In my opinion George Stevens and William Wyler are much worthier of the accolade of 'greatest living director.'" Each has more "spiritual insight" than Lean. And then, adding salt to the wound, Cook deemed their uses of music not so good either. In a passing judgment of *Great Expectations*, he declared the score not "up to Goehr's standards," to suggest now that the trouble might not have been all Goehr's fault (169–70).

In 1989, with more discretion, John Thornley looked back to a "Brave New World" that had given room in British Sound Cinema both to established and less established British composers. He approved the "reconciled serialists such as Humphrey Searle and Elisabeth Lutyens" given their adaptive capability to the "celluloid." He then quoted composer Alan Rawsthorne:

> In Britain we adopt the plan . . . of employing a composer because we think his style will be suitable for the film. We would not immediately think of asking Schoenberg to write the score of a film about rural life in England. Though Schoenberg could doubtless turn out an amiable 6/8 as well as the next man, it would be an obvious waste of his personal style to ask him to do so.

Again, the provocation regarded composers who were being asked to compromise their style or standards when writing music for film.

Jan Swynnoe reiterates this point in 2022: with *Great Expectations* the "postwar literary cinema boom really got under way." This owed partly to the superiority of Dickens's novel which displayed a "much wider emotional range" than even his *Oliver Twist*. And then:

> All the more to be regretted . . . is the rather inferior score by Walter Goehr. Coming from the tradition of Schoenberg and [Hanns] Eisler, Goehr compromises both his own integrity and that of the film by adopting a harmonic language akin to Max Steiner's. Only at certain moments of dramatic action . . . does Goehr write in a style closer to his own. If he had been as convinced as Hans Keller that "twelve-note technique is congenial to cinematic treatment" he need not have produced such an inconsistent score. (177)

Not everyone condemned the music. *Commonwealth* magazine stated: Even if the camera spoke the most, the "spoken words" of Lean's *Great Expectations* were greatly assisted by the "lovely musical score" (1947: 48, 68). *The Strad* simply reported a film series in London where Goehr conducted the Orchestre Raymonde in "two quite pleasant excerpts from his music to *Great Expectations*" (1947: 58, 77). According to my *informal* family record, Estella's motif was thought up by my grandmother, Laelia Goehr, whose rather glamorous role in a jazzy piano duo in Berlin in the 1920s preceded her becoming a photographer after arriving in London in 1933. Here, Hans Keller offered a fitting observation: "There are great possibilities in the simple tune, but it isn't a simple task to write one" (2006: xix).

When, to recall from Chapter 4, Keller addressed the musicalized newsreels, he noted the risk of a double wreckage: first, that the news and its facts would become false and fake the more the dramatization, and second, that the music would prove redundant or contrary to its nature if, by remaining true to the facts, it voided itself of its expressive capability. If music's movement of emotions was to be a proper part of a film, audiences ought to be educated so as "consciously and intelligently" to appreciate its cues. Seeking cues suited Keller's micrological method of (Viennese) analysis. He illustrated with *Great Expectations* to alert audiences to moments of unification or of detachment between music, image, and plot: when, say, the "sound track waltzes" accompany Pip's learning to waltz, or when Pip takes a step into a new stage of life. Yet, when "Romanticism and Realism" were being brought together, the musical motif was "employed sparingly, and without sentimentalism," not least to give room to noises and natural sounds. Keller noted the "honour" of the film having a score by Goehr but then asked whether perhaps he was "complimenting Mr. Goehr too much." Was he thinking that Lean might have had a say in the matter? Eschewing easy parallelisms, Keller favored the collaborative making of "like effects." Sometimes, the simultaneity spelled "disaster," but not when a master's hand was at work (2006: 27, 70, 76). The question here was whose hand was the master's.

For *Detroit Free Press*, finally, Helen Bower brought out the paradox of a wallpaper or furniture music that was both to be noticed and not noticed. Goehr's music, she wrote, succeeds in having gone by almost entirely unnoticed. Her real target was again Hollywood: "Remember the old nickleodeon days when a piano-player sat in the pit and pounded out pieces more or less in the mood of the scene flickering above his head? Times haven't changed a bit. . . . Consequently I've become a kind of music critic, too; often highly critical of the intrusive sound backdrop." And on she went to protest a Hollywood that was treating its audience as not "quite bright enough" to get a film's meaning without an obvious musical aid.

> IT WOULD BE DANDY if the Hollywood boys . . . would bend an ear to "Great Expectations." I haven't gone completely Anglophile. . . . But I do think it's smart to recognize and profit by the qualities which they undeniably do excel. A musical score by Walter Goehr, about whom I know nothing but his name . . . is never obtrusive. It never prods the emotions to a desired or required reaction. In fact, I was hardly aware of the music until almost the end of the picture, when Pip is about to succumb to a breakdown. Peace, it was wonderful! (1947: 39).

Peace after War: fear and prejudice remain despite films promising a happy end. It is a thought that will soon get us to *Hobson's Choice*, but before this and before Dickens, the thought was Shakespeare's, from *King Lear*: *About it, and write "happy" when th'hast done.*

Entering Satis House, Pip finds no sunlight. The sun is tied by Dickens to sunny days, Sunday bells and Sunday suits, the natural passing of time with the sunrise and sunset, and with lives lived in the open, released from the *dark cloud*. But in the film, sunlight is given to Pip to cry out to Estella: *I have come back to let in the sunlight! . . . Look! Nothing but dust and decay. . . . [C]ome with me, out into the sunlight.* In the film, they run into the proverbial sunset. In the novel, they part as friends, with no shadow anymore between them.

Gerald Pratley attended to the film's construction of a time made and unmade by Pip's development and the stilled clock. He saw "Lean's first postwar film" as sidestepping Britain's "postwar problems": there'd been enough "drabness, tragedy, and heartache." He liked the "intelligent escapism rooted in British character, tradition and literary achievement," comparing it to "revisiting old friends, or discovering them anew." He found a moral redrawn: "good manners and high breeding do not make human beings," that elegance and independence could attach to Pip and Estella as a couple of "the lower-middle class." He praised the innovative camerawork, even "Goehr's beautiful score," and how insights were shown so often through close-ups of reflection. Pratley asked whether "truth and reality" are found only "in hindsight, in recreating past eras or times in which few people remember what it was really like, and characters and events can be shaped into greater dramatic form" (1974: 56, 66–7, 71). Had Lean made films about the future, we would ask a comparable question about foresight, to leave only the middle, the present, unaddressed.

In "Doing Time; Undoing Time," Guerric DeBona read the film's ending "as especially enlightening in the context of post-World War II cinema." He concluded: "Has restoration to stability (read: isolation) superseded social involvement? Is it any accident that . . . Satis House looks like a bombed-out remnant after the war?" Magwitch's doing time was juxtaposed with the clock's undoing of time in a room covered with dust. DeBona found the film's finest dynamic to be the parallelism of Pip's voice-overs with the "moving 'I'/eye of the camera," so as to invest an autobiographical agency in Pip. He recalled Eisenstein on cutting: how monochrome and shaded contraries emerged of virtue and vice, kindness and cruelty. Stressing the tempo of the times, he noted the upheavals and tensions that seek moments of resolution, a way of restoring meaning and order to a seemingly chaotic or meaningless world: when Biddy replaces Mrs. Jo, and when Pip as Prince Charming awakes his Sleeping Beauty so "that the kingdom and civilization can pick up the pieces and start over again." He remarked on the postwar restoration in a victory that drove the film, however, "somewhat regretfully" into a "homeostasis," affirmed yet more "by the final tonic, harmonic resolutions of Walter Goehr's score" (1992: 85).

"Shading" was Eisenstein's favored term. As later for Lean, it captured a musicality wherein accidental grace notes shadowed the main notes to create nuances of sound, mood, attitude, and emotion. From the moving "I" emerged contrasts of a landscape close and far, a time moving and stilled, a place familiarized and displaced. Eisenstein had stressed the "affective" tempi in D. W. Griffith's Dickensian movement of key details that were carried less by the "mechanical alternation of cross-cuts" or "interweaving of antagonistic themes" than by the "organic pulse." Out of a collection of "points" on the screen emerged the modern *convergence* of a new philosophy with the new method of montage. For in film, Eisenstein wrote, every part works according to the "same great *law of unity and diversity*—lying at the base of thinking . . . our philosophy," where everything, from the "tiniest link" on, "passes into *a unity of the whole screen image*" ([1944] 1949: 195–255 passim).

In a BBC radio talk of 1947, "A Director's Approach to Film Making," Catherine de la Roche (having translated Eisenstein) expressed her aim not to fit Lean's films too neatly into "the new British school of cinema." First, because one wanted to avoid a dogmatism of method and expectation, and second, because Lean's art of integrating cuts "into a balanced whole" was "one of the great secrets" of his "movie making." Lean's cutting was moving toward "the real stuff of cinema": no "excessive dialogue" and no plodding "through every stage of a story in a kind of literary fashion." She praised Lean's non-patronizing style toward the representations of class and the craft that brought truth and reality to the audience's sense of a lived experience. Praising the "classic" *Brief Encounter*, she claimed *Great Expectations* a "greater triumph still." She saw the latter reversing the former's movement of form, where the "enlargement" of the latter came from the scrutiny of the "microscope," through close-ups that allowed each shot to record "the detail of human behaviour." *Brief Encounter* had magnified our "view of the drama," she wrote, not "the drama itself." To "compensate for the enlargement," everything had been "conveyed indirectly, by suggestion." And this had meant "mobilising all the cinema's component arts and making them play, not in unison, or even in harmony, but symphonically: through the rhythms and counter-rhythms built up from [the] tempo of action and tempo of cutting, from pictorial composition, music, and words."

In *Great Expectations*, contrarily, the movement was a "condensation": big to small. The rhythm in Pip's journey by stagecoach was "a dynamic sequence of short close-ups," carrying him "towards his new life in a spirit of tremendous elation." In London, the shots then lengthen, "the tempo eases, but the music keeps up the undercurrent of excitement." The effect was of a graphic continuity and vibrant mobility. She liked the almost magical realism in the portrayal of childhood that hadn't yet become glamorous or sentimental, and the camerawork of stronger and weaker lenses that fostered and dismantled deceptions: how Satis House, at first so vast and imposing, came to look merely old-fashioned and decayed. Between the "fairytale quality" of *Great Expectations* and the "unrelenting realism" that she would later find in *Oliver Twist* was a harmony, a poetic clarification, a compassion and rectification of social injustice: in sum, she said, a truth to Dickens.

De la Roche finally recalled that Lean had considered updating Dickens to modern dress to expose recent abuses of schoolchildren, after which he changed his mind to prevent confusing the social messages with present events and anxieties. But had he not then risked reducing the "moral purpose" only to minor (and past) incidents? She concluded with a confidence in the still young filmmaker who, being his "own most severe critic," knew the pros and cons of giving a film a too contemporary resonance.

If *Great Expectations* was well-received, *Oliver Twist*, before *Ryan's Daughter*, was broadly condemned. Made in 1948, it had its US release only in 1951. Audiences rioted in many countries, enraged by the insensitivity of offering so *familiar* an anti-Semitic portrayal of Fagin (Alec Guinness). Here, one could follow the commentators who compare the reception of Lean's film to that of Griffith's 1915 *The Birth of a Nation* or Roman Polanski's *Oliver Twist* from 2005 to consider the *all publicity is good publicity* slogan or whether controversy guarantees a box office success. Or whether, by assessing a film according to the necessary immediacy of public opinion, one loses sight of what makes the film worthy of critical attention. Or the equally thorny issue, whether we feel the offense today as it was felt in 1948.

Introducing his *British Cinema* anthology, Robert Murphy writes: "A disastrous trade dispute which led to an embargo of Hollywood films coming into Britain between August 1947 and March 1948, exacerbated the hostility of American exhibitors to British films." He then notes how the "well-orchestrated Zionist campaign against British reluctance to surrender Palestine as a Jewish homeland found a particular focus in the supposed anti-Semitism" of Lean's film (1948) (2013) (1: 4). Note the word "supposed." The outrage in the United States outdid that in Britain, Germany, and elsewhere—to a degree. Some declared the entire matter an American "tempest" in an English "teapot" (Phillips 2006: 62). Assessing the boycotts and protests through an American lens turned the defense inside Britain into a defense again of British Film against the dominating hand of the United States. To counteract feelings of offense, defenders retreated into the "art": the techniques and thematic lines, the film-noir and expressionist shadows and shadings of fear in black and white, and all the creaking of posts as warning signs of a world of crime. Overlooking the mastery of the art and craft was causing its own raw feelings on the part of the Lean team who so much wanted the cinema of Dickensian realism to be separated from the overwhelming flood of recent newsreel propaganda.

Following *Great Expectations*, the opening credits of *Oliver Twist* with musical accompaniment dissolve into an extraordinary landscape of sounds. A pregnant woman runs through a storm at night to arrive at a workhouse where she, evidently unwed, gives birth to a boy, who, then orphaned by her death, innocently pursues his identity—while everyone else pursues his identity to serve their own interests. One benevolent father figure, Mr. Brownlow, emerges to rescue the young boy who, born (like Lean's Pip) with a polished accent, stands out from all the "commoners." Oliver's surname, given to him at the workhouse, becomes marked by the first sight of him, as a child of nine years old. Scrubbing a floor, he is made to *twist* his body to come face-to-face with his less-than-kind benefactors. The film often twists bodies: first to perfect a crime, then to release the good from the bad.

Loyalty and betrayal play out through a tapestry again of thick relations that hold fast without their being fully known. Oliver must live in a corrupt workhouse of hard child labor, in an undertaker's home with equally cruel conditions (following his famous request in the workhouse for more food), and then in Fagin's den of young thieves, until, finally, he is brought to Brownlow's wealthy home: his true place of belonging under sunny skies. In each place, Oliver finds some protection from those of kind heart: from Fagin, from the "artful dodger" (Anthony Newley), and from Nancy (Kay Walsh), who, "betraying" her "family," is eventually murdered by her partner, Bill Sikes (Robert Newton). One moment of comedy has two women sharing snuff from a box shaped as a coffin. With less comedy, rough women have a rough time. When it is said that *the law supposes that your wife acts under your direction*, the law is declared an *ass*, an *idiot*. In Dickens's original, the unequal law that treated women and the poor badly was encapsulated by the idea of the law being and wanting to remain a *bachelor*.

On its release, some argued for the film's total prohibition and others for red-pen deletions of the offending scenes. Lean apparently responded that his Quaker upbringing prevented his thinking in anti-Jewish terms and that he was only representing a Jewish villain in accordance with Dickens's original description. Sandra Lean later recalled how Alec Guinness had made his Fagin be neither a "loveable semitic rascal" nor a "victim of anti-Semitic prejudice" (2001: 124). Before the release, Joseph Green of Hollywood's Production Code Administration sent a threat from across the Atlantic: "We assume, of course, that you will bear in mind the advisability of omitting from the portrayal of Fagin any elements or inference that would be offensive to any specific racial group or religion. Otherwise, of course, your picture might meet with very definite audience resistance in this country" (KB: 233). Ronald Neame, speaking for the Lean team, dismissed the subsequent public outrage in the United States as "ridiculous," and added: "Dickens created these two villains the intelligent, shrewd, witty Jewish Fagin, and the blustering bully, gentile Bill Sikes. We should have been accused of being anti-gentile as well!" (2003: 113) Pauline Kael flippantly added "gay activists" to the groups finding fault. Yet, even she, while attributing the cruelty to Lean's "fidelity" to Dickens, still balked at the "minutes of offending closeups and profiles" of Fagin's face (1982: 427).

A far less crass assessment of the proposed "cuts" came when Lean, with his team, determined that by removing the characteristics blamed for the offense, the comic ambiguity between kindness and cruelty would unlikely come to the surface. Far from assuaging offense, Fagin's censorious reduction to a one-dimensional figure would likely cause more offense, not less. But critics, dubious from the start, remain variously dubious today: Is not ambivalence really a duplicity of those who get away with abuse through acts of (apparent) kindness? (Silver and Ursini [1974] 1991, ch. 3; Mckee 2000; Paganoni 2010; MW: 53–60).

Was Lean wanting to rescue Fagin from a crass or mob-like anti-Semitism, or England from the enemy within and without? Was the "Fagin" problem as isolated from the film not a problem for so many films of the period or of all time? One early poster for the film's release seemed to turn Fagin as *der Ewige Jude* into a cowboy with a broad hat and determined face. This seems even less honest than what defenders said when claiming that Lean had used not the recent Nazi anti-Semitic propaganda as his source but only George Cruikshank's famed illustrations of the novel. Or while Dickens had used the word "Jew" countless times, Lean's script had not. This placated few, especially those who could not see past Fagin's oversized crooked nose.

Robert Tanitch reported Arthur Rank saying that "if every race, profession, and sect objected to the unflattering portrait of its members, there could be no fiction at all" (1989: 54). Some thought Fagin's portrayal so obvious or familiar that boredom more than offense was the right response. Others noted how the cruel underworld on view far outweighed any figural characterization. For the *New York Times*, Bosley Crowther defended the film: the fact that Fagin is a Jew is "mere part and parcel of [Dickens's] whole canvas of social injustice and degradation. . . . And it is this extraordinary canvas . . . of the poverty and greed which oppressed nineteenth-century England, that has been magnificently reproduced in this film." Whereas, however, some saw in the harsh workplaces a condition still dominating the news, of hard labor in the concentration camps, others turned to the survival tactics, the artfulness of children absorbing the Dickensian cultivation of keeping one's wits about one. Juliet John (2005: 206) and Christine Geraghty (2008: 30) recall Chaplin's particular fascination, before Lean, with Dickens's depiction of children. But this is the sort of fascination, they note, that risks overly concealing horror behind laughter's slapstick or sentiment's sweet expression.

Lionel Birch's *Picture Post* review of 1948 asked, "Has Lean Done It Again?" It began and ended with high praise: "From the great lumpen mass of cinemagoers," he wrote, "a film director gets hardly any credit, and no fan-mail at all. How many people in the three-and-nine pennies can name even half-a-dozen British film directors? Can you say, off-hand, who directed *This Happy Breed* or *Blithe Spirit* or *Brief Encounter* or *Great Expectations*? The man, in each case, was David Lean." Birch liked the camerawork and cutting, the uncanny and shocking emotional moments, the set construction, and how Lean gave to the finished film his "signature, invisible but unmistakable; as unmistakable as the signature on a Cézanne painting or a Tyrone Guthrie stage production"—quite contrary, that is, to the usual "thumb-mark or hoof-mark of a distributor." With Coward, Lean had learned how to "please" the public by "pleasing" himself. "I fancy," he concluded, that, in *Oliver Twist*, "the pleasure will be very much mutual."

For Alain Silver and James Ursini, *Twist* was notable for putting the long-standing Romantic principle of the "suspension of disbelief" on trial: notably, in a court scene where the straight lines of the plot detour into differently spinning planes of Oliver's consciousness. They were reminded of Laura's transport out of her living room ([1974] 1991: 4–5; Grahame Smith 2003: 145). Spinning for the injustice, the reeling perspectivism looked back to Dickens while it looked forward from Dickens to the broken promise of a Victorianism that, in the cruelest of child workhouses, got away with declaring a *Good and Just* God to be protecting the child. The lie of the workhouse had to be erased by the truth of the promise that would come out only in a caring home founded—*forever*—on working hard, as Oliver always does regardless of the task, or on persisting in a search for truth that, here, is Oliver's true identity.

As with *Great Expectations*, *Twist* was criticized beyond the political offense for masking or erasing the reality of the crime and grime on city streets by the rescue of a single individual. How, it was asked, could the film be so blind to the collective suffering of so many after 1945? Looking back, Michael Sragow saw in the Dickens films the moment of Lean giving in "to romance" to take "a glorious plunge into surging emotions and melodramatic sweep" (1985: 21). By giving in, one may now ask, how much was Lean giving up?

For *Oliver*, Arnold Bax's score featured pianist Harriet Cohen playing to Mathieson's orchestra accompaniment. Again, there is plenty of quivering music to work through the soundscape of Oliver's fright and conventionally repeated motivic lines for the locket of identity, for fighting, thieving, betrayal, and humor, and for the happy end. Lawrence Morton chided Bax for making the score "sound as though it had been written less for the film than for an eventual performance at [the] Albert Hall" (Cooke, ed. 2010: 340). Reminded of *Brief Encounter*, Swynnoe contrarily praises the punctuation as giving an "intense emotional power" to the "painfully repressed emotions" (2002: 66f). Ronald Neame, supervising the music recording while Lean was abroad, recalled a spat. New to film music, Bax was stubborn: asked for "thirty-seven seconds of music," he offered "forty-five." With the discrepancy noted, Bax huffed: "Can't alter the music . . . You'll have to alter the film." (2003: 112). John Thornley (1989) recorded the same exchange. Bax had to be coaxed, "'inveigled, not to say bullied' into writing the music." An "apostle of the Celtic twilight (he died in Ireland)," Bax found "Dickens's urban realism repellent." Still, the result was impressive: he produced some of his "liveliest and most colourful music." Thornley then picked out the piano that brought out Oliver's loneliness and the "comic ballet" for Fagin's pickpocketing lesson, which, with its pantomime, subsequently became a "trademark" of British cinema.

On the Arnold Bax website, Graham Parlett has posted notes, of which one is the composer's response in 1949 to Percy Grainger's compliment for the *Twist* score. Bax followed his gratitude to Grainger with a complaint: "I wish I could enjoy writing music for the cinema, but in England directors seem to have little or no respect for the music[;] they just turn it on or off like the 'lights' and too many hours are wasted in writing and scoring pages which are not used." For Parlett, despite "the uncongenial nature of the subject matter"—the pictorial and caricature savagery in Dickens's novel and its lack of musical reference—Bax's score revealed moods that appeared nowhere else in his output. Yet we know from Gene Phillips that Bax reused material from his 1916 *In Memoriam* dedicated to the Irish victims of the Easter Rebellion of 1916 (the background context for *Ryan's Daughter*). And if condemned for the reuse, Bax's assumption was that surely he was "free to steal from himself" (2006: 128).

Comparing two scores, for *Hamlet* and *Oliver Twist*, respectively, by William Walton and Bax, John Huntley noted in 1949 the difficulties of analyzing films when access to viewings was limited, and hence his gratitude for the new gramophone recordings of the soundtracks that at least allowed one to assess the film's coordination of sound, music, and text. Congratulating Lean's directed visualization of the music, he detailed Lean's guiding hand, as when Lean noted (Figure 13):

> Fagin raps the table with the toasting-fork and says "To work." I should like music to accompany the whole scene of Fagin donning his hat, taking the walking-stick and walking round like an old gentleman, and finally having his foot trodden on and his pockets picked, causing him to search frantically for his lost wallet and watch, which makes Oliver laugh so much.

Huntley praised the orchestration and soundscape of the opening scenes, after which he recorded how Lean had designed "Fagin's Romp" to sustain a doubleness, as Fagin moves from being "an amusing old gentleman" to a villain. The move was an unmasking:

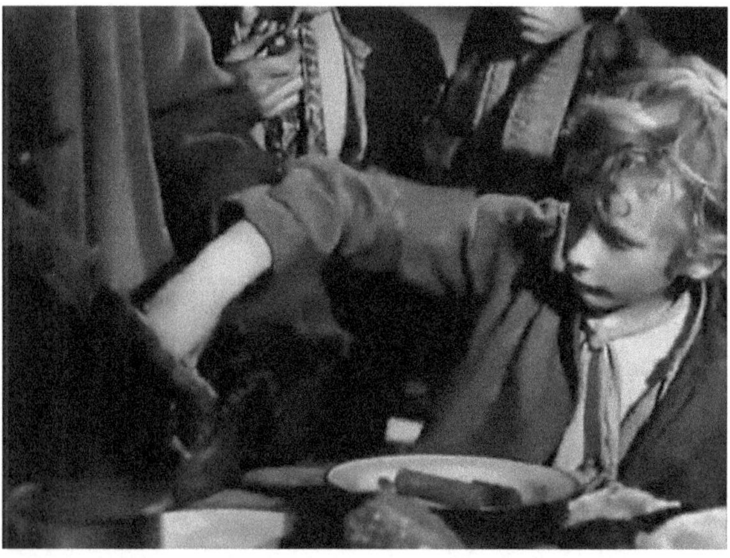

Figure 13 The right tempo for pickpocketing, *Oliver Twist*, directed by David Lean, Cineguild, 1948.

Oliver comes to sense that Fagin cannot be his true protector, because, for that, he'd have to be a true gentleman. For Huntley, Bax's music fitted perfectly, starting out with a light, sprightly rhythm to become heavier and more vulgar. The music was recorded straight through at the Denham studio, after which a "sharp roll on the side drum" was added to accommodate "the vicious effect of the kick" that Lean wanted (PFR8: 110–16).

Attending alone to the score, we might bypass a subtlety inside the film, a popular song performed in the public lodging house named *The Three Cripples*. The song "My Hat, It Has Three Corners" has its roots as a Neapolitan song, as a German song about home and suffering, but also as a song of rescue for children in the Jewish observance of Purim. A hat with three corners calls for more than a one- or even two-pronged analysis of those who, crippled by conflict, cannot walk straight.

Oliver Twist only really arrived on America's shores when *Ryan's Daughter* was made the new Lean target—in the full color of the critic's pen. Yet, as with *Ryan's Daughter*, *Twist* was not blind to the difference between mob and collective action. At the film's end, a large crowd threateningly arrives at Fagin's den, wanting to catch Fagin for taking Oliver and Sikes for Nancy's murder. Juliet John quotes Philip Collins on the murder: "(p)robably no episode in Victorian fiction has had such a stormy theatrical history" (2005: 206). But the ending matters as much. The coppers chase Sikes. Mr. Brownlow looks for Oliver. Some follow Brownlow, hoping for the financial reward he has offered. Fearing a mob, Fagin reenacts Shakespeare's cry for a once city merchant: *What right have you to butcher me*? The crowd, made from different groups, sustains a reeling of opinions or crutches, extended, then, to audiences of divided sensitivities and sympathies. A conflicted group action challenges any uniformity easily assumed or promoted for film generally conceived as a *mass art*. A reeling perspectivism forecloses any closed door on the breeding of a family where happiness is anything but uniform across the board.

From Coward, Lean learned much about the Dickensian wit of household words, the wit becoming one way to reel contrasting perspectives into his films. Catching out a conscience came not from straight mirror images. Nor with the donning of a dress, uniform, or mask indicative of a social role. Roland Barthes described the paradox that had emerged for art under the condition of a modern technology: "the more technology develops the diffusion of information (and notably of images), the more it provides the means of masking the constructed meaning under the appearance of the given meaning" (1977: 46). Emerging through a concrete history, the paradox is premised on art's technique, on its form and medium, before it becomes a truth about media: art's modern technology of distribution.

With wonderful insight, Juliet John addresses the "never-ending repetition" of Fagin images: breeding familiarity, one breeds contempt, but, much more, she says, one overly domesticates Dickens (2005: 220). Yet, a film can domesticate and be about domestication, and one needs to think through the difference. Lean's twist in Fagin's portrayal, from kindness to villainy, from craft to craftiness, was at best his refusal to reduce the character to one dimension or to a single personality trait that, in propaganda, serves a stereotype that becomes a monotype. Construed as revealing the truth of Fagin's nature, the monotype sets in. Allowing something of the kindness or suffering of a Jewish merchant to remain to the end suggests more ambiguity.

The two black-and-white Dickens films, read as in accord with a reductive or monochrome morality, were often met with black-and-white judgments. One speaks of a blanket judgment as emerging from rash generalization. Rash generalization speaks to the impetuosity and prejudice that aesthetic theorists have long argued against when demanding a careful contemplation of all that goes into a work of art or, as here, into a film. Even extreme formalists who eschew all assessment according to an external reference (to intention, biographical detail, or social situation) often do so (strategically) so as not to bring the work under an already fixed or set concept corresponding to an ideological, moral, or even aesthetic schema of conceptualization. A film, interpreted as exemplary and not as an example of a perspective already known, demands less the *tar* of the *mob's brush* than a sustained analysis of the details that bring out complexities even in the smoothest or most seamless of surfaces. (One might think here of the recent tar of the brush in Todd Field's 2022 *Tár*, with its double-trouble of fidelity to the Beethoven paradigm in the concert hall and to the loyalty demanded at home.)

Interviewed by William H. Honan for the *New York Times* in 1989, Lean staked his own claim on fidelity: "With the two Dickens films I did . . . they are, oh, pencil sketches of these great novels that he wrote, but I think they are faithful. I wouldn't have been ashamed to show him the films." Yet cinematographic details work with the reeling perspectivism of viewpoints laden with social content. Neither fidelity nor infidelity excuses a film if the claimed autonomy of its art becomes too artful a dodge of the times in which it is made.

If *Oliver* staged a tragicomic hand and footwork on slippery grounds, so, also, Lean's film of 1954: *Hobson's Choice*. It was one of several adaptations of Harold Brighouse's play that, "originally produced" in America, came to London's Apollo Theatre in 1916. Lean's film, shot in monochrome, became the best-known of the adaptations. It was much praised even as it was condemned for erasing, through its comedy, too much of the play's serious, even tragic social realism from the record.

Set in Northern England before the first Great War, though the play was written just after, the film's immediate comedy opens with Malcolm Arnold's light music for the credits, with brassy glides. We are quickly brought inside a closed shop to feel the dance and step uses of shoes, clogs, and boots (Figure 14). Together they sit in all their variations on the shelves with a Lubitsch-style anticipation for the purchases of the day. The music suggests windup mechanical music boxes, while church and shop bells define the daily rhythm. Everything Lean learned about editing, Lean would say, he learned from Merrill G. White (KB: 84; MW: 16). White had worked with Ernst Lubitsch not on the later 1940 film *The Shop Around the Corner* but on his earlier films such as *Monte Carlo* (1930) and *The Smiling Lieutenant* (1931). For Lubitsch, so much musical hall wit was connected to entering and leaving theatrically through doors. On first seeing Lean's Hobson, we see him completely drunk, entering his shop so as to effect a contrast of his collapsing onto his bed without measure, while his shoes of such perfect measure stand suddenly proud and still on the shelves.

Figure 14 A mastersinger's craft, *Hobson's Choice*, directed by David Lean, London Films & British Lion, 1954.

Something Hogarthian is seen before the camera brings us inside: a hanging boot at night with a creaking sign above the door calling up a miser past his prime, a crafty miser claiming still to be a master of his craft. Set in the 1880s, there are no modern means of transport, only striking transports of mood. Juxtapositions of insobriety (another Lean motif) show the old master (Charles Laughton) evermore inebriated while a young master, a boot-hand (John Mills), is encouraged to dream beyond his station. The musical score, produced in just days, apparently appealed to Arnold, his father having been a shoe manufacturer (KB: 307).

A music of mockery for a Sunday churchgoing morning accompanies a healthy supply of drink. Rebellious women and marriage are the worn themes for the suspect tradesmen in the Moonraker public house. Popular songs play in the background. Between shop and pub, from morning to night, Hobson belches and dances along the street with all his Lear-like troubles in British puddles of reflection. Inside Laughton's larger body is Chaplin's slender corporeal dance when ordinary things (boots or spoons) become, by use of the zither, the stuff of dreams, until the daily hangover returns with a vengeance—here, to remind Hobson that every strike of the church bell ought also to be a daughter's strike of a wedding bell. The dance and dream imagery, including a surrealist sequence of oversized buzzing bees and furry animals, affirms Milton's mockery of Hobson as the Cambridge Carrier with a choice always of a horse, "who did most truly prove, That he could never die when he could move." When Hobson dances to the moon, the coins he dreams up prove as counterfeit as the outdated principles he spouts in the pub, while, dreaming with a lighter step, the boot-hand apprentice spins his coins for a well-deserved happy end.

The film's betrayal is not an adultery but a contrived disloyalty against a Lear-like father who refuses to allow his three daughters to choose their own partners (Henderson 2019). Partnership in marriage proves inextricable from transactions of a business, this way fueling the quarrel between film as art and film as commodity. The eldest daughter, Maggie (Brenda de Banzie), reckoned by her thirty years of age to be *shelved—a proper old maid*—chooses a husband against her father's will. She picks her father's apprentice to set up a shop in rivalry to her father's. Her marriage proposal comes with an ironic romantic music. With no time for courting—*it's all glitter and no use to nobody*—passion is replaced by a steadfast commitment to a man who, in this moment, *wills* himself into a suit of dreams to sell shoes under his name. His name, being Will Mossop, suits his will and his craft that has already made his shoes the most wanted in the town. The idiom to pull oneself up by one's bootlaces is fitting, although, at first, the wit of a hanging sign warns Mossop to be *beware of the wrath to come*. In Maggie's setup, each customer will be offered a single pair of shoes: *this one, or none*. A good deal, being the only deal around, rewrites Hobson's choice as the father's no choice other than to become a sleeping partner in the firm, a family man put out like an old horse, to pasture.

A threatening trial in court follows an unintended action from Hobson's insobriety. Watching him fall from the street into a shop cellar, one feels the descent in "the looking-glass" of fantasy from *Alice in Wonderland* (prod. Walt Disney, 1951). The shop, opposite the pub, belongs to the owner who posts constant warnings against drinking. To keep the *trespass* of another person's property out of court, strong words warn against the bad publicity that comes from a trial, after which we hear: *It's a lawyer's job to squeeze a man and squeeze him where his squirming's seen most, in court*. When

Hobson, with much to squeeze, abuses the lawyer, the lawyer counters with a claim of increased costs. Their crossed words assess the damages to pocket and reputation. The out-of-court resolution is a marriage settlement for three daughters, leaving Hobson determined to fence his new family in *with the law*. Hoisted by his own petard, the proud boot hangs at the end of the film, having kicked the father where it hurts most. The shop, named for Hobson, is renamed to put Mossop's name first.

Before Hobson's daughters rebel, the shoes and boots rebel in sympathy with a domesticated wit that mocks the mastery of an industry that men believe they control. The opening chapter of J. S. Mill's *The Subjection of Women* (1869) invokes Hobson's choice to think through a suspect ethic of fit given a law that ought (or ought not) to interfere with what women are fitted by nature to do. For "they are most wanted for the things for which they are most fit." Mill described the common view that a woman's "natural vocation" is "of a wife and mother." And then the dominant complaint of the day, that, like slaves and soldiers who are "compelled" to serve, women no longer serve according to nature, but to a choice that, like Hobson's, has become a choice of "that or none." Mill's target was a fear of freedom turned into an oppressive reasoning that gave the unfree no choice other than to accept their servility as the natural order. But what happened, then, when the household furniture got rearranged?

Raymond Durgnat addressed the film's place within a feminist movement calling not yet for equal pay for equal work but for any pay for a lot of work by women already being done. (Hobson is proud to give his daughters no wages.) Maggie's victory in marriage marked the postwar labor relations wherein "affluence" triumphed over "austerity." Durgnat then found a deep flaw. He liked Hobson's dance and fall, when the universe gets its poetic revenge on the "ruthless paterfamilias." But he disliked Laughton acting so as to "humanize the old tyrant." The humanization felt untrue, as Hobson came off as "a petulant big baby." (Would one say the same of Fagin's last cry?) Durgnat thought that the Northern English air, the conditions of society and labor, were also falsely represented. More even, he saw a flaw emerging that would come to typify Lean's later portrayals of men with flawed expectations—Nicholson (in

Kwai), Zhivago, and Lawrence—for whom an "individualistic, self-destructive" idealism erased the more penetrating political and social realities. The problem assumed too many either-or distinctions hardened to erase the movement in-between: authority or independence, public or personal causes, puddle or cirrocumulus ([1970] 2011: 250).

Gene Phillips notes of Maggie and Will's wedding night how Lean subtly stopped the camera at the doorway so as not to "follow Willie inside" into the bedroom. But he finds Arnold's accompanying music for Will's nervous bodily gestures too turgidly copied by the instruments of an orchestra trying to capture something of Richard Strauss's *Symphonia domestica*. Phillips quotes from Hugo Cole's 1989 study of Arnold, how Arnold had composed a music for film very different from his "concert music" (2006: 198). But reading Cole, one finds something more telling: an appreciation of Arnold's courage to try to capture something of the spiteful comedy of Wagner's "shoemaking" act in *Die Meistersinger* (1989: 61–2). One could go far with this thought. But Arnold was already carrying his own thoughts, one being the suggestively ambiguous recollection that Lean's "advice was sound on everything except marriage" (KB: 307). Arnold would work with Lean on two more films: *The Sound Barrier* and *Kwai*.

With his own scissors, Lean's craft sustained his own identification with a young shoemaker in pursuit of the perfect fit of his product. Lean's camerawork and stagecraft were highly praised. The film won esteemed prizes, including Best British Film of 1955. England's *Picture Post* (February 27, 1954) declared that *Hobson's Choice*, like "the boots Henry Hobson made in the days of solid Victorian workmanship," is "constructed to measure"—and the measure is "Charles Laughton." Note, however, that Hobson made no solid shoes. John Mills, already highly admired as an actor, was sidelined so that the film could be congratulated for returning Laughton from Hollywood to "his proper place—as a star in British films."

Lean's film falls into a frame that we see in so many of his earlier and later films, where a dominating father is dethroned, leaving the question open as to what and who will step into his place— for a brief while or for always. The film ends as the play, with Will Mossop's surprise—*by gum*—that he owns not only his own shop but Hobson's as well. *I've done one jump in a year and if I wait a bit I'll do the other.* A chain of shoe shops becomes, like Lean's films, the promise of the future so long as one does not forget, in Maggie's words, *the truth about ourselves*—one's home, one's social origin. Happy in business, even a little in love, Maggie is glad to have pressed a single white flower from their wedding night so that the social contract will last *forever. Schooling* Will the same night, she gives him a line to write that is not for him alone: *There is always room at the top.*

I have been working with a micrological method that seeks motifs and cues for an analysis of the cutout that is both the film as a work of art and an adventure that plays to and against social forms and conventions of life. The stereoscopic analysis subverts the reduction of a picture to stereotypes. I have surveyed a range of furniture-art—the Beethoven bust, radios and photographs, stilled clocks, dancing boots—and have noted the transportive windows and puddles which, when attached to a modern transport, begin and end adventures. Windows projected *onto the soul* are well viewed in alliance with the many cuts of the cloth that *make a man*: the suit that remakes Pip in *Great Expectations* into a gentleman, the suit that raises Will Mossop to the shop floor above the basement in *Hobson's Choice*, or, still to come, the cloth that remakes Lawrence of England into a leader of Arabia. No single suit makes a person entirely. Behind the craft of every suit placed on the cutting table, we must look for a craftiness or wit that loosens the well-sewn seams to leave productive antagonisms between politics and art in place.

Chapter 6

Dream Vacations and Souvenirs

The Passionate Friends (1949), Summer Madness (1955)

Summer Madness is declared the "landmark" film that, in 1955, took Lean away from England, never to return. Still, its continuities with Lean's earlier films are striking, especially with the *Brief Encounter* "remake" of 1949, *The Passionate Friends*, where *location* already gives form and matter to a *vacation* abroad. If I am asked whether *The Passionate Friends* remained a British film as *Summer Madness* somehow did not, my answer is no. For even this film made about Americans in Italy showed so much about what British filmmaking was meaning postwar on the international screen. *The Passionate Friends*, made in black and white, is heavy with misery despite its postwar hopes for a new experience raised as high as the Swiss Alps. *Summer Madness* is a technicolor comedy with all the dreams of romance invested in a city, Venice, built upon water. Before *Ryan's Daughter*, both films bring tourism to Lean's films as a core theme. Both films ask after the cost of the souvenirs brought home, the cost to truth, or the expense account for dreaming even if only for a brief while.

When, in *Brief Encounter*, Laura dreams of traveling to European cities, her cost is calculated through books borrowed weekly. In *The Passionate Friends*, when dreams become real vacations, the repeated landscape is more glamorous but no less English given the core of the film's familiar concerns. A plane transports a married woman, Mary Justin, from England to Switzerland. Its musical score by Richard Addinsell starts with a foreign feeling of rhythm before turning to an overblown orchestral symphonism to introduce the characters into a film adapted from a novel with the same title by H. G. Wells.

The first scene shows a sailing boat on a lake in the Alps accompanied by a local music sung without words. We then see the lakefront landing and rooms of the Hotel Splendide being prepared by the staff. A cut brings us to the runway and to the noise of a seemingly private plane taking off. Mary (Ann Todd) travels with a companion, her husband's secretary. Her husband, Howard Justin (Claude Rains), is a wealthy banker and stockbroker who deals with Germany's Reichsbank and contributes to international diplomacy. Rarely is he seen not dictating a letter or receiving an urgent communication by telephone or wire. Mary's voice-over is her memory—*I remember thinking*—first, that Howard would soon join her, and second, that it was a long while since they'd had a real holiday, a *holiday in Switzerland*. One feels the adventure, the pleasure of travel after a great war, as though one were traveling for the first time. The camera's tracing of a plane in the clouds carries a music of delight corresponding to Mary's joy in eating her meal of (a no longer rationed) bread, butter, fruit, coffee, and cream. Her arrival at the hotel is accompanied by her appreciation of her very good life. We know nothing yet of her unhappiness.

Repetition is a dominant motif. Mary's memory-work puts her marriage before and after the war into question. The contradiction carried by the film's title pits the *passion*, the *big demands* of *romantic love*—*nearness* and *longing*—against *friendship*—*stability* and *affection*. Which lasts *always*? The *always* is uttered countless times. What pertains to marriage pertains to a nation-state. Lean's cuts are less subtle than those in *Brief Encounter*, and the musical moments, while telling, are also more conventional. The black-and-white cinematography captures less a creaking English fog and gloom than a wealth and sophistication for Londoners who can afford vacations in lovely places. There are a few film-noir shots for Howard—a homage to the actor playing the part—when he suspects the worst, that everyone knows about his wife's affair except him.

Mary recalls her once relationship with Steven Stratton (Trevor Howard), who, without design, has taken a room in the Swiss hotel that happens to be next to Mary's room. The accidental nature of the meeting is again significant. Steven is a professor of biology, as Alec in *Brief Encounter* was a scientist. He arrives late, by train, and has a bad enough French accent that the night porter turns to English. Mary's voice-over tells that she was thinking about him despite not having seen him for nine years; how curious the feeling was; and whether, had she known him to be so close, she would have run to him. Mary will recall the happiness they once had—*at least, for a time*. We watch his figure without words until the cutback brings us to a loud and lively New Year's Eve party for 1939. The pre-war signs, plus the postwar signs looking back, fit the setting of Wells's novel, written in 1913 on the eve of the First World War. When Mary mentions the new telephone book (published after the Second World War), the loss of so many lives feels palpable. Steven responds with how often he's seen photographs of Mary with her husband in popular magazines.

The first view of Mary's husband at the party is of him standing in a rather sinister fancy dress on a balcony surveying the New Year's Eve dance below. (A dance shown on a lower level is a Lean motif: revelers of the lower class have fun.) When Mary returns from the dance floor, having run into Steven, her husband says: *I thought I'd lost you*. (Another Lean motif.) Many such remarks carry double connotations. A later business dictation in Switzerland has Howard addressing a political failure of goodwill, while his anxious secretary substitutes the phrase *financial considerations* by *irrational considerations* as she watches his jealous fury rising at seeing his wife bidding Steven farewell a little too enthusiastically. Believing that on this holiday, nine years later, Mary has taken up with Steven again, Howard's fury is at odds with the facts—although *facts* alone are what interest him. Having chosen Howard once over Steven, Mary will keep choosing him, only Howard doesn't fully get this.

How he hands a political *matter* over to his *legal advisors* foretells his businesslike filing of the divorce petition. A little too wary for one allegedly so uncaring, Howard regards Steven as an *enemy*. Leaving the New Year's party, he says: *One should never let the enemy know when he's being observed*. When Mary repeats *The enemy*? He replies: *All right, then, dear. Friend*. It is a clue that Howard will always take Mary home in his expensive car (once a horse-drawn carriage) if he comes better to understand what his marriage means to him.

Hidden in the film is the original passion of Christ turned into a passion of and for a very great piece of music. Wells's more complex novel comprises a father's letter to his son, who thinks about his father who did not write such a letter to him. It is a story of upbringing, of learning, of science and art, of generations who learn or fail to learn from each other. It is also about Lady Mary Christian, who entered the life of Stephen (originally spelt with a "ph") Stratton: "Why not make the adventure of life with me? Dare!" Throughout, love (and that Nietzschean daring) comes into contact with war as an embattled passion that turns with urgency to destructive jealousy. "There are times when that solicitude matters no more than a spring-time sky to a runner who wins towards the post, there are times when its passionate urgency dominates every fact in his world." The passionate friendship is expressed with a gravity of memory and music. "Faintly in our ears sounded the music of past and distant things. We pretended to hear nothing of that, tried honestly to hear nothing of it. . . . 'Yes', she said, 'a friendship.'" The friendship comes with a prayer corresponding to Mary's profound experience of the music and architecture of St. Paul's Cathedral. She writes to Stephen:

> The temples beguile me and the music, but not the men. . . . Such dreadful little *arguing* men! . . . All the really religious people seem to be outside nowadays and all the pretending, cheating, atheistical, vain and limited people within. . . . Do you know Saint Paul's? . . . the most beautiful interior in all the world. . . . The other day I went there . . . to hear Bach's Passion Music, the Saint Matthew passion. . . . The whole place is music and

singing. . . . Latterly, Stephen, I have been reading devotional works and trying to catch that music again. I never do. But at times I put down the book and it seems to me that surely a moment ago I heard it, that if I sit very still in a moment I shall hear it again.

The musical air sustains the motif of repetition, as expressed in her repeated locutions and at the novel's ominous end. Their last meeting happens in the summer of 1911 when "immediately after the coronation of King George there came one of those storms of international suspicion that ever and again threaten Europe with war." The novel concludes with the destruction that brings Mary to suicide by a drug overdose. Her husband threatens divorce with the necessary naming of the lover. She wants most to save the life of Stephen, who is now married and with children. Her children play a lesser role in her life, as told by Stephen. (The film erases the children.) When, finally, Stephen and Howard agree that her death was their doing, her spirit becomes a symbol of society's emancipation from slavery, stupidity, suspicion, and "dull hatreds." The feminine spirit promises a new dawn of understanding. Stephen writes of women's emancipation less as their dependency on men than as a dependency of men compounded as they turn women, as subjects of love, into objects of possession. Resentful that Mary is able, despite her deep passion *for him*, to live independently *of him*, Stephen writes:

> beneath the respectable assumptions of our social life[,] there is an endless intricate world of subterfuge and hidden and perverted passion,—for all passion that wears a mask is perversion. . . . We Strattons are daylight men, and if I work now for widened facilities of divorce, for an organized freedom and independence of women, and greater breadth of toleration, it is because I know in my own person the degradations, the falsity, the bitterness, that can lurk beneath the inflexible pretentions of the established code to-day.

Gene Phillips observes that because Wells's novel was not so well-known, Lean felt "freer to depart from the text while still maintaining the spirit of the literary source" (2006: 146). Untruth to Wells proved, however, less telling for most commentators than untruth to Coward, how far Lean would depart from *Brief Encounter*. Brownlow fills out the story: because Wells's novel had already been adapted to silent film in 1922 by Maurice Elvey, a new version was called for. Leaving Coward then meant, for Lean, leaving England (KB: 250). Yet, much of the film is shot in London despite the frame of the holiday in Switzerland, and the London scenes cannot be overlooked. And while *The Passionate Friends* tells "one woman's story," it reveals a lot about the two men. From Wells, we know everything through Stephen's pen. The film dramatizes only the novel's last chapters. Characters are changed and details are lost to abstract a triangle, as in *Brief Encounter*. If, moreover, in *Brief Encounter*, no one listens to the Rachmaninoff, and, in *Blithe Spirit*, no one is allowed to listen to it, then, in *The Passionate Friends*, Bach's *Passion* is silenced as a religious and musical motif. However, and this is true of all Lean's later films, traces of his earlier films and the originals he adapted remain, often through passing musical details, to produce potentially revealing cracks in the surface.

Mary Christian (her pre-married name is not in the film script) is now Mary or Mrs. Howard Justin. The film is written for Mary. She will consider suicide, but she will not die, so that the independence she has always desired from the *clutching* and *gripping* of relationships can be reworked in keeping with a marriage to a man with whom she will end up loving with presumably the destructive passions removed. In the United States, with the censor striking out the word "passionate," the word "friends" was lost also. The alternate title *One Woman's Story* erased from the triangle the needed contradiction of terms. While "passion" and "friendship" hardly ever appear as terms in the film script, the triangle is staged through the perspective that each character takes on another, against the background of a music and a song that play for a first and last love. Which love will last *always* and for the right reasons? . Are there "right reasons" in matters of love?

The clutching motif is first introduced following a dance of love between Mary and Steven to a record on a record player. Howard's reeling into anger when he thinks he has *lost* Mary for good then becomes an outpouring of what it means for him and Mary to have failed thus far in a marriage based on *cold* satisfaction: *I'd have been well satisfied* had the *love* not been what *you'd give a dog*, the *kindness* what *you'd give a beggar*, and the *loyalty* that *of a bad servant*. Wells's novel had told through the lover's voice: "We try to love as equals and behave as equals and concede a level freedom, and then comes a crisis,—our laboriously contrived edifice of liberty collapses and we perceive that so far as sex goes the woman remains to the man no more than a possession—capable (only) of loyalty or treachery."

The meeting nine years later in Switzerland becomes the recollection of Steven and Mary's affair nine years earlier, with added flashbacks to when they were both unmarried and first in love. Visiting his London home, she, now married, appreciates his arrangement of furniture and mementos: *I never knew you had this photograph of me*. She notices how his books are *still mixed up*, how *Sherlock Holmes* has gotten in *amongst the Aristotle*. (Holmes reads cues while Aristotle thinks about friendship.) All the while, the coffee pot, the cup of coffee, and the sugar lumps maintain a thread of the normal time passing after lunch. Steven says: *There are some books of yours here*. One is a Christmas present from him to her, but which he kept: *remember this one*, she says and then reads *In the beginning God gave to every people a cup of clay*. He finishes the line: *and from this cup they drink their life*. Sometimes, he adds, it takes years for some things—like their love—to be understood. Mary goes to the piano to press the keys and to ask whether he still plays, and he says *quietly* for his *own private satisfaction*. Looking away, she says: *From the music they love, you shall know the texture of men's souls—Do you remember that too*? And he says: *of course*. When she says that the line came from one of his letters to her, he recalls having copied it from John Galsworthy to impress her. She sits to play only the first notes of an old and familiar melody—not Bach; it quickly dissolves into their orchestral music of youthful love (Figure 15). They recall his aspiration to be a *knight in shining armour* and never to become *predictable*, after which the darkening sky tells them how long their lunch has been. The music continues, increasing in volume to carry all the passion that they suddenly now remember. The scene ends with a passionate kiss. St.

Figure 15 At the piano, *The Passionate Friends*, directed by David Lean, Cineguild, 1949.

Paul's Cathedral stands in the distance. A series of quick cuts take us through the many meetings of their evermore passionate affair.

Melanie Williams traces the cup of clay to a Native American proverb used by Ruth Benedict to preface her *Patterns of Culture* of 1934. Benedict's preface told of the "chief of the Digger Indians," who described the grinding of mesquite and preparing of corn soup. "In the beginning," the chief said, "God gave to every people a cup, a cup of clay, and from this cup they drank their life." Williams feels Lean's "special resonance" of the Dionysian-Apollonian contraries of frenzy and restraint, bestiality and civilization, sensuality and morality: "the traces" of the "division and repression," Williams adds, "are writ large" (MW: 8-9).

When Mary quotes Steven's quotation from Galsworthy, the words are subtly amended. In 1918, Galsworthy wrote *Indian Summer of a Forsyte* as part of his *Forsyte Saga*. He used for his epigraph a "summertime" quotation from Shakespeare's sonnet of comparison to a summer's day: "And Summer's lease hath all too short a date." Lean could have used these words for his own "summertime" film. Galsworthy then wrote: "The light was just failing when they went back into the music-room. And, cigar in mouth, old Jolyon said: 'Play me some Chopin.'" After which came: "By the cigars they smoke, and the composers they love, ye shall know the texture of men's souls" ([1918] 1933: 325). No Chopin, no Bach.

In Lean's film, the only explicit reference to smoking recalls *Brief Encounter*'s suggestion of the *wrongness* of women smoking in public. Steven reasons that sitting in a park doesn't count—this way showing a way out of a prohibition. Her *way out* becomes, by the film's end, the explicit sign at the London Underground station that almost results in Mary's suicide, a repetition of Laura's Anna Karenina moment of almost jumping in front of an approaching train. Not departing from Coward here, Lean distanced himself from Wells. Determined to kill herself, Mary lies to Steven, saying the divorce petition has been dropped. Bidding farewell, she (accidentally) keeps his cigarette lighter, a keepsake different in mood from a holiday souvenir. A space is opened for her husband to welcome her home.

Eric Ambler remarked: "The story is so slight that you could write it on a postcard" (SS: 83). But we already have a sense of Lean's wanting to keep his scripts sparse. Ambler's script also hardly mentions music. Still, key musical moments allow Steven and Mary not to attend the musical comedy ironically titled *First Love* at London's Royalty Theatre, Howard goes there to find their seats empty, while the light song plays eerily in the background: *I knew from the first it was you / East love and West love in Springtime or Fall / My first love's the best love of all*. He takes a program home to catch them out. When Steven brings Mary home from their secret dinner, he enters the house by Howard's invitation for a nightcap. Howard tells of his having been in Germany and Italy, and how *the taste for intrigue* is an acquired taste. He lectures them on the Teutonic high culture that has turned from sober sentiment first to a romantic hysteria and then to an angry mob that has come to *believe that a big enough lie is not a lie at all*. The failure to contain romance or frenzied feeling, to let it be acquired or find expression, is supposed to encourage the restraint that repeatedly aligns the personal with the political. The radio's light *mellow* music, put on by Mary, fills the background. Sitting on the sofa, she sees the theater program that Howard has placed there, and onto which he deliberately places her drink. She, in turn, had left the theater tickets behind to clue Howard into their deception. Mary whispers to Steven that Howard knows they *weren't at the theater*, which forces Steven's hand to admit that he and Mary *have always loved each other*. They had wanted anyway to tell Howard. Switching off the radio, Howard cannot contain his rage and tells them that, in such circumstances, one *even* thinks of *killing*. With the love revealed, Mary must choose. Her choice, feeling like a no-choice if made between the two men, becomes her decision to continue a marriage now premised on the independence without which she cannot live. That Mary in the film seems less sure about what this independence means diminishes the more explicit emancipation narrative in Wells's novel.

Karel Reisz heard the music in this scene as "a sharp, raucous South American dance" that, capturing the mood, did not intrude and, suddenly silenced, allowed Howard's outburst to shock Steven ([1953] 1966: 98–9). I find the radio music less raucous than preparatory for the turn of Howard's sweet revenge into a fury. As Steven leaves the house, a clashing orchestral dissonance paves the way to Howard's eventual cold petition for divorce. Steven's shocked face is accompanied more tellingly by a close-up on Mary's face, suggestive of a music that will finally return to its home key. At the scene's conclusion, we do not know yet that the cold climate will turn warm as Howard finally discovers that he has fallen in love with his wife: *I fell in love with you.*

The film shows a marriage of separate beds. The affair, contrarily, is made from intimate moments usually interrupted (as in *Brief Encounter*) and accompanied by little (big) lies told to Mary's husband. In place of eros is a knowingness claimed by Howard: he alone knows his wife. At first, his knowing belongs to a *bloodless banker*'s perspective filtered through the binoculars that keep him at a distance. Thinking that he sees the "lovers" returning from a day in the Swiss mountains, he loses his reason. Steven's perspective is that of a biologist with a heated poetic tendency. On top of the mountain, he grasps the ideal of romantic love. Humanistic learning is what Wells gave his character, who, lifelong unsettled by his constant yearning for Mary, read and traveled in search of understanding. Careerwise, for Wells, Stephen had become a successful and influential publisher. In the film, the panoramic scope and all-around sound of music contrast with the friction of the crossed paths when the two men meet. In one encounter, an ominous wind blows papers around on Howard's desk while a ticker tape brings in ominous news of the world. The technology on display signals the emptiness of modern human communication. The ring of (Rachmaninoff-like) bells, separated from St. Paul's, comes to feel hollow when attached by wires to telephones and telegraphs.

Petitioning for divorce, Howard tells Mary that she has made him despise himself and he wants out of the marriage. She runs out of the room and misses the apology that follows. She passes the ticket office and the *way out* sign without stopping to reach the platform. Leaving her handbag on the chair clues Howard into what her departure means, and he runs to rescue her. Throwing his arms around her, he says: *It's all right . . . You're all right now*. Mary sobs. he says: *Shall we go home now? Home?* she repeats. *If you want to, that is*, he adds. With her choice acknowledged, they walk away with linked arms, as though this were their first real gesture of love. She slightly smiles—perhaps in recall of having earlier told Steven that she had *never really known the pleasure of walking arm-in-arm with a man before*. Steven was the first; Howard is the second. A platform guard whistles. An orchestral music announces the film's end. There is no more vacation or Switzerland on show, only a restored security back home in England. But what it means for a marriage to have both love and independence is leftover as the hanging matter.

Reviews of the film were lukewarm. Most felt bored by the remake-feeling of *Brief Encounter*. Many then laughed, or cried, at the "life imitating art" trope when Lean and Ann Todd, having had an affair on location, encouraged their spouses to petition for divorce. The tabloids were thrilled: the marriage duos were playing out an angry quartet for the film world. Lean felt less the thrill than the cuts that made the film feel a little too like the analysis he was undergoing at the time. Too many visual and sound cues come off as crude psychological clues.

The next chapters will find more quivering telephone wires spreading across Europe and the world to signal great uses and abuses of humanity's scientific achievements. Before that, *Summer Madness* addresses the sightseeing that, while in full color, casts a shadow over a woman who, transported by plane and train, seeks a souvenir to take home as a remembrance of a world now past.

Summer Madness of 1955 turns an affair into a confrontation with a city and a country. The woman who arrives in Venice falls in love with the city as Lawrence, from England, falls for Arabia. The brief encounter is between a middle-aged, Midwestern single woman and a questionably honest Italian shopkeeper. Their trading of a likely counterfeit, eighteenth-century red goblet both triggers and undermines the promise of a transformation indicative of the capability of cinema itself. Immediately, there is something false in what Jane Hudson (Katharine Hepburn) wants most: to find the wonderful, mystical, and magical *miracle* of romance at the end of *the rainbow*. What the married lover, Renato De Rossi (Rossano Brazzi), offers her as an affair cannot translate back into ordinary life. The misadventure is as beautifully cut as the red goblet from Murano, a place name that rhymes with Burano, the island of *Tristan*-like winds to which they will travel by boat for their romantic getaway weekend. There is wit and music throughout: the island once named for the rainbow is met with a momentary dissonance of worn sounds and sights.

The red goblet is like the Beethoven bust: it alerts us to a paradigm of fidelity that has seen better days. The broken record of true love stands for the promise and the premise: a loss of sanity, normality, or control only lasts between the first and last lines of a summer season. Throughout, Jane carries a home movie camera (something Hepburn made famous in *Adam's Rib* dir. George Cukor 1949]). When, in the famously comic moment, she falls backward into the canal near the antique shop that has so attracted her attention, she warns the viewer: beware of the camera, this could happen to you too. Like the radio and gramophone, the camera makes and breaks the affair. Jane's camera, and the camera that follows her, presents the city and her *pensione* as a place of dreams and as a trap for susceptible tourists. The *pensione*'s guests play out their parts, like those in *Brief Encounter*'s station room. Venice is a dream location in *Brief Encounter*, made no more real in *Summer Madness*. It is mapped as a landscape for the untruth in the promise of love, the more the touristic gaze snapshots the economic abuse of the city's beauty. Its colors are as significant as the strains of music, operatic and popular, in making for an adventure that is as outdated as it is contemporary, of which the end is the object(-lesson) that Jane takes home as a souvenir. The screen credits name David Lean as director in front of a cartoon of Jane arriving by train. Leaning out of the window, she looks ahead. Perhaps this is how Hepburn got equal billing.

The film doubles up on the camera to question the construction of a city of dreams. Whatever the continuity between Jane's and Lean's gazes, the divide is as palpable as the film's music within and the more conventional film score without. The divide is reeled and revealed through cuts that show the city through Jane's eyes and what she would see had she another perspective. The cuts show what a camera catches and what it catches out as a crime. But the crime is, again, a misdemeanor made small, and certainly smaller than the indiscretion of the disabled voyeur in Hitchcock's *Rear Window* (1954), where an overly large telescope in search of a crime replaces, Hollywood-style, the discreet binoculars of detection on the other side of the Atlantic.

Summer Madness cuts its landscape with city noises: train whistles, the hustle and bustle of tourists, the bells of Piazza San Marco marking time, the call of traders, peddlers selling musical mechanical monkeys, and gondolier water drivers. The first bus journey by canalboat (because Jane does not want to pay for a water taxi) is photographed as a tour of Venice's sightseeing destinations. One is reminded of the opening of Paul Czinner's *Escape Me Never* of 1935, a film about musicians and lovers, which Lean had edited. The persistent whirring of Jane's camera begins with the first picture she takes of the Venice guidebook on the train, the first promise of romance. The invocation of sounds and colors for the imagination—a city coming alive—cuts the romance off from all the witty quips about the real and the endlessly crooning melody of heavenly violins off from the city sounds. Whenever a gondolier sings or a violin plays, the sounds signify Jane's desire to find something that's been *missing all her life*. The faultline cuts through a life that has not given someone quite enough, where the British moderation of the middle-class "quite" is resourced to a sadly moralizing middle America: Akron, Ohio.

The conventional film score is cut by key musical moments for script and plot. The temporality of aging is channeled by the radio and record player that plays a popular music. But more, it is worked along Venice's canals through the eyes of a woman who fears that her time is past. An early conversation has Jane describing herself as wanting still to be a *girl* with a *dream*. She speaks in the third person about a desiring self detached from her ordinary self. Will they meet? Behind the character, however, one feels Hepburn refusing age or gender to get the better of her: Wasn't she, after all, the actor who redressed the filmic figure of *woman*? Lean declared Hepburn his favorite actor and *Summer Madness* his favorite movie.

> I enjoy working with really good actors. Someone like Katharine Hepburn. During rehearsals you tell her, "Try to act a little more ironic, a bit more sentimental, or a little more this or that." She does it. Like a beautiful instrument. . . . [I]t's the second-rate actors who are the most annoying. The stars are easy. I always say that if you're a young violinist and you need some help, you'd do better to go see Yehudi Menuhin. (DL: 112)

Alison McKee quotes Hepburn's recall of the film staging "two love affairs," of which one was Lean's affair with the city (2021: 26–7). She draws from Laura Mulvey's (2006) diagnoses of the anxiety regarding the ephemerality of cinema and human life. Unable to hold onto what passes, one compulsively seeks in cold repetition the *always* of a reward that lasts.

John Orr says that "Lean could easily have given us kitsch, syrupy imitations of landscape photography." But no, what Lean achieved was an inextricable linking of the "romantic sublime" to "the découpage and sense of place" so that the image would assume "its own power of conviction" (2010: 69). Orr's praise demands less interpretation than the thought of a director easily giving us kitsch. In 1964, Susan Sontag reminded us that when kitsch is offered, it is rarely delivered with an ease of thoughtlessness. It rather gets delivered in small and neatly folded packages under the touristic consciousness of the souvenir. She described the zeal for debunking high culture in favor of a conscientious courting of a vulgarity where commercialism turns every promise of transformation into a document equally of civilization and barbarism. For the film, the commercial terms, with all the syrup, allows little things, like snapshots or popular tunes, to be taken home in suitcases as well-purchased remembrances of little things past. Turned to metaphors for a worn art, souvenirs sustain the economic payoff that comes at best to equal the aesthetic investment in the director's cut. This is the return that renders worthwhile the hours one spends watching and rewatching Lean's film back home as another sort of home movie.

With *Summertime* proposed as the title, the worry arose that it could mislead audiences into thinking the film was an adaptation of George Gershwin's *Porgy and Bess* (1935). "Can you imagine anything so ridiculous," Lean quipped, "Kate Hepburn in a Gershwin operetta?" (SS: 85). The film was an adaptation of Arthur Laurents's successful Broadway play of 1952, *The Time of the Cuckoo* (1954). Laurents was a New Yorker, witty, Jewish, gay, and blacklisted after the war. Working with Lean on the screen version, he was deeply dissatisfied. H. E. Bates took over the script. Laurents declared the film a *half*-adaptation: too much of his original had been changed or excluded.

Laurents said this in a 1965 television interview following a second adaptation of his play into a musical *Do I Hear a Waltz?* This title reminded everyone that the transformation that comes with falling in love comes with a dance. Titled for the cuckoo's cry, Laurents's play wittily conjured up the "summer visitant" proclaiming its arrival in Europe to herald "the season of love," only then, with Shakespeare, for a husband or wife to be cuckolded when an egg or sperm was laid in the wrong nest. Laurents specified a Venetian blind named for the window that lets insiders look out while outsiders cannot look in: *If possible, there should be a scene curtain: a half-closed Venetian blind through which the beginning of each scene is glimpsed, and by which the end of each scene is shadowed out* (Think again of *Rear Window*). The inequality of gazes reinforced the inequality in the affair between two persons, one married, one not. Laurents's unmarried woman was cynically named Leona Samish, perhaps to mimic her need always to hear the same explanation—to ensure that nothing would change her mind.

When Leona Samish was renamed as Jane Hudson, Lean's film took on the grit of Laurents and Hepburn in the East Coast landscape along the Hudson River. This is as telling as the fact that Lean was a British filmmaker taking on Americans in Italy. Financed partly by an American production company, the film was made to less fit than mimic the Hollywood genre. Lean described his digging at the US film industry in a postwar Italy where dollars were replacing the local currency. Finding Laurents's play "almost plotless," he took liberties without any feelings of guilt for the sake, he said, of making a good cinema (KB: 312–14).

When the critics offered their backhanded praise of Lean's film as at least better than Laurents's play, this little impacted their appreciation of the fact that, with this "landmark" film, Lean (in his own words) left the "pitch-black mine" for "the sun" (Phillips 2006: 204–19; KB: 330). Still, whatever the departure, one cannot bypass the combined wit of Coward and Laurents that stands behind this film to make it a remake of something done before. In *Summer Madness*, the breakout from daily norms extends the travel route from Ohio to Venice; in *Brief Encounter*, the intentionally *plotless* travel comprises brief stops between middle-class English towns on a local train. In *Blithe Spirit*, conjuring up another world requires only the choice of a song and where to place a table; in *Summer Madness*, the world is remade through a tourist's guidebook. For Lean to develop his style was for him to keep cutting and recutting an already-borrowed material anew, in film after film.

Note also the quip from *In Which We Serve* where a stranded sailor blames the Germans for the torpedoes because *you'd never get the Macaronis to tackle a job like that, not for love nor money. The Eyeties will do anything for money. Anything but fight. That's why they were so lousy in the last war. That's on account of their warm, languorous southern temperament*. A slang turn of the word "Italian" into what *ties the eye* anticipates what the allies wanted most to retrieve postwar: a highly charged purchase of an Italian cosmetic. Laurents wrote of the love of money as defining Americans at home and abroad. Lean took the American money for a film that wanted to bite the hand that was feeding it.

In Laurents's play, when June and Leona think of going to a movie, June says: *movies are movies* and movies, like *Chesterfield* cigarettes, are best when American and dubbed in Italian! Would Lean's movie be the kind of movie that Leona, during her brief spell in Venice, would or would not want to see? And what would it mean to see the film dubbed?

In *Runaway Romances*, Robert Shandley seeks a definition to bring all his film examples under a self-contained genre. He seeks not a closed definition but one that is more pragmatic, cluster-like, family-resemblant, accordant with a "paradigm model." Films are treated, then, less as examples than as exemplars, so that, more than judging the perfect fit of their characteristics to the model according to shorthand "industrial explanation," they throw light on the genre as a living body of production (2009: xix–xx).

So what happens when an old city calls attention to itself under a modern advertisement promising nothing more and nothing less than romance? The recent surge of critical literature on tourism, travel, and transport addresses the transfiguration that occurs in foreign or strange lands when, suspending disbelief, the ideal holds only so long as the reel of the illusion lasts. Behind the romance of the 1950s was the lack of license for married persons to divorce, meaning the affair had nowhere to go. The same literature addresses the many new deals made by the victorious allies wanting to make films abroad in war-ravaged (formerly enemy) countries. What was brought to the depressed and defeated nations by way of economic deals and technological advances had to be reassessed according to what had to be rescued by way of a culture and nature that couldn't be destroyed: sun, sea, and skies filled with music, opera, and song, all of Italy's *natural* splendor and beauty (McInnis 2020). From all the postwar touristic narratives, one gleans far more about how the tourists thought about themselves at home and abroad than about the Italians, as though the Italians were being denied the right to self-representation. When they spoke, they had to speak English with a foreign accent. For Lean, Englished-foreign accents rendered differences of class, opinion, and morals easily recognizable for international audiences. Alison Light notes one consequence of the evermore frequent experience of hearing one's voice technologically reproduced: how a sort of standardized British emerged, a BBC English that, minding its Ps and Qs, left behind some of the extensive theater of wit in favor of a moral standard (1991: 215; Donnelly 2005). From the other side of the Atlantic, Anderegg described Hepburn's Connecticut accent rubbing like "wrong notes" against the conventionality of middle America, all to suggest a critique of the role from within (MA: 88). Lean did not try to disguise the contradiction.

In one episode, the lovers are dancing to the violin melody that is the film's leitmotif. He croons (not too well), allowing her to note the Italian's propensity to sing. Sealed with a kiss, their dance ends with an explosion of red fireworks. Praising Italians to the skies was how postwar films denigrated but then displaced them as the target, to make the real target the blinkered United States, producing a mirror of the world to prove its moral and commercial interests universal. The more the runaway romances, described as *Ameritalian* or as *Britalian*, transported mirrors of desire and duty to foreign grounds, the more the former wartime isolationism gave way to a parochial love affair with Europe.

Shandley describes the United States as "liberators, conquerors, tourists, capitalists, and colonialists," while Europeans (as former enemies) were made into "war criminals, victims, children, sexual amusements, or merely attractive but blank slates onto which Americans could project a range of fantasies." Yet, the pictures of Europe were always double-sided to serve also as "the arbiters of sophistication, erudition, beauty, and social legitimacy" (2009: xvi). Capitalizing ROMANCE (as in *Brief Encounter*'s crossword), the United States produced its guidebooks according to generic conventions and common characteristics: the arrival and departure by a modern means of transport of a tourist carrying a visa of sufficient wealth to live comfortably enough in a *pensione*, to eat well, dress well, and to go sightseeing with eyes seeking souvenirs. In listing such conventions, Shandley stresses the new ways of doing things, only to end with the inevitable return home (ibid: xxi–xxii).

The runaway romances were about the tourists and less the artists who arrived abroad, so that falling in love with a person or a work of art assumed the form of a dream or wish-fulfillment—not to make something but to find something ready-made. The end of the affair was often tinged with a sense of betrayal, an untruth that, bitter in the mouth, turned sweet as a souvenir—especially when a gentle lady and gentile purchaser (Laurents's Jewish wit) insisted, as Jane does, on paying the full price. If something was learned by returning home, little was changed by way of the ideal that was Italy other than perhaps the recognition that it was only ever an ideal. A sense of an Italian city as an aged or ruined beauty suggests souvenirs of faded color, while yet *Summer Madness* stands out for its extraordinary color and brightness. As in *The Passionate Friends*, the postwar thought is of a vacation to a new location being experienced for the first time. While grateful to them, Lean described the Venice shopkeepers as "a kind of blackmail ring" (DL: 132). Grateful to Lean, the merchants of Venice perhaps did not see the suspicion into which they were cast, a suspicion reminiscent of those older mergers of the city's merchandise with its visual and auditory landscape.

The city of Lean's film is Venice, while its subtext is the taking-back, postwar, of Italy's culture, history, and arts: Italy's ideal and promise. "Tourism" is the modern term for what was once the Grand or European Tour for those who, with wealth or artistic aspirations, aimed to make every sort of purchase on art. American tourism was construed as a pitting of the New against the Old World, while British tourism carried the contestation of a parent country extending its embrace of a commonwealth in new and old distant terrains.

Allied, the victorious countries drew from the rubric of romance to carve out a new aesthetic and economics of art that had earlier been sent home as their impressions of Florence, Rome, Naples, and Venice by the likes of Dickens, Ruskin, Henry James, and Edith Wharton. The extraordinary number of early dispatches was quickly matched by the equally extraordinary number of postwar films of high romance that allowed English and American tourists to fall in love with persons, cities, and countries. But always only for a specified duration. First time tragedy; second time farce. The point was not to remain abroad with the object of love but to purchase it as a souvenir, a reevaluated value to be drawn back into the forever-abiding sentiment that there is "no place like home" (Bordwell 1993: 96f.).

When Dickens offered an "Italian dream" in his *Pictures from Italy* of 1846, he described his "(f)loating down narrow lanes, where carpenters, at work with plane and chisel in their shops, tossed the light shaving straight upon the water, where it lay like weed, or ebbed away before me in a tangled heap." And then of how "it floated me away, until I awoke. . . . I have, many and many a time, thought since, of this strange Dream upon the water: half-wondering if it lie there yet, and if its name be Venice" (1891: 264–5).

Naming Venice as the last word allowed Dickens to move on in his waking life, and Henry James to pick the word up for his essay of 1882. James described what was "strange and fascinating" in the "mysterious impersonality of the gondola." The gondoliers were "the children of Venice," standing for the idiosyncratic and essential: the silence and melancholy of the city's voice. A city of conversation: people talked without fear of being caught or caught out. But as a city of stilled waters: a melancholic voice said that Venetian life had "long since come to an end," that its present "resides simply in its being the most beautiful of tombs." No longer flowers in hands: only "money and little red books." The shopkeepers and gondoliers, the beggars and the models were collected by the "custodians and the ushers of the great museum" to become "objects of exhibition." Piazza San Marco was "the lobby of the opera in the intervals of the performance." Inspired by Ruskin's *Stones of Venice*, James addressed the *disloyalty* that Ruskin had felt when describing the city in a way untrue to the principles of form. Through *misdescription*, the city became less an object loved than a beloved object "disconcerted and abjured" (1909: 5–45 passim).

What, then, could or would rescue the city? Not an old master's voice, but a new voice, perhaps? A voice singing perhaps for *the vanishing lady* standing before a scene of Venice reproduced in every shop window to put a girl's dream of another place over the rainbow on sale (Maxwell 2018). Rebecca White describes the postwar films of Venice as paying homage to the nineteenth-century writers while turning Venice into "a postcard of itself" traded cheaply by Malraux's "museum without walls" (2012: 159–60).

Eisenstein and Balázs theorized the modern landscape with regard to music's movement as how to bring out the plasticity of emotions in what appears stilled before one's eyes (Füzi 2012; Webster 2003). Simmel likewise drew from the rhythm of the mood—*Stimmung*—that brings persons to a feeling of unity or love. In his "The Philosophy of Landscape," the "Landschaft" drew from *schaffen*, to create or make a relationship or condition as in Goethe's *Verwandtschaft*. The *Landschaft* might carry the air or convey the atmosphere of Venice, but only when "the experience and interpretation of the world" called up an internal universe to liquidate all that is falsely compartmentalized by science. Simmel's liquidity was the other side of the breakdown of unity corresponding to the modern liquidation of society. It was the desirable energy in the artwork that, with its unifying power of form (*Gestalt*), brought shape to a soulful feeling in the mind (*un état d'âme*) that far exceeded any merely cognized or conceptual accumulation of parts. To speak of "pieces" of nature was a contradiction of terms. Similarly, error arose by speaking of the landscape as merely cultural if this contradicted the thought of the landscape extending the differentiation in time and space into an unbroken and infinite extension. Culture, Simmel concluded, was not then to be exhibited in discrete mechanical parts but made from flowing or moving entities (selves and things), which, through the confines of an adventure, would bring a purity to an ideal disentangled from the "turbid randomness of [everyday] life" ([1913] 2007: 20–9). With the analogy between an artwork and an adventure again on the table, Lean's film *about* tourism eschewed the finely cut experience in favor of a souvenir from the get-go. The tourist arrives to take something home. Doubling up on the unreality of the experience, the film, to extend the repetition, becomes an experience of a film that, as in Lean's string of *affair* films, keeps remaking itself.

Summer Madness aligns itself to the Hollywood films made in Italy in the Fifties: *A September Affair*, but also William Wyler's *Roman Holiday* (1953); Vittorio De Sica's *Indiscretion of an American Wife* (1953), and Douglas Sirk's *Interlude* (1957) (with Brazzi playing a married orchestra conductor in Germany and Austria). *Roman Holiday* announces itself as a "romantic comedy," which one feels too in *Summer Madness* with every contradictory cut of vision, sound, and text, or with every mechanical doll or record player placed on a shelf of romance. Standing on the bridge listening to a romantic song near the film's start, a bucket of cabbage waste is thrown into the canal. Clear water, dirty water: Venice is made from both.

As in *Hobson's Choice*, cartoon credits set the film's mood, only now we are offered a red London bus arriving as a tourist bus in a foreign country. One of the credits announces the composer, Alessandro Cicognini, with the words added *recorded in Rome* (Figure 16). Cicognini's first notes dissolve into the noises of a crowded city. No heavy tug of Rachmaninoff's church bells, only lighter tugs of violin strings to bind an American to Italy with a sentimental song. Nevertheless, commentators, like Gene Phillips, find the Rachmaninoff still there, remade for mandolin and guitar to give the film "a Mediterranean flavor" (2006: 204–19). James Clapp describes the soundtrack oozing out "Vivaldi and Rossini" (2009: 52). It sounds like a contagious disease. McKee hears in the strings and horns "the majesty of Venice and Jane's reactions to it," set against the persistently "ironic musical note" for "boarded-up windows" (2021: 39). The irony plays to what Anderegg earlier heard in the Rachmaninoff remade: the "ambient and non-ambient" tugs and resistance of a camera engaged and distanced, a way for an audience to be brought in and kept out, as the tourist seeking an experience but holding herself at a distance (MA: 90).

Figure 16 Music arriving by a London bus, *Summer Madness*, directed by David Lean, London Films, 1955.

"On location" in 1983, Gerald Kaufman described Venice as a "far too celebrated" city for filmmakers. He saw the location making the film while the film was remaking the location. But he also saw in Lean's "painstaking detective work" a way for an "accidental" tourist to become "obsessive." Was the obsession more Lean's than Jane's? In 1990, Richard Combs found a "tourist trapped": a gentle woman who, for all her yearning, came across as empty. Not really knowing what she was looking for, her entrapment by her own camera was very unlike the "angst and spiritual isolation" that was expressed later, in 1990, say, by Paul Schrader in *The Comfort of Strangers* or by Bernardo Bertolucci in *The Sheltering Sky*. With safety, the travel-movie genre was turning against itself, just when the epic was becoming anti-epic. Combs recalled Luchino Visconti's *Death in Venice* (1971) and Nicolas Roeg's *Don't Look Now* (1973) as far more nightmarish in their fantasies of betrayal. Lean, by contrast, was becoming a "professional tourist," on his way to "the full-blown desert madness of *Lawrence*." For now, with his "parochial angst," he was embracing a city's gifts with all the New World's "travel-brochure loveliness," only then to reject the gifts with an Old World "philosophical" asceticism, the more they proved counterfeit or of no worth (TL: 31).

Lean said his film was about loneliness. Unlike love, "we speak less about it. We are ashamed of it. We think perhaps that it shows a deficiency in ourselves. That if we were more attractive, more entertaining and less ordinary we would not be lonely" (KB: 312). "Less lonely" meant "more love" for Jane at least, only then for the calculation to be falsified by her surrounding cast, a cast that played to Laurents's thought of deficiency: the (American) desire only for the sort of company that must always make more money. Between love and money stood Hepburn as a woman who did not fall for the *always more* promise of anything, except perhaps for a good part to play. Many see the conscious exaggeration and wit of her gestures, her postures of reserve and passionate outbursts, as a carryover of her early Hollywood days. C. A. Lejeune (1955) congratulated Lean for letting Hepburn play a "dubiously moral heroine," who, in a delicate trick of storing up her memories, recalled Greta Garbo in Rouben Mamoulian's *Queen Christina* (1933).

Many shots show Jane at a table made for company where, however, the company leaves or does not show up. She is often near tears, vulnerable, desiring experience, yet lifelong *independent*. Sitting alone because one is independent and feeling lonely are different thoughts, of which one, the first, was the theme of *The Passionate Friends*, while the second plays to the outdated rhetoric of spinsterhood, where threads of love and marriage are rewound back to the first looms. McKee (2021) finds a portrait of *woman* released from the clutches and crutches of cinematic conventions of the lonely *spinster*. For Williams, the same portrait is painted over with the hysteria she finds also in *Brief Encounter*, only in *Summer Madness*, she finds it brought to the "knife-edge" of absurdity (MW: 123).

Santas finds in Hepburn's overt display of sentiment Lean's way to displace Romanticism's naive impulses, all those pantheistic or Wordsworthian outbursts, by a distancing camera of aged reflection. He finds the passion denied in *Summer Madness* transferring the English reserve in *Brief Encounter* to a Midwestern puritanism. He finds a "plain Jane" on the plane, arriving in Venice, already "enraptured by the carnival atmosphere, lushly living in the land of the lotus-eaters for a brief while" (2012: 178–9). But how plain was a Jane who had really arrived from the Hudson River? Lotus-eating in the *Odyssey*, and then in Tennyson's romantic borrowing, was about erasing all desire to return home. How did Jane on the plane reinvent the wings to make returning the only safe option?

The red goblet, like the Beethoven bust, carries contested values. Made from glass, it is the pride of the city, as Edith Wharton noted in her chapter "Italian Backgrounds" from her book of 1905 with the same title. "Escaping the obligatory romanticism of the hero and heroine," one sees "the crowded picture of a world as bright and brittle as a sun-shot Murano glass." The brittle technique of Murano glass extended back several centuries, most fittingly to a single *adventure*, to a chance occurrence when metal shavings were accidentally mixed into an unusual chemical compound. In the film, Murano is a running motif, with mentions from the first water-bus journey to the first view from Jane's window, and then to her arriving at a shop window.

The *accidental* encounter carries all the risks of not knowing the outcome in advance, however much one designs the outcome in preparation for one's trip. Whether the goblet is authentic or fake is what the *fancy secretary* asks about her Italian lover. The fact that he is a shopkeeper and keeps reminding her of this means that she, as an administrator, ought not to expect more than an ordinary trade, assuming that he's a trader of the real thing. In Laurents's play, Leona's preoccupation with trade is made to stand for, even to define, what makes someone an "American": a self-worth countable in coinage. The red goblet is soon displaced by a deal of counterfeit money, a gamble to secure some equally suspect red garnets: *Garnets. Real. Bite 'em.*

Lean's film runs away more with the romance of the goblet than with its value. It shifts the mercenary matters to a Cinderella complex. When Jane expresses her desire to take home a red goblet, her prince tells her that Venetian glass might not be enough, that something nicer might be *better*. (*Better* is an oft-used term.) Is *living* not *better* than *buying*? Perhaps—but only for a brief moment. When Jane succumbs to her lover in a night of bliss, she drops a single red slipper on the veranda, hoping for a restitution of the pair. The red shoe pairing matches her purchase of the red goblet, conditional on the shopkeeper finding a second. It is a pairing for a fidelity that is then jeopardized when a third party interferes. Seeking a second goblet, Jane is confronted with a third, a fourth, and a fifth when a pair of American tourists, the McIlhennys, return to the *pensione* one day with six ready-made red goblets (Figure 17). Cut by a machine, the *cutest* goblets impress more than all Venice's *pictures—All done by hand*. The name McIlhenny likely alludes to the manufacturer of Tabasco sauce, whereas the other *arty* pair living in the *pensione*, the Yaegers, recalls a German hunt, as well as, with more irony, Diana's references in *The Merchant of Venice* to a hunted woman who says she'd rather die chaste. Both accompanying pairs claim a purchase on romance when the economy of relationships is brought into foreign and unfamiliar fields. The most cutting comments are directed to the McIlhennys, who, childless like all the other visitors to this *pensione*, expose their barrenness in philistine purchases of cheap goods paid at high prices—all one and the same.

Figure 17 Too many red goblets, *Summer Madness*, directed by David Lean, London Films, 1955.

In Laurents's play, the red goblet is first mentioned by Leona when, cynically, she describes herself as a *Girl Tourist*, who must

> *take a picture of everything. Even those bloody pigeons in front of San Marco. And that was a narrow escape, too. Anyway, this afternoon, I bought a goblet. 18th Century Venetian glass, fellas. The wildest dark rose. And the only one left, damn it. I got it in a cute little shop Di Rossi's. . . . I wanted to get a picture of the shop where I bought the goblet, but a plain simple picture wouldn't do. I never owned a Brownie before this trip, but I have to have composition in the lousy picture. An authentic old Venetian church on one side and an authentic old Venetian lady on the other. So . . . I start backing up. I back up and up, and right in back of me was an authentic old Venetian canal.*

And into the canal, she falls. The canal alone is authentic. The next mention occurs at the *inexpensive pensione* where the play is entirely set. The question arises whether Leona has been trying to purchase the goblet or the shopkeeper, Di Rossi—who arrives at

> Forty-odd, he has slightly tired good looks made striking by prematurely silver-grey hair . . . invariably at ease . . . a worldly

man, his knowledge is a product of experience and his senses rather than of his mind and thought. He is so very charming, so direct, so simple (like a child) that it is difficult to believe he might not always tell the precise truth. At any rate, since he always believes it is the truth when he is saying it and since there is so much truth in what he does say, does it matter?

In Lean's film, *Di* Rossi becomes the *De* Rossi whom Jane tries to resist on her arrival as anything but a tourist: *So happy to be here. Instead of a hotel full of tourists—like me*. The *pensione* feels a little more expensive in the film than in the play. Jane offers the hostess a cocktail, half Italian and half American, to show her willingness to let half of her engage in the local custom. When, however, having traded for one goblet, not two but too many appear, she suspects that she has been part of a suspect deal. Even if, with her red sash and shoes, she enjoys watching the peddling of mechanical toys with their red ribbons attached, she is unnerved by De Rossi's tricky suit to keep distracting her. His name perhaps echoes the Rossinian lover advertised in the little red guide book. He offers a promise that she will eventually take home as a musical souvenir. A romance begins, he tells her, when one hears the music. Seeing her resisting, he chides her for choosing *beefsteak* over *ravioli*. Beefsteak is for those who dismiss romance morally as adultery. With the final chord, he leaves her with a souvenir: of an ideal moment that never again can be unpaired from or impaired by reality. Jane returns home as what: no wiser, a little wiser, or, crossed by Hepburn, more determined than ever to remain independent: *Let me go. . . . I must catch that train*. De Rossi is left with his marriage intact, on the lookout for the next purchaser of the promise: a *gondola friend*, as Jane describes his always newly traded object of affection. As the play puts it with a more Jewish itch: *there was once a seven year drought*–and it keeps repeating itself. If this is one itch, then other comes from those who refuse the double bind of heterosexual desire brought under the rubric of bourgeois moderation: that gratification comes only in small packages. Then there are those sublime torments of the Schopenhauerian Will turning to little packages of kitsch when confronted with the (bourgeois) satisfaction that goes as fast as (or faster than) it comes.

No part is given to the lover's wife. We meet only his son (at first introduced as a nephew). In the play, the lover is forthright about being married with many children and having affairs. In the film, he conceals the marriage, knowing that American Jane wouldn't agree to the adultery. When Jane tells Renato that she's going home *because you and I will only end in nothing*, he responds with sincere words that cost him nothing: *I shall always love you. Yes.* she replies, *If I go*. Throughout, a young urchin, Cookie, follows Jane around and befriends her. Through a youthful mirror image of the lover (with shared bodily postures), the almost Dickensian child aims to become a perfect *guide* for tourists. Truth and lies mix with skepticism and care.

Along with the camera, the red of the red goblet, like the red of the red slipper, controls the traffic and transport for Jane. Relinquishing control only briefly, she stops recording so as to participate in her experience. When one has passion or happiness, said Nietzsche, one is in it and not standing at a distance. Participating, she lets the purchase of the red goblet be displaced momentarily by a white gardenia, white (in this Lean motif) for her virgin demeanor and for her dream of innocence when, as she tells Renato, the flower once proved too expensive (two dollars apiece) for the college boy who was meant to take her to her graduating dance, Sashing red around white signifies something Jane wants both to lose and to protect. The gift in white wrapping paper that Renato runs to give her as the train departs will never reach her hands. Is her experience real, a fantasy, a counterfeit? Does the truth or reality matter if, on location, the entire construction is an outdated city of dreams?

Delivering eyefuls of all the must-see sites of Venice, Lean displays James's "money and little red [guide] books" in the shop windows. Cutting through the culinary surface, he supplements the camera's looking with a listening. Noting all this as a fatal weakness in the compositional excess, Des O'Rawe sees in Jane's extreme wonderment "a magical, musical utopia of heterosexual happiness and harmless irony" (2005: 224–5). But in the magic, what exactly makes the utopia musical?

"Gondolas, lights, music . . . my soul, a stringed instrument . . . Did anyone hear?" In *Ecce Homo*, Nietzsche described what he could really exact from music. Striking out against a German understanding, he looked to all that was strange and foreign, reaching finally Rossini and then Venice. "When I look for another word for music, I only ever find the word 'Venice'. I cannot tell any difference between tears and music" (2005: 94–5). Such thoughts were alive in the first musical souvenirs, so-named in the early nineteenth century, as later in Tchaikovsky's *Souvenir de Florence*, where the takeaway from a journey abroad became a contribution to one's own national music back home. One might consider, with Christian Thorau (2019), the musical itemizing of souvenirs as part of a project on the musical tourist's little red guidebook, the Baedeker of music-reception: how we are led by programmatic critics to hear a symphony as a passionate sightseeing trip. Music, in Lean's films, contributes to a sightseeing that is always also a sound-seeing.

Jane's welcome to the *pensione* is interrupted by the maid Giovanna singing a popular Italian song. When not singing, Giovanna is always *playing that terrible machine*. Jane says that she likes *the machine; it's Italy isn't it*. The wit lies with the music box as a gift ready-*made in America*. In the Piazza San Marco, when the bells are not chiming or pigeons circling, an open-air band performs Rossini's overture to *La gazza ladra* (*The Thieving Magpie*), so that we can ask after the theft. In Rossini's opera, as in so many more operas, a bird who flies nearly always lives by the wings of a desire to be set free from any sort of arranged or caged marriage. Edna St. Vincent Millay's poem of bitter memory, "Souvenir," asks: "Why do I remember you / As a singing bird?," to which Hélène Cixous offered an answer that could serve as an epigraph (or should it be an epitaph?) to all of Lean's films:

we've lived flight, stealing away, finding, when desired, narrow passageways, hidden crossovers. It's no accident that *voler* has a double meaning . . . [that] women take after birds and robbers just as robbers take after women and birds. They go by, fly the coop, take pleasure in jumbling the order of space, in disorienting it, in changing around the furniture, dislocating things and values, breaking them all up, emptying structures, and turning propriety upside down. (1976: 887)

Leona says in the play: *The bargains some people expect on a hot six-week vacation!* And then Di Rossi: *There's a concert in Piazza San Marco questa sera. They're playing Puccini, all Puccini. You like Puccini.* Left alone to write a letter to her friends back home, she writes that *Venice is as unbelievable as a musical comedy.* What this line means is as ambiguous as the gramophone that jukes out Italian tunes with scratches. When we hear that music is always good for getting *girls*, the *girls* are compared again to the trading of American cigarettes. *Everything in America is better. . . . Many Americans come in . . . marvelous. Everybody has money.* When Leona resists this claim, it is because she wants to prove that the object of her desire is authentically Italian. But then: *We invented it: the installment plan and the installment man.* When Di Rossi does not arrive to court her, the record player falls silent. When the arty June tells about one of her failed affairs, this time with a musician, she quips that at least she was *faithful to the arts.* At a cocktail party, when the record plays "Would you like to take a walk?," the dance is interrupted when Leona learns that the money paid for the red garnets was counterfeit. Di Rossi, accused, forgets his English words. With the spell broken, she shouts: *Turn off that damn music!*

For the New York writer and for the English filmmaker, the city canal offered a pool of reflection for a doubled and divided consciousness. The comic opening and the splicing moments of music and wit turned the romance into an aged world picture. Another "one woman's story." Freud theorized the one who falls victim to the object of love as unable to give it up—unless one changes gear to write about it as an experience of the uncanny (*Unheimlich*): of suddenly not being at home. Insisting she is no writer, Jane returns home with the red goblet. Yet, will the souvenir, like the Beethoven bust in *Ryan's Daughter*, be put on the mantelpiece, or will it remain in its box? The petrified paradigm for romance and for Venice, like the Beethoven bust, feels outsized and cracked. In the cracks, however, lie the cues for something perhaps different to happen the next time around. We never step in the same canal twice, or, with all the wit and irony trodden into the path of reflection, Henry James put it thus:

Venice has been painted and described many thousands of times, and of all the cities of the world is the easiest to visit without going there. Open the first book and you will find a rhapsody about it; step into the first picture-dealer's [shop] and you will find three or four high-coloured "views" of it. There is notoriously nothing more to be said on the subject. Everyone has been there, and everyone has brought back a collection of photographs. . . . It is not forbidden, however, to speak of familiar things.

Chapter 7

Trials of Home and Hard Labor

Madeleine (1950), *The Sound Barrier* (1952), *The Bridge on the River Kwai* (1957)

For their innovations and locations, Lean's films are considered landmarks. Their unresolved endings have brought them, however, to a court of extreme criticism. For some, given increasing compromises with Hollywood, Lean swapped a thoughtful ending for something saccharin or spectacular. For others, he brought the trials and tribulations of postwar filmmaking to subtle reflection.

Finding in his philosophy of cinema the traditional allegory between love and art, Alain Badiou sees a *forever* marking a resistance to any ordinary notion of dying. Whereas many consider *Brief Encounter* exemplary of the allegory, Badiou focuses on Kenji Mizoguchi's 1954 *The Crucified Lovers*, where the lovers smile as they go to their deaths. He draws from Arthur Rimbaud to pursue the poetic thread that cuts out from ordinary life the choice to resign oneself to prohibitions on passion—or to resist. What, he asks, will philosophy say to this choice? And the answer: "We must think the event. We must think the exception" beyond "the ordinary." He finds in philosophy a daring akin to how cinema draws its strength over and over again in trials "to be won" (2013: ch. 27).

In Lean's films, even when trials end up in courts of law, they trigger alterations and abstractions of a troubled consciousness tending to the philosophical: a sense of trespass and property damage in *Hobson's Choice*, a theft of persons and things in *Oliver Twist*, and a sense of redemption in *Great Expectations* when Magwitch is figured as an outlaw standing for the good against the English law that brands him a common criminal.

Chapter 7 continues with combustible motifs of music and technology. It focuses on the trials and tribulations in *Madeleine*, *The Sound Barrier*, and *The Bridge on the River Kwai*. The films share in constructing spaces of confinement. *Madeleine*'s Victorian murder trial ends with an almost smile, corresponding to the trial's famously unresolved verdict. *The Sound Barrier* questions the English family as an unbreakable unit through a wife's loyalty to her father, husband, and son. Both films ask what a woman owes herself. *The Bridge on the River Kwai* explores and exploits different modes of disobedience and sabotage as a bridge is built and then destroyed under caged conditions of hard labor.

Released one year after *The Passionate Friends*, *Madeleine* takes on an aged code of morality drawn in black and white. As in *This Happy Breed*, but not with technicolor, the camera pans over a city to close in on a well-to-do square in Glasgow until reaching one home in particular. The credits overlay a city of 1950 before it cuts back to a century earlier to the highly publicized trial in 1857 of Madeleine Hamilton Smith (Ann Todd), who may or may not have poisoned her lover. The film script drew from the trial transcript, newspaper reports, and the secret letters sent between the lovers. It drew also from Harold Purcell's play of 1944 titled (after Shakespeare) *The Rest Is Silence*. Having acted in this play, Ann Todd, now married to Lean, urged Lean to adapt the story. At first, the film's title referred to the *trial*, then to Madeleine. The cut of the main figure turned the court trial into an investigation of a young woman's confinement within a Victorian household.

The film opens with a family moving into a house (a Lean motif). The strict father wants to marry his daughter (off) to a respectable suitor. A perfect suitor is on offer: William Minnoch (Norman Wooland) of unquestioning fidelity until almost the end. Madeleine, however, is already devoted to a Frenchman (actually from the Channel Islands): a moneyless dandy and eventual blackmailer. Before *Ryan's Daughter*, Emile L'Angelier (Ivan Desny) is the sad shadow of a Byronic figure. Comporting himself with a walking stick, he comes off as a man of French fashion but also increasingly as disabled. The plot focuses not on the making of the illicit relationship but on its unmaking. Whether or not Madeleine poisoned her lover with a cup of laced cocoa comes out as *not proven*, a "bastard verdict" given an insufficiency of evidence. One would expect the film to convey this insufficiency to a tee. The film was generally disliked, even by Lean (Tony Williams 2000: 180f.). Coward complained: one can't make a film "in which you, the writer-director, don't know in your own mind what was the outcome. In other words, did she do it or didn't she?" (KB: 275). But which side should Lean have taken?

Melanie Williams finds similarities between the final almost smile of Madeleine as she is whisked away in freedom by carriage from the court, and Lawrence's final expression as he is driven away in a car (MW:71). There is also Adela's last smile in *A Passage* when she is back home in London. Williams is interested in how the public eye detaches from the camera's eye that tracks Madeleine's attempts to break free from the conventions of her historical time and from a cinema a century later when it refused to display Victorianism as out of date. More commentators who approach the trial as about a "young woman too respectable to convict" find a match of the smile with the public's approval of those who believed that *getting away with it* reinstated her born privilege (Jenkins 2019; Rance 1998: 227). Other critics think Lean was too much repeating strategies of his earlier films, so that more than the criticism of Victorianism coming over as "enigmatic," in Pauline Kael's words, the final uncertainty comes over as "superficial," "numbing," and "stiff" (1982: 350).

If, however, superficiality suggests a mere surface appearance without due cause, then it is telling that Madeleine on trial comes off as preoccupied more with her look than with her life-threatening situation: her appearance and dress before the court, the public, and, by implication, the camera. Perhaps we are being shown a beauty that impresses alone as, and for the sake of, appearance. Little lines pass by: *I wonder if Madeleine is wearing her new dress*. The poison that allegedly kills Emile by Madeleine's hand is purchased from the pharmacy to kill *a rat*, as she tells the pharmacist in registering the purchase, but, in an aside, also as a cosmetic for her *skin*—to which the retort comes: *Maddy, you are vain*. She later begs for the truth to be known: *I bought arsenic for my skin. Tell them that*. Is this a woman's film, again, about the norms of looking at women (on screen)—a film about women reconsidering the power and powder of their own image? What does it mean for someone to be vain or to act in vain, where vanity produces the nothing of no consequence, the biblical naught of no offspring? When Madeleine brings her family to *shame*, her father declares the family *naked*, stripped bare of its reputation and public image. He will demand newspaper reports to be burned. Remember that for film to put film on trial is for film to scratch beneath the surface where the scratching is laden with (Freudian or analytic) doors and keys of admission and exclusion.

Feminist scholars investigate what it has meant for women in film to kill their husbands or lovers as their only way to free themselves from a patriarchal cage of social propriety. Melanie Bell draws femininity into the frame to find women of a certain class "held up for scrutiny and examination." She refers to Mary Ann Doane's work (1987) to show how the threat of "the femme fatale" gets reworked as "a secret" to be "aggressively revealed, unmasked, discovered" (2009: 57–9). *Madeleine* comes to stand alongside *Daughter of Darkness* (dir. Lance Comfort, 1948, after Max Catto's play *They Walk Alone*, 1938), where a dark secret is revealed under conditions of domesticated exoticism. Looking back before film into bourgeois society and opera, Horkheimer and Adorno, together and separately, addressed the skewed rationale for women of "dark" skin (as in Bizet's *Carmen*) to be killed through an aestheticized exoticism. In a darkened space, the aesthetic distance allowed the audiences to be unnerved, yet to return to their brightly lit homes with no real damage done (Horkheimer [1936] 1982; Adorno [1955] 1999; Goehr 2021: 202–3). More comparisons are drawn, as by Williams, with Alicia's poisoned drink in Hitchcock's *Notorious* (1946) (MW: 67). But there is also Hitchcock's *The Paradine Case* (1947) where Ann

Todd, not yet playing the accused murderer in *Madeleine*, plays the suffering wife of a lawyer who falls for the strikingly beautiful woman on trial. Here, the trial is really that of the lawyer, of his professional duty and marital fidelity, so that his wife can have the last word for a happy restoration of their relationship (Orr 2010). *Madeleine* further finds a direct cinematic predecessor in the "loose" adaptation titled *Dishonored Lady* (dir. Robert Stevenson, 1947). Alternatively titled *Sins of Madeleine*, the film portrays the woman's guilt as the "natural sin" of being beautiful, because beauty triggers a desire that cannot be tamed, and men must (as again in *Carmen*) kill whatever causes the loss of their reason or control. *Dishonored Lady* leaves little doubt as to the "lady's" natural innocence: her infidelity and then murderous action have a due cause: a brutal and abusive husband.

In Lean's *Madeleine*, Ann Todd was criticized as coming off as cold and one-dimensional, unable to carry off the part that required the character to carry so many sides of a woman at once. On this note, a telling phrenological analysis of Madeleine was appended to the transcript of the actual trial indicating an unusual "force of character," a "magnetism" with "masculine and feminine qualities," a "great talent for engineering, architecture," a "great love of travelling," and a "[g]reat love for the Fine Arts," with the addition that "Martial music" would "please her." (1905: 292). We don't hear martial music in the film.

Lean's black-and-white camerawork, when color could have been used, draws the film back to film-noir expressionism. Weather patterns play to extremes of moods and norms. The film ends with a male voice-over: *Madeleine Smith, ye have heard the indictment. Were ye guilty or not guilty*? But of what? Doesn't her father arrange a marriage to maintain the family's reputation? Doesn't she get rid of her lover as collateral damage or as an analytic substitute for killing the father? If she did it! Madeleine's preferred life in the basement separates her from what is expected of her upstairs and positions her to see her lover, his footsteps and walking stick, or his notes or letters, arriving at illicit times of the day. Doesn't Emile then guarantee his fate the moment he enters the living room upstairs for the first time and with a paternalistic air? No longer hidden in the basement, he seems to open the door to his death, this way granting Madeleine her only way out. If she did it! Suicide is not an option: there is no thought that Madeleine purchases poison to kill herself.

In court, a close-up of the staircase leading from the cell signifies a threatening social mobility, her willingness to lower herself to a lover with ambitions to raise himself. The home and court run parallel in their cues: how doors are opened and closed, how basement and cell windows are barred. Keys and locks hold the evidence in abeyance: sure facts are staged as uncertain. As in the Dickens films and *Hobson's Choice*, a Hogarthian theatricality allows the closed quarters of the court to stratify the accused, the judge, lawyers, jury, and spectators according to rank and class. Todd expressed pride in being descended from William Hogarth (1980: 16). The court, and even more the home, feels haunted by the dead spirits of *Blithe Spirit* and *Great Expectations*. Close-ups of faces and feet in shoes contradict the broad swaths and banners of public opinion inside and outside the court, as when a preacher cries out against the artifice of *woman*. Madeleine's polished face gives little away. The crowd scenes recall and anticipate Lean's earlier and later films. A certain relief that the lover is dead is expressed by a crowd who fears the invasion of anything foreign, and the lover is viewed as "foreign" in so many ways.

In a questionably consensual sex act, Emile throws Madeleine to the floor. Released from his walking stick, he seems (as in *Ryan's Daughter*) suddenly to be a man of capability. In a battle of wills, he takes her down, as earlier, she takes him down in a gypsy dance. That he calls her *Mimi* fits her theatrical inclination to be part of a village revel that, staged at the bottom of the hill, suggests a happiness denied to those who live with propriety above. We see this upstairs-downstairs contrast on the wedding night of *Ryan's Daughter* and at the New Year's Eve party in *The Passionate Friends*. In the dance of a reel, prohibited passions are released. Here's the reeling perspectivism again. Madeleine throws Emile's stick for their bodies to move and then fall. From consent to non-consent, the different falls insitigated by each anticipates his final fall from the agonies administered perhaps by her poison.

William Alwyn composed the film score. Muir Mathieson conducted the Royal Philharmonic Orchestra. Alwyn reworked the Scottish reels and a French chansonette for the dance scenes. In 1951, for *Sight and Sound*'s special issue for the Festival of Britain, Ernest Lindgren devoted an article to Alwyn to certify the decade-long "supremacy" of British film music. He liked how "millions of people" could access "good music" even if only unconsciously, because meeting cinema's demand for looking, he said, one did not listen. Thanking Mathieson for engaging distinguished British composers, Lindgren noted that, by not making film music out of a concert music previously composed, Alwyn found his way to set out "untrammelled by tradition" (in his own words) on "an adventure into an uncharted and enchanted celluloid world." Lindgren named *Madeleine* as one of Alwyn's many film-music achievements.

Ian Johnson forefronts Coward's complaint to declare Alwyn's intention confused because Lean's intention (by his own admission) was confused. Johnson hears an overly "syrupy" motif accompanying the titles, which then continues as Madeleine pursues a "dalliance" that finds her happily waltzing down to the basement (2005: 224–6). For Johnson, there is a missed opportunity for the music to capture a complexity in the double standard that puts a woman on a pedestal while preaching against her from the podium. For Brian Jenkins, the court evidence as presented turns the case into a more interesting game of musical chairs (Jenkins 2019: 187). Was the Victorian furniture subtly being rearranged to Madeleine's advantage? Douglas MacGowan records the real Madeleine in Glasgow's North Prison repeatedly asking the prison officials for access to a piano (2007: 82). Eleanor Gordon and Gwyneth Nair take on the "too much waltzing" in Glasgow's musical life to which Madeleine and her suitors contributed (2009: 75–95).

Madeleine taunts Emile at least twice from his point of view. Standing outside the home near the start, he watches Madeleine playing the piano and singing in French to appease her father and suit her official suitor. She later pleads against his jealousy that her French song was really for him, her French lover. Sidelined and excluded again later, he watches her dancing with the upstanding English Minnoch to whom now she is showing more affection if not yet acceptance. The sense of Madeleine playing something forbidden on the piano turns the piano keys into keys of detection. Todd, to recall, was known for her "Rachmaninoff" moments in *The*

Seventh Veil, a reputation already passingly acknowledged in *The Passionate Friends*.

Between her French lover and English suitor, Madeleine spins on a reel controlled by her father. Almost exactly halfway, she demonstrates the genteel art of music-making to accord with the proper sentiments of persons well-bred. In the father's chair with all his assumed airs of entitlement, Emile sits and ominously says: *I shall be gone by the time your family returns*. A close-up on the cocoa cup shows him drinking. At first, she does not drink, so that it remains uncertain whether she has poisoned his cup of cocoa. Their conversation is polite but threatening. *Is that the instrument you play? Yes . . . I have true passion for the pianoforte* (Figure 18). Her playing of light music lasts only a few seconds, after which an undetermined cut of cause and effect finds Emile back in his living quarters holding his stomach in pain. Again, did this lover, made more jealous and hence possessive every time he was made to stand outside to look in, not somehow bring his death upon himself? The windows, like the Venetian blinds that render views unequal for those inside and out, guarantees an uncertainty equal

Figure 18 Poison and passion for the pianoforte, *Madeleine*, directed by David Lean, Cineguild, 1950.

to the historical court verdict. Maybe Madeleine smiles at the end because the front door to her home has been locked for good.

The Sound Barrier of 1952 is similarly reeled through the perspective of a woman finding faultlines in the alternating perspectives of men. Men are tested as they feel the call to take planes beyond the sound barrier. Women are tested for trying to break through a solidly bricked ceiling. A wife feels the betrayal of a husband whose calling seems supersonically to supersede his commitment to her: *I find now I'm married not only to a test pilot but married to an explorer as well. . . . Darling, I hate it.* The British pride from *In Which We Serve* is countered by her passionate doubt until, at the end, the moderation of British reserve kicks back in. She tries to be gung ho, but her doubt is palpable throughout.

Terence Rattigan's script tracks the confidence and the doubt. The subject is the dawn of the Jet Age when Britain and the United States were competing for domination of the skies. Adrian Smith details the Churchillian commitment to airpower and civil aviation in the building of the variously named biplanes, airships, and flying boats. He notes the camerawork and choreography of adventure as invested in the film's documentary tendency to put the science of industry and machine construction on display with a poetry of passion. Lean's team aimed "to get the feel of the immensity of space," to move from close-ups of a pilot to "the cloudscape" (2010: 492; MA: 74). Art and science give both form and subject-matter to the film.

Before the credits, Malcolm Arnold's music opens dancelike, for a British plane to move through the changing clear and cloudy sky. The motor's increasing volume dissolves into the orchestral score. Below are the remains of a broken Nazi plane with a swastika intact enough for an audience to recognize a defeated enemy. English soldiers are lying in the sun near the white Seven Sisters cliffs at Seaford. The film suggests epic thoughts while the music carries traces of film noir mixed with an increasingly eerie science-fiction motif. A plane and a telescope are proclaimed literally and as metaphor to have put *man* into a dangerous competition—a *fight*—with nature and the skies.

Ann Todd plays Susan, daughter of the obsessive scientist of the skies, Sir John Ridgefield (JR) (Ralph Richardson). She is sister to a brother who does not want to fly, wife and widow to Tony Garthwaite (Nigel Patrick), her father's test pilot who only wants to fly, and mother to their son, whose future she wants to redirect away from the skies. The home is an immense, stately house outside of London, aristocratic by design, yet a little too large, befitting an owner who made his money in oil. Oversized, antiquated busts and the largest possible telescope dominate the spaces of a living and a research that Susan wants to pull apart.

Susan declares the universe *unfriendly*. JR retorts that even if nature is *unconscious of our existence* and seems to have the upper hand, conscious humanity always wins the battle with its weapons of *imagination* and *courage*. If a plane's mechanics cannot break the speed of sound according to their *natural* design, then a reversal of the gears is humanity's answer, a revision and advance of the technology. Susan's doubt confronts JR's certainty or his possibly *evil* ambition as the death of loved ones becomes the price paid for scientific progress. The ending cannot rest with her condemnation. She comes to see the loneliness of her father's genius: *How alone you must have been*. Having left her father's home to protect her son's future, she returns—her last words being *We've come home*. With the door closing on the great battle, Susan's smile stands not for independence but for the forever of England's family. Meanwhile, an English plane breaks through the sound barrier to forge the reconciliation of the new world with a very old one. But still at the end, the eeriness in the music remains. The film was admired far more for its artistry than for its unsubtle messaging.

An almost *Gone with the Wind* moment kiss shows Susan accepting Tony's marriage proposal. An interrupting truck has just passed by, singing the war song of 1917: "Bless 'Em All," with hints of a change to "Fuck 'Em All." Once married, her passionate objection to his giving his life not to her but to her father as something a test pilot must do is expressed as her inability to bear the sound of a test plane in the sky (Figure 19). Her brother, entirely unsuited to their father's project, hates the sound so much that he kills himself by letting his plane crash. Susan goes to the local *Palace* cinema because there *you can't hear the sound so clearly*. The film she distractedly watches is given to us through its rousing British victory music. The cinema is a false bolt-hole: her husband's plane crashes

Figure 19 Anxious listening, *The Sound Barrier*, directed by David Lean, London Films, 1952.

to produce an enormous crater in the earth. Widowed, she turns to her son, who, now fatherless, *doesn't seem to mind the noise at all*. Her unhappiness at his future being scripted is palpable. She fears for the son what she saw in her husband, his stopping in his tracks whenever he heard a plane engine, only to wave away the danger as a *piece of cake. . . . I think it's the most exciting sound I've ever heard*.

Susan is far more prone to cover her ears. Tony's death is construed as necessary to sustain a generational dialectic of age and youth. Having been in the war, he's a bit too old and not quite smart enough to know what is needed postwar. Only a younger pilot can achieve on a fourth run what was not yet achievable on the prior runs. Were there no younger pilot around, they'd have to design a *pilotless* plane: *Ever heard of pilotless aircraft?* In 1952, that was *the* future. Meanwhile, England must depend on its *sons*.

One evening, Susan plays the piano—very briefly. It marks a moment of her wanting to move out of her father's house and to share her news that she is pregnant. Had she her freedom, she would play a *modernist music* that she likes quite as much as modern art. Her tastes favor not the prison house of *experiments* in science but a freer *experimentalism* in art (Goehr 2008: ch. 4). She detests her father for his having despised her for *not being born a son*. He snipes at the dinner table: *I sent her to Oxford to get an education and all she comes back with is a passion for donkey-tailed daubs and modernistic music*. Her taste is said to come from her mother. The donkey-tails likely came from the mockery of the daubing or color-splashing of the so-described "jackass" painting in Moscow and Paris around 1910. If the orchestral music for every plane in flight is juxtaposed with motor sounds and warning signals in the air-control tower, the poetic revenge brings out humanity's design faults. While a futurist could add a donkey tail to a dove, a plane so tailed would be grounded. Artists make impossible, but more humanistic or morally less objectionable, objects of fiction and fantasy. As in *Kwai and Lawrence*, what comes naturally to birds in flight comes only with a necessary and often destructive artifice in human machines. What can art or cinema do to counteract the destruction?

Planes are named for humanity's myths: *Vampire* and *Prometheus*. Even the *Comet* suggests something unnatural about the plane's tail. Susan must explain the myths to Tony, who only understands the flight paths of scientific ambition. *Prometheus? Who was he? He was a Greek god who stole from heaven. . . . Came to a sticky end, didn't he? He did. But the world got fire*. Their shared flight to Cairo for a day's holiday comes with an advertisement: a destination in only five hours! Over continental Europe, the flight path covers England's white cliffs, Paris's Arc de Triomphe and Eiffel Tower, the Alps, Athens's ruins, and the pyramids on the approach to Cairo. Close-ups on great antiquities pit the ruination that lets human achievements endure forever against the violent combustion of modernism under the banner of scientific progress. Susan feels the smallness of the earth below. Tony chides her for being *old-fashioned*, for worrying *about the poor old Earth. Look up there. There's our future. Space. You can't make that insignificant. Down there's had it*. Returning to England, the pouring rain replaces Cairo's sun. Tony asks: *Who . . . said, "Oh, to be in England?"* Susan answers: *Browning. But he wasn't* (in England but in Venice). Tony's literary and romantic ignorance seems suddenly to be another reason for denying him a future. A future in space cannot outwit a future, carried by the cinema, that links the forever of nature to the ideals of love and art.

With the US release, the film's title was changed to *Breaking the Sound Barrier*. Why stress the achievement? Lean said that he had

> always been fascinated by adventure. I always think of the first man who went off in a boat and disappeared over the horizon, not knowing what he was going to find. I suppose I'm a romantic, but I find that frightfully exciting—the fact that we're still reaching out, trying to discover what we are, what the world is, what the universe is. (KB: 296)

What, however, did a fascination with adventure mean beyond a scientific project of which one result had so recently been the atomic bomb? The film won many prizes. Mostly, the film, replete with clichés, is forgotten today. When it is remembered, it is for its supersonic effects or "flying hardware," as Clancy Sigal put it, only then wittily to add: "as long as it stays up in the air *The Sound Barrier* still crashes through" (1984, TL: 35).

When Lean chose the young Malcolm Arnold to do the music, conductor John Hollingsworth offered some advice: "I know David well, he'll ask you for a big tune, romantic feeling and all he wants is Rachmaninoff, but it'll be Rachmaninoff and Arnold." Arnold recalled producing a score with "much more" than Rachmaninoff. Making a spitfire dance for the credits, he composed something in the style of a "Tchaikovsky-ballet," after which he asked Lean for permission to recompose the music as a work for the concert hall (2011: 33–5; KB: 292). At least one critic, writing in 1952 for *Picture Post* with the title "Great Expectations Fulfilled," found an "ultra-modern man" skydiving to "a modern screen ballet" akin to the *symphonie chorégraphique* that was Maurice Ravel's *Daphnis and Chloe*. The kinship to French modernism would have appealed to Susan.

Regarding his music as superseding the "commercial soundtrack," Arnold allowed for a doubleness to cut across that old chestnut that refused a music intrinsic to a film (song, opera, or play) to fly away into an independence of production. Independence never meant cutting all ties, in music or in relationships. Relative autonomy maintained a healthy friction. This issue assumed pertinence when Maurice Jarre gave *Lawrence* and *Zhivago* separable musical overtures and intermissions without word or image. Before Jarre, however, there was already Arnold, as Roger Manvell confirmed in 1955:

> Most films have brief overtures played during the sequence of credit titles. . . . This music can set the mood for the film, . . . as in *Of Mice and Men* or *The Sound Barrier*, where the action begins behind or even before the credits themselves. . . . The opening music to films is one of the more fascinating details in film technique. (1955: 58)

Arnold went on to compose the music for *Kwai*.

The Bridge on the River Kwai (1957) is an adaptation of the 1952 novel of fused fact and fiction by the highly (war)-decorated author Pierre Boulle: *Pont de la rivière Kwai*. The film's chief confrontation is between Colonel Saito (Sessue Hayakawa) and Colonel Nicholson (Alec Guinness). The dialectic between construction and destruction is staged as a *madness! madness!* on both sides. British prisoners build a bridge for the Japanese according to principles of British skill and honor, after which an allied commando group blows it up. Whether the destruction makes sense of the questions surrounding the construction is unresolved. The historical background regards the horror of the number who died in prison camps and the horrendous condition of a labor of servitude. In the cinematic reconstruction, the location and climate (in Ceylon/Sri Lanka) made for its own hard labor: a bridge had to be built and then blown up. A 1958 "short," *The Rise and Fall of a Jungle Giant*, documents the labor and the financing to celebrate more Sam Spiegel as producer than Lean as director. While brought into the familiar river of extreme critical opinion, the film won several awards.

If the film is a "one man's story," which man's story is told? Commentators usually name Nicholson first: his having made an epic mistake in demanding British honor of his men whatever the cost. Loyalty to one's (British) army superior isn't meant to translate into serving a (Japanese) slave driver. By tracking Nicholson's mind, the film stages an epic (Aristotelian) reversal to hold up a Shakespearean mirror to the conscience of the one who asks: "what have I done?" Enduring the extremes of torture as a model to his men, Nicholson finally falls to his death on the detonator that blows up the bridge. Is this an action or an accident? An extension of Lean's camera, Nicholson is seen, in Michael Sragow's observation, "like a director who falls in love with the stage so much that he forgets his reason for being there" (1985: 24, 1994).

Several commentators remark on the too thin veneer of a political questioning—what should I do?—as revealing a much more personal or poetic "What have I done?" The ignorance to knowledge trajectory of epic tragedy shows a "stiff-necked colonel," in Santas's description, rising to the "heights of conceit and self-deception" as British engineering skills are paraded as superior to Japanese inefficiency. Santas employs a musical metaphor of "choruslike reverberations" to compare Lean's move from the political to the poetic with the once Homeric objectivity that approached bloody massacres on the battlefield through the lens of art. With "a slightly changed atonal musical note or two," any wisdom that could have been gained is re-reversed to reveal the repetitive blindness of human folly. Even if aimed at ambiguity and irony, the ending comes over as "slippery" (2012: 15–17; 2008: 40–4). Here is another little note change, a "grace note" to bring out the smallest detail or ornament in an overwhelmingly seamless whole (Crowdus 2001: 50–1).

The film's cast is of counterpointed figures, with a script replete with quandaries about the human condition. First, there is Nicholson's double, the camp commander, whose (Japanese) brutality is measured against his appreciation of both America, symbolized by a pinup calendar on his wall, and England, symbolized by the whisky and cigars and the fact that he earlier studied art in London. A reluctant soldier, he tortures Nicholson while sharing with him a well-mannered meal. Is he meant to be rescued by his Western ways?

Then there is "American imposter" Shears (William Holden) spotlighted in the film's advertisement. He, too, is of two minds: to serve or not to serve. Is he lazy or despondent? Does his final death signal a rediscovered courage? Sitting back often as an onlooker, does he better assume the distance of Lean's camera? When the *soldiers* first arrive at the camp, close-ups are offered of their worn boots or bare feet. The camp guards issue orders in broken English. Saito describes the new arrivals as *prisoners*. Shears spits out the word *slaves*. Recalling *The Rules of the Game* (dir. Jean Renoir, 1939), Shears interrupts Nicholson and Saito's spat over the Geneva Convention. Saito tells the prisoners *A word to you about escape. There is no barbed wire. No stockade. No watchtower. They are not necessary. We are an island in the jungle.* Whenever contradicted by Nicholson, Saito counters with a *Don't speak to me of rules. This is war! . . . not a game of cricket.*

Well-named, Shears cuts chains to prove he can escape, only then to return to camp when his lie about his army rank is revealed. In his interactions, a world-weary fatigue with having to survive contrasts with the timely survival urged in Coward and Lean's war films. Mostly, Shears wants to relax and trade rationed provisions. Santas calls him a "cynical pragmatist," even perhaps the film's real hero (2012: 22–3). Raymond Durgnat placed him at the center of the tragic crisscross in the modern epic. A hero who refuses to be one corresponds to the *American* who challenges the norms of class and rank for the sake of leveling democracy to an equality of all values. With all and no one claiming certainty, the repeated *madness-madness* spoken as the last words leaves the world at best with an unsettled order. Being a film that simultaneously condemns and condones, it is no surprise for Durgnat that its criticism matched the double perspective ([1970] 2011: 103, 118–19).

Interspersed in the script are quick-witted snipes. The snipe comes from a bird whose targeted beak turns into a spray of bullets. Birds of natural beauty become vultures of prey when humanity tries to master and manipulate nature. The camera pans and feeds an anthropomorphic schema of human cruelty and waste while reeling perspectives sustain competing ironic and slippery camouflages of meaning. The contrast of the two world wars is palpable. The first was made for *an officer and a gentleman—when officers fought with only a swagger* stick—but the second for the madness of a mass and the madness of a leader. In the crisscross (as in Coward's crosswords), a reeling perspectivism emerges to leave no single view safe in place.

A parade of clichés at a camp lineup rings hollow: a good end justifies the means or that work makes you free. Saito says: *Let me remind you of General Yamashita's motto: Be happy in your work*. In 1957, newspapers were still reporting the false promises nailed on the gates of entry to concentration camps. While Lean stood proud in having told a good story, critics stressed the historical infidelity and concession to Hollywood's commercialism. In Chapter 1, I quoted Lindsay Anderson's description of *Kwai* as a "huge, expensive chocolate box of a war picture." The description stuck. In France, François Truffaut dismissed the film as "two old men arguing inside a hut" (1978: 86–7. Santas 2012: xviii). "Old fogies" is a closer translation. The wastage of time anticipated the condemnation of the later Falklands War, so-named from Margaret Thatcher's British side, as "two bald men arguing over a comb."

With a false upright posture, the weariness and waning of the British Empire is the theme. Standing on the completed bridge, Nicholson leans with a stick of his disability against the railing (as Hamlet on the ramparts). Nicholson drops his stick into the water, somehow between intent or accident. Melanie Williams asks whether Nicholson in this moment is freed from the crutch of his British confidence so that, with Saito standing by him, he can face the enemy that has become himself, face-to-face. She notes how Lean allowed his "stroking" camera to capture what it means for someone suddenly to lose their grip and how Lean was borrowing from a film on which he'd worked in 1927, Maurice Elvey's *Roses of Picardy* (MW: 149–50; KB: 48). Losing grip of one's stick is the motif of dependency in *Madeleine, Ryan's Daughter*, and *A Passage*. In the last, Frederick Weatherly and Haydn Wood's 1916 war-song "Roses of Picardy" is also used. "Leaning" is a Lean motif wherever great ambitions call for their deflation. In *Great Expectations*, the fall demands a great fire; in *Ryan's Daughter*, dynamite. In *Lawrence* and *Zhivago*, battles leave bodies lying in fields of blood. Early reviews of *Kwai* addressed the combustibility motif as actions and attitudes rise too high only then to fall in a great tailspin.

One outstanding review, "Bridges Over the Kwai," was written in 1959 by a former prisoner who made his firsthand experience count. Ian P. Watt used Boulle's novel to expose Lean's muddles. Boulle's novels, including *Planet of the Apes* (1963), treated "the destructive consequences that arise from the West's [technical] mastery of means but not of ends." Boulle had served as an engineer and secret agent regarding the *Death Railway* in Burma. He wrote a memoir, *My Own River Kwai*. Watt read Boulle as taking on England and Nazi Germany as a Western background of "archaic" educational traditions, to make "the harmonious simplicity" of the Malayan villagers stand out (where, following the dialectic, the harmonious simplicity was itself a projection of the West). Watt appreciated the film's opening: "the vultures, the narrow cuttings, the bedraggled prisoners on the [railway] line." He liked the excitement, humor, and visual beauty: "Technically, Mr. Lean had obviously shown his old accomplishment." He felt the repetition of Pip's first fright at Magwitch when Shears mistakes a child's kite for a monstrous vulture. But then came the false notes: the bridge could not have been built with the resources shown to be available, and, shot in Sri Lanka, the landscape and climate were all wrong. The "most perfectly photogenic compositions" revealed the perspective not of one who'd *been there*, but of one who had arrived later with "the distant perspective of the tourist." Watt was overall unforgiving of the general portraiture: the all-American cowboy; the soap opera pin-ups; Saito as "an incompetent and sadistic drunkard" repainted into "yet another of those frustrated artists with unhappy childhoods." Worst of all, Lean betrayed Boulle by blowing up the bridge, this way erasing the original "central irony," that the allies would build a bridge to be used against their own cause. Watt wondered whether cinema could ever surpass its surface display to reach any really significant insight: regarding, say, the "cumulative effects" of "humanity's blindness" (TL: 216–18).

The bridge blowup was the film's first thought: "You can't present that [sort of idea] in a movie and then not do it" (SS: 125). Brownlow, contrarily, reports from the 1989 interview of Carl Foreman, the scriptwriter, that Boulle had wanted to destroy the bridge but couldn't see how to do it and so encouraged Lean's team to go ahead (KB: 11). Advising on the film, relations became strained. Santas notes more abstractly: "film, like music, is set in time. . . . Time restrictions . . . require condensing the contents of a lengthy novel, cutting characters, simplifying plots and authorial reflections." If this is obvious, so, too, is the observation that actors can never exactly look like starved and tortured prisoners. (That's why acting matters, I would say.) Nevertheless, considering Charles Laughton for the part of Nicholson, the Lean team found the portly stature just a bit too unrealistic (2012: xxx, 11).

All this means is that *fidelity* with a little *infidelity* thrown in better brings the desired *realism* to its productive *illusion, artifice, artistry, and effect*—and vice versa. André Bazin knew this in his review titled "High Fidelity." He regarded the film as "far superior" to the book in its having not thinned but thickened Boulle's adventure and moral psychology. Even if Lean had stretched certain elements by introducing women, the resulting erotic aura felt right in preparing for the final scene of heroic death. Nevertheless, while appreciating Lean's "perfect equation between ambition and execution," Bazin did what he often did: he expressed a final preference for the French and Italian artistry of Renoir and Fellini (1997: 225–30).

Watt had appreciated the fact that Lean had not even tried to show the stink, chaos, decay, and monastic condition of the camp. But he wondered, then, whether he had conceded too much to Hollywood by allowing Shears, with a "stupefying indifference," to lie on a beach under the sun to ask: "What's a nice girl like you doing in a place like this?" Also reading Watt's review, Williams views the beach episode differently, as a filmmaker's ironic homage to the silent movie, W. S. Van Dyke's *White Shadows of the South Seas* (1928), where masculine desire finds its orientalized object (MW: 147–52). Focusing on the conflict between "intention and actual effect," Victor Perkins asked: How could an audience be educated about war's "futility" if drawn into a glorious, magnificent, and spectacular landscape? Did this epic film *about* self-deception not deceive itself? (1972: 149). Gary Crowdus similarly recalls Boulle's novel as an "over-the-top anti-British satire" combined with "rabid anti-Japanese racism." The bridge that wasn't blown up in the novel brought home a "battle of wills" that, in the film, told that "war is hell, yes, but it's also incredibly cinematic" (2001: 50–1).

To build a bridge only to pull it down tracks the pathos, the tragedy, and the old Shakespearean wit of digging one's own grave. To dig one's grave is to sabotage one's self-standing, one's construction of a self as a bridge or scaffolding over troubled waters. When eyes are closed, it doesn't matter, or it matters less, how much or little is placed before them. Eyes turn inwards as ears retreat into a selfhood—so that the film becomes a satirical allegory of the building not of a bridge but of character.

A 2013 remake of *Kwai*, by Jonathan Teplitzky, *The Railway Man*, is a "return" story, the return to the torture of an English soldier at the camp. Beyond referencing *Kwai*, it references *Brief Encounter*. The former soldier and engineer loves trains and meets the love of his life on a train. Passing Carnforth station, she tells him the love story. The film shows the lovers in bed and the prisoners being tortured. Crudely psychoanalytic: one has to *relive* the experience to *relieve* the pain. We watch a therapeutic return with the help of a passionate lover. Noting how many films were making so much ado about trains, writer Philip Oakes wittily surmised that perhaps more than the trains, it was the train stations that were really *stoking* the passions (1990 TL: 10; also Huntley 1969).

Kwai opens with a train delivering prisoners and ends with a train trying to cross a bridge. As in *Brief Encounter*, the first and last station for the train gives form and frame to the film. And there is the residue again of Coward's wit and military experience. Lean never served. When Coward's "Mad Dogs and Englishmen" draw *Kwai*'s prisoners into the madness of the midday sun, one feels the line that conveys the "shame/When the English claim/ The earth/ That they give rise to such hilarity and mirth." England's *forever* is still in ironic play. When prisoners who try to escape are put in solitary confinement to bake in the sun, the soldiers respond with a gutsy rendition of the courage of a *jolly good fellow*. The radio tells the news and broadcasts a music to encourage toasts to King and Country and to bolster British pride in overcoming adversity. We hear that elm trees built London Bridge and that the bridge lasted 600 years. Only a few scenes show the hard labor that would build a bridge to last. With less labor shown, the bridge can be made more easily to fall.

The confrontation that divides the allies over whether the bridge should be destroyed little erases their shared ability to have fun, as when, one evening, a drag entertainment chimes out with: *If you were the only . . . girl in the world*, the song also used in *In Which We Serve*. The *drag* contrasts with the soldiers' first *bedraggled* appearance. Howard Maxford notes of the scene how "violin and drums can be heard, yet they're never shown"—nor is a gramophone player—making one wonder where the music is actually coming from (2000: 102). The music further recedes into the background as the stage is juxtaposed with secret nighttime activities. A victory music ends a film with very little scored music. The end circles back to the beginning. The audition of marching feet is crosscut by a river still flowing and a bird still flying, because nature will *always* sweep away humanity's floating debris. Bits of the bridge float down river, specifically the celebratory sign of its construction. One could fish the sign out and take it home as a souvenir (Figure 20). Today, climate change calls for a humanity that will last for the sake of future generations: a generous gift.

Kwai is known less for Arnold's atonal or dissonant undertones than for the determined step and beat in the whistle of the "Colonel Bogey March" by the soldiers arriving at the camp. One commentator notes "the epic that whistled itself around the world"; another, the self-respect of those who "whistle while we work" (Santas 2012: 62; Durgnat [1970] 2011: 102). Lean and his team encouraged the "real swagger" of "grandeur" and "pride" (MW: 147; KB: 16). The longer the march felt, the more Lean tested the limits of how long a director could keep a motif going. Lean wanted to use "Bless 'Em All," as in *The Passionate Friends*, a First World War song, but the cost was prohibitive. So rights to use Kenneth J. Alford's 1914 "Colonel Bogey March" were secured, but only by granting Alford's widow her wish that the march be played without words because the words had been rewritten as rude. So the song became a whistle (because a whistle is never rude!). The whistle repeats itself as an auditory signal alongside other auditory signals: as when *Radio Tokyo* signs off with a reminder: *This is your friendliest enemy reminding you to take it easy . . . and never volunteer for anything*. The radio's joke gets redirected to a soldier who observes that had the broken radio remained broken, they'd never have known *about the train*. Unexpected moments can change the course of all things, the timetable: *There's always the unexpected, isn't there?* (Figure 21).

When Arnold brought the whistle to the orchestra, he offered a "counter melody" as a subtle variation on a theme. He was excited by the experimentation and the speed of composition that film

Figure 20 Humanity's debris, *The Bridge on the River Kwai*, directed by David Lean, Horizon Pictures, 1957.

Figure 21 Fixing the radio, *The Bridge on the River Kwai*, directed by David Lean, Horizon Pictures, 1957.

made possible. *Kwai*'s 34-minute score was composed in a couple of weeks. It was appreciated for its unobtrusive presence. Hugo Cole heard in the menacing orchestral and natural sounds not a quotation but an allusion to Hunding's horn so as to raise the (once Wagnerian) tension almost to a "breaking point." With the music made so integral, no "musical quotation" would have worked (1989: 57, 62). Cole had said the same regarding the Wagnerian strain in Arnold's shoemaking music for *Hobson's Choice*

Arnold said a lot about working with Lean. One interview allowed him to offer *Kwai* as a desert island disk to express his luck in having worked with directors, and above all Lean, who were "terribly conscious of the value of sound and music." He recalled the scene accompanying the opening credits when a bird flying and swooping down into the jungle tracks the camera that closes in on the graves of soldiers who have died building the railway to their own prison. "The distant sound of a train, gradually getting louder," gives way to the trucks from which new prisoners are pushed out by the Japanese captors who have "made them trek for many days through the jungle under appalling conditions." Arnold noted the transition that began with the noises of nature and machines to move on then to the "harrowing" music that began precisely when the train stopped in its tracks (2011: 33–4). In this moment, one certainly sees and feels the weight of soldiers having come a long distance: their subsequent march lightens the mood. The machine gun that points *at* the prisoners, who are laying down the tracks for the train to move on, converges with the camera that points the hard labor *out*. When Lean's name appears as director, the camera turns away from the violence to a seamless auditory-vision of a beautiful river and mountainous landscape.

Arnold also described the "celebrated case" with "many headaches," where the reality effect of the "Colonel Bogey March" only proved the power of film's technological artifice, how for "four minutes" soldiers had not only to whistle but to march in time. Given the heat, their rhythm proved as wobbly as their pitch. The effect had to be created in the background and then attached to the image. To fit the whistling, an independent march was then composed as an orchestral extension (2011: 31–2).

Arnold was wary about placing his music into the many hands of recordists and cutters but thought Lean a true master of the team. Most composers found Lean terrifying, he added, but he didn't. He recalled offering music lessons to Lean when, in *The Sound Barrier*, he sensed "a frustrated musician." To no avail. Receiving an Oscar for *Kwai*, Arnold was happy but thought the "Colonel Bogey March" more prizeworthy in cocking a "snook" at the Japanese. If, as a composer, he was calling for Lean to take notice of the score, so the "bogey" captured the exact moment in a fraught match when a golfer caught the attention of his adversary. If enemies became counterparts in a productive-destructive doubling, so Lean's sometimes antagonistic team brought their hard labor to a film well-constructed. But the end, as ever unresolved, left more work to do. Arnold praised Lean's "other" composers: William Alwyn and Richard Addinsell, yet felt his pride of place in having worked on three of Lean's films (2011: 37, 73, 93, 99, 120). Was it not "the oldest joke in history," he quipped, "to call me Master of the Lean's music"?

Chapter 8

A Myth, a Gift, and an Echo

Lawrence of Arabia (1962), *Doctor Zhivago* (1965), *A Passage to India* (1984)

This final chapter treats the three films for which Maurice Jarre composed the music: *Lawrence of Arabia* (1962), *Doctor Zhivago* (1965), and *A Passage to India* (1984). It is the most epic in its length. It brings out a running thread: how every composer was tested by Lean for a music made *for his* films, a score to complete a film's integral musicality and soundscape. An almost operatic myth works through *Lawrence*, the gift of a musical instrument through *Zhivago*, and a sustained echo through *A Passage*. Countless shots and cuts produce crosswords of clues that rarely yield set solutions. Questions of (in)fidelity pertain to individuals, families, and countries, and to original texts of which the films are more or less adaptations. Epic questions place political agency in conflict with personal agency. Lean expressed pride in taking new risks the more drawn he became to characters who refuse "to face defeat even when they realize that their most cherished expectations may go unfulfilled" (Phillips 2006: 96). Lean sought ever more defamiliarizing places for a filmmaking about the literal and metaphorical transport required for an adventure. Yet, home away from home, he carried along with him every film he'd ever made.

When Lean introduces Sherif Ali or Ali ibn el Kharish (Omar Sharif) into *Lawrence*, he makes a dark figure on a horse approach from a far horizon. With words, noises, and no music, the tension of who he is—a Turk? Bedu?—mounts over the flat landscape for three minutes—a mirage, perhaps, in an arid heat. We watch Lawrence and his guide, Tafas, watching. The great silent expanse suggests a desert awaiting its remapping by a human hand, a foreign force. When Tafas recognizes Sherif Ali, he aims his handgun but is shot by him in return with a rifle—to make weapons a motif. Ali explains that a member of one tribe may not take the water from the well of another, and this water well belongs to him. Water becomes another motif—from the water that relieves thirst to the cocktails in the English clubhouse, and to where the desert meets the sea. With Tafas dead, Lawrence, referred to by Ali as *English*, names Ali first *murderer*, then *friend*. As Saito doubles Nicholson with recognition and resistance, Ali doubles Lawrence. When friendship means sharing water, the friendship endures, and the naming is renegotiated.

Lean regretted making the long shot shorter than first conceived (Sandra Lean 2001: 170; also Turner 1994). It became, nevertheless, a quotable moment for this film and cinema in general. Lean recalled: "Nowadays you don't hold a shot like that. But if you think of it . . . in terms of the second movement of a symphony, it's got to have that kind of weight. I don't say that I'm writing music. . . . But flow, music, creating images, it's in the same line of country" (SS: 27). Typically, a symphony's second movement is weighted by a slower tempo. From symphonic form, one soon feels a setup along Wagnerian lines. By pairing Lohengrin and Lawrence for a suggestive moment, we see that naming a man or cutting him a suitable cloth according to an indeterminate or unknown identity can bring lines drawn in the sand for a modern nation-state almost to a standstill. Before film, opera and theater dominated the construction of a drama with all the tragic and comic elements that turned the hero into an antihero and the epic into an anti-epic.

The cloth for Lawrence (Peter O'Toole) is white, as his skin is white, while his eyes are blue, as Lawrence's eyes were really blue. One senses a divination of a prophet or man-god of Arabia drawn out by the Christianized West. An early advertising poster contradicts the light-skinned complexion and then withdraws the face behind the white headdress to bring the question of *who this man is* or *was* into focus. Williams notes the allegory to cinema's origins: "The gradual transformation of Ali from abstract black shape on the horizon . . . to a real flesh-and-blood man is a remarkable cinematic achievement. It also alludes to the origins of cinema itself" (MW: 166). In the long shot, the something or someone indeterminate that comes to living form is set against an empty landscape where an individual like Lawrence, now paired with Lean, comes face-to-face with himself with almost a divine directness.

John Mack, in *The Prince of Our Disorder*, is one of many historians wanting to separate history from myth (1976; also Hodson 1995). Lawrence was five and a half feet tall and wanted to be taller and was more a coordinator of the Arab Revolt than its leader. Contrarily, a tall Peter O'Toole charges ahead of all others with a role-playing encouraged, before Lean, by Lawrence's reconstruction of himself. Lawrence made himself and was then made by others into an epic would-be hero, where the "would-be" captures the increasing doubt as to the mission. In the film script, constant exchanges dominate as to what makes a man be of England or of Arabia, what makes one *interesting* enough to be *written* about or be followed about by a journalist, what counts as being educated in *several languages* or *music* and *literature*, what it means to be able to quote from the Koran, or, finally, to sleep in a bed *with sheets*. Dressing the man is the issue for the representation of Lawrence as a member of the British army and for his transformation into a leader of Arabia at odds with British order and rule. His mission, to bring political strength and liberty to *Arabia*, inverts itself to become a mission to secure the fidelity of a country to him.

Before Lean, others tried to make a Lawrence film. Alexander Korda tried in the 1930s until the project was abandoned given censorship policies and wartime sensitivities regarding the representation of "the Turks" (Richards and Hulbert 1984). Nazi Germany's Josef Goebbels oversaw the making of *Uprising in Damascus* to make Lawrence into "a cunning agent of British Imperialism and Zionism" (Jackson 2007: 39). The Cold War and

Suez Crisis further compounded the difficulties. Only Lean, it was said, really succeeded in bringing to film a figure who had never wanted a film to be made about him.

As a contradictory figure, Lawrence serves two masters, two countries, but where his self intervenes to render his adventure a service to the self. The theme of betrayal or treachery is premised on the passion for illusions and for the disillusionment that comes from looking at oneself through the refracted lens of a country to which one does not belong: through an Arabic knife that he is given to carry. He is described as a *sword with two edges*. The film script forefronts the master-servant dialectic as a personal struggle within a tribal conflict and the First World War. When Lawrence claims a personal cause for giving up on his mission, he is told that such a cause is a betrayal of the one who serves, even when the master is a shifting target.

Commentators claim *Lawrence* the most unsettling and most memorable of Lean's films. They trace political and personal motifs of domination and loyalty to a country whose identity is as much contested as the man's. They assess a film given over to a touristic and panoramic spectacular, what it meant to shoot on location in difficult terrain, and what more it meant, from a British perspective, to let inauthentic accents play to the multiplicity and indeterminacy of identities for the characters. Omar Sharif, capable in many languages, expressed pride in playing "a foreigner without anyone knowing exactly where (he) came from" (Caton 1999: 24, 56).

Fidelity through infidelity sustains the reeling perspectivism that splits a singular mind into competing drives. The split produces mirror images, again, of doubles and counterparts. Yet, increasingly, the mythification renders the figure an empty vessel. The void is not the *man of all seasons* (played by Peter O'Toole in 1966 with a script by Robert Bolt) nor the alienated modern man of no *shadow* or *qualities*. It is the would-be turn of an *ordinary* mortal man of *flesh and blood* into an *extraordinary* figure whose divined assumption becomes an under-determination of a private personality, this way allowing a public persona to be all things to all *men* and for all *men* to invest all things into the one who leads them. (Similar words are claimed for a brief while by the Revolutionary leader in *Zhivago*.) Being *of Arabia* is to be *of a desert,* which the script describes as a *nothing* for the English who take it over, and as a place that, with a great past, can become great again: *you were great. Nine centuries ago* (when *London was a village*). *Time to be great again.*

In his *The Seven Pillars of Wisdom. A Triumph*, T. E. Lawrence concluded his preface by assuming no pretense to impartiality: "I was fighting for my hand, upon my own midden. Please take it as a personal narrative piece out of memory. I could not make proper notes: indeed it would have been a breach of my duty to the Arabs if I had picked such flowers while they fought." After the fact, he reconstructed his experiences of the broad landscape to cover 1916–18, to draw, as befits a midden, more pillars of wisdom than monuments to victory. Likewise, Lean claimed his license to rearrange chronology and facts to capture Lawrence—and himself as director—less as a maker of history than as a poet of a man's figuration (Bolt 1962). Part of the filmic figuration drew from the messy question of Lawrence's birth. When Lawrence is told: *you are free to choose your own name. El Aurens* becomes his name: it sounds like Lawrence but assumes an otherness as he adopts the dress of a man of Arabia.

Technology persists as a motif in the film, as radio and telephone wires track the trains for the literal and imaginative transport of a nation seeking its identity. Script lines tell of telephone wires that have been broken, so that it can be asked whether a communication or a negotiation without all the modern machines might not better resolve human conflicts. Broken lines spread a humanistic doubt over the military confidence in weapons. As in *Kwai*, telephones, radios, and weapons *depend* on English engineering. The skill is brought into and imposed upon a foreign land where East-West battles of will and skill allow the English to betray the *Arabs*. At the same time, different Arabic groups are described as borrowing or stealing from the English, only then to betray each other.

With crossed lines drawn in the sand, Lawrence allows truth and lies to blur. Much gets lost of words in translation. Colonizing and imperialist tactics sustain a cinematic criticism of all and any nation or empire, East or West, extending its limbs into places already settled. Plundering foreign lands is met by a snide: when you've got what you want, you'll go home. Having just blown up a train, Lawrence refuses the snide on the grounds of being neither a *fool* nor a *deserter*. If the *desert* can be home to no one, then everyone will eventually seek a place with *water and green trees*. Lawrence will go home but not because he got what he wanted.

Lawrence arrives in "Arabia" as a figure of contrast and antagonism to the standing British army. At first, he is an army officer with an unspecified *minor function*, playing like a schoolboy with a map of army maneuvers laid out over a table. Mapping is a motif, as are English schoolboy tactics. He is prone to tricks when using a match to light a cigarette, to feel the pain of the heat without letting on that the burn hurts. If it hurt, he'd be an ordinary man of flesh and blood. Testing his flesh reoccurs when, later, he is badly beaten. Commentators make much of Lawrence's self-punishment for his forbidden homosexual desire—beginning with Coward's quip to retitle the film, with so "pretty" a male star, for Florence and not Lawrence (Jackson 2007: 95).

What has feminization to do with the failure of heroic formation: Does it save or undo him; does it play to a hero who'd rather be a *poet* than a *man of action*? As in so many Lean films, self-knowing shifts between public service and a *happy breeding*. Critics note the absence of women, despite passing sightings of the backs of women bidding farewell as their men go off to battle or of female corpses strewn in a village massacre. The absence plays to an abstraction of an ideal feminized figure to capture another way that Lawrence is seen and sees himself.

Lawrence opens with a musical overture of quickly alternating motifs: percussive, symphonic, jaunty, and march-like. The Lawrence motif is marked for memory, to remember a man as myth. The credits acknowledge Lean as co-producer with Sam Spiegel, co-scriptwriter with Robert Bolt, and director. Jarre is credited for the *music composed* and Gerhard Schurmann for *orchestrations*. The Lean team wanted to repeat what Arnold had done in *Kwai*, to orchestrate a score around a recognizable march. They landed with Kenneth J. Alford's "The Voice of the Guns" (1917). The team interviewed several composers: Arnold, William Walton, Aram Khachaturian, Benjamin Britten, Richard Rodgers, and others. A young Maurice Jarre got the part, with the instruction to complete the work in six weeks. Adrian Boult was to conduct the London Philharmonic Orchestra but allegedly felt taxed in fitting the music to the film. For "prestige," his name remained in the credits (Jackson 2007: 55, 89–91).

As the credits pass by, an almost monochrome Lawrence, dressed in an English suit, prepares for his motorcycle ride. The black-and-white cuts to color. A warning sign of road construction interrupts a quiet English country lane. Recalling *Blithe Spirit*, Lawrence speeds to his death. The crash stops the music. The motorbike engine roars as the bike skids to avoid two oncoming bicycles, anticipating *A Passage*. The bike flies into a field. Eye goggles hang on a tree to affirm a blindness to be investigated by eyes *wide open* — or *wide shut* as this becomes an idiom for the camera shutter of cinema. Whether the blindness is of a poet who acts on inspiration or of a man of action blinded by ambition becomes the question to be carried on a camel's back.

A decisive cut is made to the memorial service at St. Paul's. (It offered a model for Lean's own memorial years later with the word "cut" serving as Lean's epitaph [Cassidy 1991].) Taken briefly inside the cathedral, we see an oversized bust of Lawrence. A bystander declares Lawrence to be *the most extraordinary man I ever knew*. Not wishing to speak ill of the dead — *nil nisi bonum* — a man of the cloth questions whether Lawrence *really* deserves *a place in here*. The organ music inside subsides as the camera pans outside over the departing guests. The press rushes forward to determine what is known of Lawrence. The praise from British dignitaries rings hollow as they admit to not ever having really known the man. The American journalist, Jackson Bentley, declares that it was he who made Lawrence known to the world. He was a *poet, a scholar, and a mighty warrior*, while yet (in an aside) *the most shameless exhibitionist since Barnum and Bailey*. While a dignitary is offended, the audience is alerted to the power of the media, how the press, like cinema, makes the news and shapes public opinion. A cut draws away from the final notes of Lawrence's life to pursue the story of his life. The not-knowing at the memorial signals a former British club of army officers refusing to own the man who'd become a myth.

Unsuited to army service, Lawrence is fully supplied with all the suspect wit of speedy retorts. He leads a group that is also *unknown*, yet represented as stereotypically duplicitous (*a nation of sheep-stealers*). A sort of blind leading the blind, except that those who follow the leader have their own goals, ideals, and military experience. The clothes that make the man soon turn Lawrence's repartee into an unabated hunger for power. Lean recalled the actor before the character he played: "Peter is given these robes fairly early on when he's accepted by the Arabs, and then the rot starts to set in. He gets the sort of power mania." He then described how the material of which his Arab clothes was made to become thinner and thinner "until it was just muslin." And this was because "the rich silk" at the beginning had to dissipate for the figure to look "almost ghost-like" at the end: "a kind of faded look" for a worn figure. "Nobody," Lean said, "ever spots" this (DL: 126).

Withdrawing weight and substance to leave a transparency—almost a colorlessness in his white skin—serves the myth that remakes the man in search of a country and an identity. The transparency serves the abstraction of the land- and soundscape: an arid atmosphere, an empty expanse of sand and sky, and a sparse script. From the emptiness emerges a pathos of the biblical proverb that feminizes the *wisdom* that *hath builded her house* as it hews out *her seven pillars*, only then for the desert sand to become a quicksand into which a young Arab boy falls. The quicksand becomes a Babel of meaningless words. At the memorial, we hear: *Could you give me a few words. . . . What, more words?*

When the adventure is over, *home, sir* are the car driver's last words to Lawrence. A motorcycle, periodically appearing in the film, overtakes the car to recall a beginning and an end in England. The final scene sets the sun on Arabia. No one walks or runs, as in *Great Expectations*, into a happy end, only into a stalemate. At the end, negotiators fail to come to a peace treaty. A crossroad between new and old remains for people and embattled nation-states. Prince Faisal (Alec Guinness), who appears in several key scenes because Lawrence's mission by order of the British is to find him, says: *Young men make wars, and the virtues of war are the virtues of young men. Courage and hope for the future. Then old men make the peace. And the vices of peace are the vices of old men. Mistrust and caution. It must be so.* T. E. Lawrence wrote correspondingly in *Seven Pillars*: "When . . . the new world dawned, the old men came out again and took our victory to remake it in the likeness of the former world we knew" ([1935] 1997: 6–7).

As Lawrence gets promoted through the army ranks, the mockery of his experience increases in proportion to his self-promotion. Accused of betraying his outfit by failing to follow orders and assuming a new cloth, he presumes a disloyalty to right a wrong. With seven pillars come seven conflicted stakes.

The film became iconic in cinema's history both despite and because of the first slate of negative but witty reviews. Critics complained of a history and theology abused, a story of an imperialist mission turned into a cowboy western. A "huge, thundering camel-opera that tends to run down rather badly as it reaches its third hour," declared Bosley Crowther of the *New York Times* in 1962; and worse, or better: "We know little more about this strange man when it is over than we did when it begins." Roger Sandall began in 1963: "From the director of *Great Expectations*, a galumphing camelodrama in debut de siècle style. From the producer of *The African Queen*, an Uncrowned King of Arabia suited more a jester's cap than a coronet." Disliking as much the accents as the "unspeakably turgid score," Sandall expressed relief whenever "an eruptive camel-grunt" came over like a deflating "fart at a coronation."

Penelope Gilliatt titled her review "Blood, Sand and a Dozen Lawrences" to draw out all the "incompatible" Lawrences living "under the same skin, and two or three women as well." For all Lawrence was, he was not "a good soldier," which made for the film's real "difficulty." The film's form was "solidly heroic," with "music bracing enough to be played by a Soviet army band" (an odd comment!) while a puny protagonist, an old British Tory, "resolutely refuses to be a hero." She was targeting cinema's tendency to equalize the feminine to a weakness of intellect. She disliked the desert's obsessive cleanliness, its smell of disinfectant. The strong color coding in Freddie Young's photography was sumptuous but hollow, while the pithy messages in Bolt's script became emptied through ever longer shots of sand. Too many inventions of artifice and not enough of the "bolder liberties," she concluded, that good art demands (1962: 25).

When, late in life, Lean recalled the harsh criticism, he smiled at Gilliatt's Sunday paper's subheading "the two and half pillars of wisdom," after which he defended as "sinless" the many liberties he'd taken, how, say, he'd shown Lawrence learning to ride a camel as a way of his discovering a new world (DL: 103). But it was Eric Rhode, I believe, who actually reduced the seven pillars to "two-and-a-half" in his *Listener* review published just days after Gilliatt's review. Rhode quoted Hannah Arendt on imperialism (with words included in her eventual book of 1968):

> No matter what individual qualities or defects a man may have, once he has entered the maelstrom of an unending process of expansion, he will . . . cease to be what he was and obey the laws of the process, identify himself with anonymous forces he is supposed to serve in order, to keep the whole process in motion. (1973: 215–16)

Rhode further invoked Arendt's systemic distinction between "the bureaucrat" and "the secret agent," so that we can "all detest" the one and "love" the other. Lean's film had delivered our "nostalgia for lost glory" on a plate, with "the picture of imperialism we all crave for," while yet sopping our conscience with existential doubt. Rhode admired the persistent haunting of Lawrence in our popular imagination. While praising the photography as oppressively brilliant, he thought, finally, that Lean had run away with the desert to let the "glamorized symbol of the maelstrom" overly dominate. Had not the psychological complexity been reduced to serve a tourism to which then a journalist could only respond by sending a feed home like a cheap souvenir?

The "flesh and blood" theme gave Carl C. Curtis his title for an article tracing the classical and biblical, Homeric and Messianic, allusions to the prophets or man-gods who variously pursued passages through the desert or wilderness. Mythifying Lawrence reflected the biblical or epic opacity demanded of a man who was to become more than ordinary. What did Lawrence want to accomplish? A miracle, a military victory, a martyrdom, as proof, "to borrow a Homeric phrase, that he (was) something 'more than man.'"? Curtis reads a key episode—the Turkish Bey's attempted rape of Lawrence at Deraa. (We see only the seduction and then the beating that follows.) The moment marked not the "climax" of a "career," but a "defining" moment when Lawrence is suddenly confronted with his great "deflating failure." All the terms, *climax, career, defining, and deflating*, are loaded, as is Curtis's likening of the seducer, the Bey, to a Herod or Pilate who wishes to deflate an enemy to a mere mortal. So, also, the likening of Lawrence's beating to Oliver Twist's beating over a barrel, but to suggest what became well documented, that Lawrence (unlike Oliver) had always craved a painful punishment for a biblically forbidden sex act. Curtis quotes from *Seven Pillars*: "A man who gives himself to be a possession of aliens leads a Yahoo life, having bartered his soul to a brute-master" (2012: 274–87). Lawrence would describe his own brutality as when, as master, he twisted the will of others when exploiting environments both known and unknown to himself.

Other critics turn away from English schoolboy traumas toward the feminization that signifies more the fragility of desire than the certainty of reason. A man stripped bare reveals not reason's unwavering logos but the impossibility of revealing a wisdom whose truth must remain veiled. Williams joins with Anderegg and Stephen Caton in finding the film's absence of women drawing the *category* of woman into a divination of Lawrence as a "white goddess" (MA: 110; Caton 1999: 205–6). She further contrasts the large-scale sand spectacle of an "all-male utopia" with the "quintessentially feminine form" associated more with Lean's early "small-scale soap" operas (MW: 155–6). Is the soap for cleansing, disinfecting, or does it have a cosmetic purpose? One is reminded of Catherine de la Roche's early appreciation of *Brief Encounter* and *Great Expectations* as indicative of cinema's movement between the miniature that becomes magnified and the magnified that becomes small.

Stripped and beaten, Lawrence is thrown onto a dirty, wet street. Already on arriving in Deraa, he steps into a filthy puddle when borrowing *dirty clothes* to *pass for an Arab in an Arab town*. Disguised, he assumes an *invisibility* as the all-white, divined leader of Arabia. Face-to-face with the Bey, his *interesting face* isolates him from the *cattle* surrounding him. The Bey's recognition equals the seductive identification by a Turk of a man born and bred in Britain. Leaving the dirt behind, Lawrence travels to the mountains to be cleansed in clean water. Arriving in Azrak, Ali nurses him back to health with the punctuated eating and sleeping that befits an ordinary mortal. Lawrence addresses his imposture. Ali says: *You have a body, like other men*. Lawrence replies: *I'm not the Arab revolt, Ali. I'm not even an Arab*. He determines to go home. In reversal, however, he takes the road to Damascus to exact revenge on the Turks: the *tragic flaw* of a *bloodbath*. The blood from his beating forever seeps through his British army uniform. His (Wagnerian) wound renders him a *servant* of use no longer to anyone, not even to himself.

Of desert miracles and mirages, words like "oasis," "spring," or "pool" seem fitting for Lawrence's *Seven Pillars* and certainly for *Psalm* 107.35: "He turns a wilderness into pools of water, And dry land into water springs." But anticipating *A Passage*, Lawrence will speak of a *storm in a teacup* to bring home what he takes to have been merely a sideshow *theatre of operations*. And the puddle scene, beyond recalling *Hobson*'s transformational dream sequence, captures the British preoccupation with rain and with the waterworks, at *Lawrence*'s end, over which a contested flag flies. Behind the scenes and screens of British propriety walks a man with another walking stick. Named Dryden (Claude Rains), he is the *chief architect* in search of *compromise*. When he ironically quips that the waterworks will soon fly an *Arab flag*, we get an ironic aftertaste of *Kwai*'s ending and a foretaste of *Zhivago*'s beginning: a great dam built to serve a Revolution.

The script is filled with verbal and visual snipes against telephones, electricity, weapons, bombs, and warplanes. It allows a tribal barbarism to emerge with every imperial gesture of British civilization. Were Lean and his team effecting a poetic revenge on a history that could not be documented merely as record? Following an exchange about the profits of war, evidenced in gold and guns, Moses is called up as crossing the Sinai with his children. Lawrence leaves for Jerusalem with two children in tow. Had the allusion also been to Moses at the Red Sea, we would have been given a water source for first the Genesis and then the Exodus watershed moments in a very hot climate. The film's many sunrises and sunsets on the horizon recall the Moses iconography of his crossing bodies of land and water (Goehr 2021:

ch. 9). Arriving at the shore, having *taken Aqaba*, Lawrence sees a garland of flowers floating on the water. Ali says: *The miracle is accomplished. Garlands for the conqueror. Tribute for the prince. Flowers for the man*. Lawrence replies: *I'm none of these things*. But in this moment, he expresses his overwhelming *love* for *this country*.

In *Projecting Empire*, James Chapman and Nicholas J. Cull find "the apotheosis of the cinema of empire," "the high water mark of the epic" that gave cinema a *before Lawrence* and an *after*. They see "the first celebrity whose image was created by the mass media." Regarded as one of the "greatest British and American films," *Lawrence*, they affirm, is "also one of the most troubled films in cinema history." And then: "If, as film theorists like to claim, all films are really about cinema itself, then *Lawrence of Arabia* is even more so than most." They report the difficulties of bringing Lean's project to the screen. Not liking Michael Wilson's script, Lean and Bolt took over, after which Wilson's screen credit was denied allegedly for more reasons than that his name was "blacklisted." The action-packed feeling of the first script was displaced by Lawrence's relationship with Ali as "an unconsummated love affair similar to the one at the heart of *Brief Encounter*." Lawrence was then given his place in a "lineage of visionary outsiders," including "Nietzsche, Dostoevsky and Van Gogh," where the singular man stands alienated against the conventional and ordinary. With Nietzschean stakes of transformation hammered out, every warring side comes over as distanced and voided of due cause, and every individual, and Lawrence most of all, voided of personality to convey less a failure or fragility of agency than a "futility" (2009: 87–113; Hodson 1994). A film allegedly about the politics of empire yields, for the unhappy critics, no lasting impression or point.

Many follow Edward Said's writings on imperialism with his more particular observation of Lawrence as having constructed a questionable background to sustain an adventure of "fairly fluid possibilities." Peter Lennon recorded Said's cartographical remarks regarding how the map for "the large and undifferentiated mass of the Southern Ottoman Empire" was redrawn postwar by the West (which, presumably, construed the Empire in these "undifferentiated" terms in the first place). Lennon was dissatisfied with the crudity of staging two cultures at war through unequal power relations (1986 TL: 29–31; Said 1978: 195–6; 230–1). Alexander Lyon Macfie addresses Said's work but stresses more Lowell Thomas's Nietzschean reconstruction of Lawrence as a "modern romantic hero, an inveterate dreamer, a great writer, an anti-imperialist, a surrogate woman and even a god." He recalls the silent era when Rudolph Valentino, half-clothed, appeared as the virile sheik of "Araby" (2007: 77–78; 83). Lean would refer to Valentino again in *A Passage*. More tellingly, Jackson Bentley, the journalist, was partly modeled on Lowell Thomas. If Thomas, in Macfie's view, was turning Lawrence into an *Übermensch* caught between Apollonian and Dionysian drives of order and frenzy, then Bentley, in my view, was inflating the man more to accord with the American poster image of the "most wanted."

Hadrien Fontanaud reframes "the imperialist hero" by drawing out the cowboy myth of the American western, where individuals remake themselves through law and order against a landscape of human lawlessness. The drive toward unifying Arabia becomes the *manifest destiny* of sunrise and sunset that is always driving uniting states setting and newly rising suns. Seeing tribal warfare all around, the cowboy arrives with banners of justice, order, and unity. Fontanaud looks back to *Clive of India* (dir. Richard Boleslawski, 1935) and *Rhodes of Africa* (dir. Berthold Viertel, 1936) to place *Lawrence* in a "transnational history of cinematic imperialism." The script only invokes Gordon of Khartoum as a *desert-loving Englishman*. Fontanaud points out the misrecognitions and misrepresentations of tribes in Arabia to find in the film a colonial empire-building falling from its self-defeating fears of disempowerment and disability (2022: 118–22). And the result? A film that so inflates its signs that the signs come over as reduced: seven to two-and-a-half.

Inflation is the issue when Lawrence's *destiny* is presupposed to be written already for him. Then comes the deflation: *for some men nothing is written unless they write it*. Becoming an agent of Arabia, Lawrence assumes an increasingly brutal stance, to mow down enemies and leave no prisoners. A shocked Bentley takes a *rotten bloody picture for the rotten bloody newspapers*. Lawrence loses his *compass*. In really losing his compass, he wonders where he should place his trust: in the sun or in the path laid down by

Moses as a *pillar of fire. . . . My compass. No matter*. When a child proclaims the fire to be but *dust*, the fast-approaching dust storm makes their passage more difficult and more doubtful. When Lawrence finally arrives at a very blue Suez Canal, he finds a theological lifeline overwritten by a modern river of trade. Outside Damascus, a wooden signpost on the road shows the divine way in the wit of three languages. With every theological conceit comes a put-down. Standing in his office filled with oversized pieces of art, Dryden tells an overexcited Lawrence: *only two kinds of creature get fun in the desert: Bedouins and gods, and you're neither* (Figure 22).

When Lawrence shows his drive as unstoppable, it is by camel and horse when not in a military car. Transport is everywhere: planes attacking Prince Faisal's community; cars and trains speeding. Lighting a match to set off the explosives that will blow up a train, Lawrence has the fitting face of a naughty schoolboy. After its derailment, the train is plundered for its oversized Western goods: the *toys*. In this moment, Bentley arrives to represent the *Chicago Courier*, hungry for *a story to tell*. Or so he has already explained in requesting permission to go after Lawrence: *we Americans were once a colonial people, and we naturally feel sympathetic to any people anywhere who are struggling for their freedom*. A hero is needed to bring the United States into the war in Europe, the First World War, while, in 1962, more wars in a long string of bloody wars are at stake for every filmmaker. Bentley makes his presence felt further when the topic (as in *Kwai*) turns to the Geneva Convention.

Figure 22 Oversized busts, *Lawrence of Arabia*, directed by David Lean, Horizon Films, 1962.

To pursue Lawrence is for Bentley to catch him on camera. It is to take a snapshot, as Lawrence shoots his gun and as Lean shoots his film. All shoot with an ambition to blow a truth out of the sand or, following the idiom, out of the water. Truth, carried by the moving camera, is also carried by a wit and a suspicion, especially when Bentley arrives on a truck advertising *T. Mikopolous & Son. Finest Fresh Bread Delivered; Gordon St.: Jerusalem*. Curtis reads the sign as feeding the one who stands for the "new bread of life" (2012: 248). When Auda Abu Tayi (one of the leaders within Lawrence's *army*) smashes Bentley's camera, Lawrence explains that photography for a man of Auda's faith is tantamount to stealing *his virtue*. Stealing property is one thing; stealing a soul is far worse. The theft is motivic in its questioning of what it means to steal from one's enemy or friend and what, if anything, is justly taken in war. Bentley takes his shots with an American comeback: *Yes sir, that's my baby!* —an allusion to a 1925 song controlled by the rhythm of a mechanical pig. When the Arabic forces follow Lawrence into battle, they chant his first name, not their cause: freedom for Arabia. Lawrence does not correct them. Only Ali resists. A final scene shows appalling conditions for the injured Turks in a hospital that has no water or electricity. Lawrence collapses in hysterics. A newspaper lies nearby: his picture as a hero appears on the front page. More of humanity's debris (Figure 23).

In *Overtones and Undertones*, Royal S. Brown published his interview with Maurice Jarre on September 14, 1991. Brown had

Figure 23 Spreading the myth, *Lawrence of Arabia*, directed by David Lean, Horizon Films, 1962.

heard in *Lawrence*'s "big theme" a melody from Edouard Lalo's Piano Concerto in F minor. The interview revealed more: Jarre did not want to be known only as the Oscar-winning maker of big tunes for the big screen. He recalled how Arthur Honegger had instructed him best on "musical philosophies on the human level" and how to put music together for a film as a task different from straight composition. With Lean's invitation, Jarre ended up in Hollywood. There he discovered the extensive labor in making music for film, a labor that he thought French composers were not sufficiently appreciating. Jarre acknowledged Lean's lack of technical know-how while admiring his intuitions and insistence on the hard work being done before the shooting began. Asked about his best movie experiences, he replied: "The scores I did with David Lean." He liked other directors also. Yet, when asked about film composers, he quipped: "Certainly not film composers, because the composer I listen to the most is Mozart." He didn't comment on composers who had worked on Lean's earlier films and, much more, he expressed pride in being the "first" to use "the *ondes martenot* in the United States"—the piano-lookalike analog synthesizer for making musical waves (1994: 71, 305–13 passim). It is striking how consistent or repetitive were the claims made by composers over the forty years of Lean's filmmaking regarding the music for Lean's films.

Kenneth LaFave assesses Jarre's contribution in his book *Experiencing Film Music*. He regards Lean's films *about* war not as war films but as epics striving to become erotic through a musicality wherein visual dynamics of tension and resolution meet with the Straussian-inspired orchestrations or machine-produced harmonies and dissonances. For LeFave, *Lawrence* is the "epic of all epics," with its overture being "arguably the finest such piece ever composed." Yet, for this critic, this being Jarre's first film with Lean set Jarre on a troubled path: What could possibly follow? Jarre became "the composer of *Lawrence of Arabia*," and that was that (2017: 55–72 passim).

To assess *Lawrence*'s music as equal to Jarre's score, we miss a suggestive musical background that Lawrence described in *Seven Pillars* but which Lean's film only vaguely echoes. One description regards the British fatigue with Turkish music and their wanting more German music, not perhaps the band's "flabby" rendition of

"Deutschland uber Alles" but more "Eine feste Burg." A second description questions a long thread of history and theological prejudice that attached the glories of German music—with its "tang of humanity and real love"—to a vision of Christ "which Judaism and Islam could not achieve"—in part for their Bilderverbot and in part for a stubbornness in not changing as the seas of change demanded ([1935] 1997: 60, 347). In private correspondence, when Lawrence expressed his great liking for Mozart and Beethoven, it was for this music as it was coming over "on the box." "Music? We have none here [in the desert]. Wireless is a very false-toned caricature of music, I think. Gramophone is my stand-by, and a magnificent stand-by, surely" (Garnet 1938: letters 197 & 344).

In Lean's film, we get not German music but Coward-like snippets of popular music. When the British Waterworks is hoisted by the Arab flag, Dryden says: *On the whole, I wish I'd stayed in Tunbridge Wells*. It sounds like a refrain from a popular song. When Lawrence is being driven home, a truck of soldiers going in the opposite direction sing in an image reminiscent of a comparable crossing of paths in *The Sound Barrier*, only now the singing is of the American marching song of 1900 made popular in the British music hall: *Goodbye, Dolly Gray—I must leave you, Though it breaks my heart to go*. The lyrics that follow are known but not sung: *Something tells me I am needed at the front to fight the foe. See, the boys in blue are marching and I can no longer stay*. Lawrence is no longer needed in Arabia.

Appreciative critics remark on the soundscape of music and noise that produces perfect merges of nature and human-made things. Then come the usual knockout punches. In 1962, in a piece titled "El Aurens," John Coleman wrote: beyond "the obligatory, contemptible music," the film's real failure is its inability "to make up its mind." Williams, contrarily, reminds us of the watershed moment when Lawrence hears a voice (Lean's own) calling out, *Who are you?* (MW: 161, 167) A river always has two sides. The unanswered question echoes the ride earlier taken through the mountainous landscape when, way too loud, Lawrence sings "The Man Who Broke the Bank at Monte Carlo." At the water well, Lawrence only whistles this song. Later, to break the (river) bank, he gambles with stakes high enough to break a camel's back. The song's words reverberate most at the moment of desiring to "be a millionaire." The song, from 1891, was parodied in 1916, the year of Lawrence's adventure: *The Tanks that Broke the Ranks out in Picardy*. Breaking out of rank is what Lawrence does when he calls out to a more superior British officer: *Hey you*! Bombs reverberate in the distance: *Not again—They simply will not understand what modern weapons do.*

In 1984, Jay Cocks stressed the construction of a "great adventure" as made not by politics but by and about "a poet who wanted to be a regent, a scholar playing at warfare" (DL: 60). Cocks's words pave our way now to *Doctor Zhivago*, where the extremes of freezing snow replace *Lawrence*'s extremes of heat and sand. A man of medicine and poetry considers his life and the life of his country as in and out of time. The pen and paper for the writer of his life makes the political situation be first about him so that the political can meet the personal in a great adventure that becomes an intimate affair. From the affair comes the question of identity framed by questions of loyalty and infidelity written under the condition of poetry. After *Zhivago* comes *A Passage to India*, originally written by E. M. Forster out of the poetry of Walt Whitman. Whitman's "passage" celebrated the opening in 1868 of the Suez Canal, a wedding of the Mediterranean to the Red Sea through a song sung for technology and trade, science and engineering, democracy, and the uniting of nations: "Passage O soul to India!" (Goehr 2021: 28–30). But Whitman also penned a "Song of Myself" for his *Leaves of Grass* that refused to erase the contradictions of a self-knowledge constructed between yesterday, today, and tomorrow by words of poetry. When Lawrence poeticized a song for himself, only at moments of the greatest inflation did he stop his ears from grasping all that Whitman had meant in writing: "I am large, I contain multitudes." Lohengrin could have sung the same words. To contain the inflation brought doubt and downfall to the certainty.

There is a witty Rachmaninoff moment in Lean's *Doctor Zhivago* (1965), a piano recital of the *Prelude in G minor, Opus 23–5*, at a wealthy doctor's house that has a most significant interruption: an urgent call to save the life of a woman, the mother of Lara

Antipova. The musical moment is swift. The doctor's wife says, *Boris, this is genius*, and the doctor responds: *Really, I thought it was Rachmaninoff? . . . I'm going for a smoke.* The interruption allows for an accidental crossing of paths for star-crossed lovers. Although Boris Pasternak knew and admired Rachmaninoff, he did not mention him in the novel of which Lean's film is an adaptation. Chapter 20's description of the evening party and concert prepares, however, the scene in the film:

> Beyond the open side doors of the ballroom the supper table gleamed, white and long as a winter road. The play of light on frosted bottles of red rowanberry cordial caught the eye. . . . Not to delay the pleasure of earthly food too long, the company got down hastily to their spiritual repast. They sat down in rows. . . . [T]he musician took his place at the piano. The concert began. The sonata was known to be dry, labored, and boring. The performance confirmed this belief, and the work turned out to be terribly long as well.

After a too-long interval of a too-long piece, the concert resumes, only to be interrupted with a call to a doctor that meets with a snide not against Rachmaninoff but toward those of a lower class who feign illness to get attention: "There's a relative of his dying. So now they're dying! I can imagine."

The cuts made for the film match the novel's episodic form even as the film omits and changes details. The film stresses the cross-roads and cross-words for lives unfolding according to bloodlines of love and violence. Recalls of epic poetry, theater, and opera carry the tragic motif. Lean and Bolt envisaged first a Beethoven carving a model for a young doctor-poet—Doctor Zhivago—out of a muse and then a "Tristan and Iseult situation, a great, grand passion" for poetry to overcome the political lines of separation as "the crown of the film" (KB: 501, 507).

As with *Lawrence*, the film has an overture and, given the length, also a musical intermission (Entr'acte). The overture opens with percussive drum rolls before a grandiose orchestral sound takes over. Chords become dissonant before dissolving into a revolutionary song hummed without words. Later, the words are sung. The soundscape is suggestively Russian, and all the more so as it is drawn into long journeys taken over a vast landscape. Journeys are by train or by horse and carriage, when once the lovers travel to the country home that stands now in ruin. Lara's motif echoes a Wagnerian turmoil of passion. Described in the credits as *original music*, Jarre's overture lasts for several minutes without any images. When Lean's direction is credited, it, like the other credits, is pictured against a color-saturated landscape of a sparse forest, only now the sun has arisen: a reminder of *Lawrence*. Borrowings from his earlier films and from Russian cinema help to carry a film history into what some, but not all, critics regard as another Lean classic. Playing to the popular imagination, the film is said to define fashions—notably the fur hat—and to offer a cultural iconography that rescues Mother Russia by bringing her to the West. The film exaggerates the drama in gestures, accents, words, and design that are often too exaggerated.

The first scene, shot before the sun has risen, is of a moving train of walking girls *in and out of reformatories*. Brought into an office of oversight and administration, we hear that it is not *cost-effective* for *human beings . . . to move earth*. When the need for more heavy construction *excavators* is expressed, patience is called for: *You're an impatient generation*. The office frames the drama, part in and part out. Its overseer is Zhivago's half brother, Yevgraf Andreyevich Zhivago (Alec Guinness). Through a voice-over, he tells the love story of the parents of a young woman, Tonya Komarova (Rita Tushingham), who is invited out of the workers' line into the office. She is shown a photograph printed in a book of poems written by Yuri Zhivago (Omar Sharif) for Lara (Julie Christie). Her face suggests no recognition of her parents, so that her uncle can draw her back to her childhood. Befitting an analysis, the film reconstructs her story. Lara's pregnancy is told only in our last vision of Lara: taking a train, she departs from Zhivago, never to see him again. Zhivago, in turn, cut off from this child, is also separated from the children born to his wife, Tonya Gromeko (Geraldine Chaplin). Releasing the memory of the daughter Tonya's separation from her mother repeats her father's loss of his mother at a similarly early age. Knots are duly tied in a family string of belonging as also between those of Lean's films that thematize lost children coming to know the identity of their parents. Lean's opening to his film is, as in *The Passionate Friends*, the novel's ending, in this case Pasternak's.

When Yuri Zhivago's life story begins, a balalaika with a strikingly red middle is the only gift he receives from his mother (Figure 24). It is given to him by the Gromekos, who will take him back to Moscow, where, later, he will marry their daughter. They say, *I thought all the people in this part of the world could play the balalaika*—so that Yuri's mother can be recalled for having stood out for her ability to make the *little instrument sound like two guitars*. Upset because he doesn't know how to play the instrument, Yuri is quieted (through the voice-over) by the thought of finding his own gift, his way of being true to his inheritance. As Tristan, qua poet, found his muse in the musical Isolde, Yuri will find his muse for poetry in Lara. Still, as we should expect by now (of Lean), Yuri's love for his wife and family runs very deep.

Ian Christie thinks the running sight and sound of the balalaika recalls Carol Reed's zither in *The Third Man* (1949) (2015: 32–4). The balalaika does much more work: it is the gift of inheritance that ties people together and brings a film to its highly strung connectedness. The image of Zhivago on my book cover tells a lie, for the instrument is more a gift handed down than an instrument he plays. With gloves, he could not (easily) play, and nowhere is it suggested that he has learned how to play. When Tonya enters the office, we do not see the instrument and are not yet made to know about it. A black plastic bag is slung over her shoulder. But we do

Figure 24 Can you play the balalaika? *Doctor Zhivago*, directed by David Lean, Carlo Ponti/MGM, 1965.

know by the end, as she walks away with her boyfriend, David, with the balalaika now in sight. We do not see her take the instrument out of the bag either, but she must have at some point for her uncle to call out: *Can you play the balalaika?* David calls back: *Can you play the balalaika? Can she play? She's an artist!—An artist? Who taught you?—No one taught her—Then, it's a gift.*

Is her balalaika her father's instrument? Did the red paint in the middle fade to signal a world-weariness? For Tonya and her uncle, whatever the change of paint (as with the ship of Theseus), no doubt remains as to the family line. In Pasternak's novel, the balalaika appears only in a passing line of a rude peasant song, while another line tells about a dance music that, while played, makes life assume a feeling of eternity. Lean used the second thought more than the first to draw the instrument away from the rude song to become a lifeline for the entire story. Lara's theme, partly played on the balalaika, expresses what Laura saw in her mother's painting in *Brief Encounter*, something that can't be taken away.

Wherever Yuri is, there is the balalaika to be taken back or handed down in key moments. Its red middle symbolizes the poetic thread. Sometimes, a balalaika shows its wear as bare brown wood, as when played at a crowded railway station, when the Zhivago-Gromeko family is leaving Moscow. We see a balalaika played by a poor man with a mood different from the melodic motif that runs through the score. The mood in this moment contrasts with the terror of the train's chugging that, day after day, makes for the long journey for families, soldiers, and political prisoners. Closing in on Zhivago's family waiting for the train, Zhivago's red balalaika keeps his family connected. By the end of the journey, the quarrels en route among all the passengers have turned to a frenzied dance.

The balalaika is the property most protected. When Zhivago's family is confined to reduced quarters in their former great house, they find themselves sharing with several other family units—*Fifty square meters for a family of less than five persons*. The reference to a "family" contradicts the revolutionary condemnation of the family as having become a mere tool of bourgeois capitalism. When the revolutionaries claim to be storing the family's belongings, Zhivago proclaims their confiscation a theft and grabs back his balalaika. The instrument signals his conscience as a humanist. You can't take away the gift of poetry, or the family feeling that sustains the personal happiness of *individuals*.

By title, name, and musical instrument, the film comes across as "one man's story," but, motivically, it is crosscut by the story of a *woman*. Repeated accidental meetings occur over great expanses of place and time. But large emotions and thoughts are drawn into small spaces: a room, a bed, a kitchen. The woman is sometimes Zhivago's wife; more often, the woman is his lover, Lara. Combined, the figure of mother comes to stand for Mother Russia. The film shows bits of guilt or the shame of infidelity in small expressions of a body or face. Morality is not the issue, although a brief moment in a church allows a priest to chide Lara for the weakness of her flesh and to encourage her to secure the sacrament of marriage. This moment is sharply juxtaposed by an exchange when Lara's lover/seducer, Victor Komarovsky (Rod Steiger), whom Zhivago despises for *using* women, offers Lara to Zhivago as a *wedding present*. There is a lot of doubling: two sorts of men and two sorts of women. Victor tells Lara: *There are two kinds of women and you, as we well know, are not the first kind. You, my dear, are a slut.* One is reminded of Dryden's chiding of Lawrence.

Zhivago refuses political commitment and action so that his humanity can allow him to demonstrate what, for others, are only extreme standpoints. The black-and-white sides of the Revolution are made into a battlefield between the red and the white, contra the yellow daffodils that poetically promise a new spring. The all-too-familiar color symbolism allows Lara to wear red when seeming to be a *slut*, but soon she will wear white. The white of her goodness contradicts the white guard who mow down the reds to spread their blood, while the reds summarily execute those whom they judge to have betrayed the Revolution. Lean and Bolt negotiated the relative weight of the love story and the political narrative: Lean favored the first, Bolt the second. As in every Lean film, the political, traced through the personal, rendered the opposition uncertain. Critics again were divided: Was this a productive doubt or a poverty of ambiguity?

When (recalling *Great Expectations*) Zhivago watches from the balcony revolutionaries being mowed down, the violence is mirrored in his horrified eyes. The confrontation begins in monochrome and then turns red with the waving of the red flag and with the spread of blood. An abstract pattern of killing gives way to the aftermath of bodies, weapons, and band instruments strewn over the street. Music plays against the eerie silence. A snipe against the Revolution, heard at a different moment in the film, regards a song sung at a demonstration: *No doubt they'll sing in tune after the revolution.*

An anachronism in the novel, as much as in the film, allows us to consider the revolution in the First World War period through the aftermath of the Second, given a very cold war contestation of human values. Values freeze in a country house that has turned from warmth to age and ice, in recall of the Satis House in *Great Expectations*. Patterns of crystal and chandeliers in wealthy homes become fractured mirrors and windows of social and self-reflection. Freezing time carries the *forever* of values associated with love and loyalty to a Mother Russia betrayed by the authoritarian hand of the (faithful/unfaithful) son: the Soviet Union. Zhivago's poetry echoes the Shakespearean "winter of our discontent / Made glorious summer by this sun." Is there a son who won't betray the sun?

Gift-giving, linked to inheritance, is part of the adventure that carried, for Simmel, a tentative distinction of gender: "A love affair contains . . . two elements . . . the adventure characteristically conjoins": what we have control over and the luck that is beyond our control. Perhaps, however, he added, the adventure is "only for men," given their activity contra the passivity of women who accept their lot as a concession or as a gift ([1911] 2002: 227). In Lean's film, passivity and activity characterize lives regardless of gender. Zhivago, like Pip in *Great Expectations*, responds to situations in which he finds himself. Lean thought about *Zhivago* as the doctor whose heroism is premised on doing nothing: "He doesn't do anything really" (DL: 16, 25). In the old battle of the sword against the pen, to write is not to act.

Scholars say that Zhivago treats the Revolution like an earthquake, hence seeming to naturalize and neutralize it of a political stance for which individuals must take responsibility. Zhivago tells his half brother how the Revolution has dismissed the poetic pen and the medical knife to make the sword alone cut out *all the tumors of injustice*. The uncle likes the poetry secretly but thinks, and must think, it insufficient for the actions demanded by the realities at hand. As in *Kwai and Lawrence*, Lean allows the half brothers to hold onto a doubled doubt given their understanding of what destroys an agent of political action when the wrong sort of hubris gets the upper hand of human ambition. Faced with the risk of betraying one's political agency, is it better to return home, as Zhivago is shown returning, to tend to one's own garden where the world cannot then touch him? The film ends sadly and badly for Zhivago, and for Lara, although we see only the end for the man for whom there is no back garden left.

The existential thought dominates, that passivity cannot avoid value, that doing nothing is an active response to the situation one finds oneself in or has made for oneself. Meeting the revolutionaries, Zhivago is told that the Revolution has put the personal aside, that family and personal love are but selfish products of a bourgeois or capitalist structure. Even happiness is no longer a reason: *Happy men don't volunteer.* There is no longer a happy or an unhappy breeding. Poetry is dismissed as a bourgeois art of individualistic feeling. Fidelity to the Revolution becomes the rewriting of society. Zhivago's love affair, like his poetry, is his quest to cut out a brief moment of freedom from the everyday landscape overwritten by another No Exit sign. Fantasy and romance are Lean's counterpoints to history's baser realities and facts—for a brief duration.

Crossing paths without yet meeting, Yuri and Lara sit almost side by side on a tram. The visual cue is accompanied by a little spark of (Goethe's) electricity as the tram follows its path along the tracks—the sort of "grace note" that marks a key moment in the precision and perfectibility of Lean's design. Lean recalled from his childhood "the clop-clop-clop of horses' hooves on cobbles and the noise of tram bells and the tram wheels on the tracks," and particularly "the exciting flash and crackle as the arm travelled along the wire—I used that in *Doctor Zhivago*" (KB: 16).

In the city, pre-revolutionary class divisions divide Lara and her mother, who live near the train tracks, from an educated bourgeoisie and aristocracy. If the musical instrument divides classes, so, too, does the iron that Lara uses because she has been pressing clothes all her life, whereas Zhivago's wife will learn only after the revolution what it means to iron and to work. The wife's still youthful adaptability, her courage, and her willingness to keep having children: all of this allows her to remain faithful to her family even under the Revolutionary condition. Contrarily, her aging father (Ralph Richardson) stages in every stubborn gesture his fidelity to an old world.

When, after the early Rachmaninoff moment, Zhivago turns up with his adopted father to attend to Lara's mother, we learn that her attempted suicide follows from Victor having replaced her with her daughter. Zhivago is distracted by Lara's presence. With train noises turning to the main motif, he watches her through a door pane, sleeping. A close-up shows her hand tired from work, though it is no laborer's hand. He watches her embracing Victor. As Zhivago and Tonya announce their engagement at a grand party, Lara's hand is shown shooting a gun aimed at Victor, the same hand shown just prior as suddenly powerless to resist Victor's seduction. Hands upon musical instruments and everyday tools are split between great care and great abuse. When Victor is shot in the arm, and Zhivago attends to him as a doctor, Victor reads this as a sign of their *destinies* being *interwoven*. When Zhivago writes to his wife about Lara, it is to acknowledge Lara's hands as naturally gifted to help others. The weaving of hands means the weaving of an entire cast for the pull and push of human relations. (Recall the hand on Laura's shoulder in *Brief Encounter*, Madeleine's alleged hand-washing in poison, and all the hands in the piano-films about crossed keys.)

Lara uses a gun that belongs to Pavel (Tom Courtenay), Lara's husband-to-be. She will have a child with him before he leaves her for the Revolution. Renamed Strelnikov, he becomes a leader who forgoes family to live by *bread and water* alone. His name speaks to the depersonalizing and mythologizing of a leader, as in *Lawrence*. Family relations are suspended as currents of chemistry: chosen and forced affinities produce crossed paths and cross words between Zhivago, Victor, and Strelnikov, all of whom possess Lara in some way. She is their connecting thread. Understanding the danger Lara is in, her being still married (now without legitimacy) to Strelnikov, Victor—an *ignoble Caliban* of these tempestuous times—claims alone to be able to save her from summary execution.

Feeling love for his wife, Tonya, who is about to bear him a second child, Zhivago runs to town to tell Lara: *I'm not coming back . . . never*. There's the *never* again of the *always*. Returning home, he is captured by revolutionaries to serve as a medical officer. Escaping without requisite papers, Zhivago's journey of return is tormented. Arriving at the train station of Yuriatin, frostbitten and diminished, he learns that his wife and family have gone to Moscow (and are soon to leave for Paris). Through his wife's kindness (conveyed by a letter), he has a brief moment to live and love Lara in the old country house at Varykino. Yuri impregnates Lara and writes poems in her image, an ideal image that she at first does not recognize—partly because the ideal lives forever without aging. A wooden horse from Yuri's childhood keeps Lara's daughter (from Pavel) occupied. Sitting at his writing table, Yuri hears wolves howling, as does Lara, to signal the imminent danger. Jarre's music of their days and nights carries *Tristan-like* strains of waiting. The passing of real time is overpowered by the stilled time that allows the book of poems to be completed.

To complete the book is to allow something to endure beyond death, a gift that, combined with medicine, eases the suffering of others (Moscrop 2011). Through poetry and medicine, Zhivago becomes another sort of guardian of a ship, the guardian of doubt when and where doubt is most needed. Parting from Lara after six months together in an army hospital, Yuri bids her goodbye, after which, like the captain in *In Which We Serve*, he bids farewell to hospital workers with the now-forbidden personalization of names. When the White Guard promises to take care of the revolutionaries they have just mowed down, Zhivago refuses to go indoors. He wants to help. Seeing typhus all around, he cares while the Party denies the problem, so too regarding the *other disease we don't have in Moscow: starvation*.

When Victor arrives to take Lara to safety, Yuri gives Lara his balalaika: a sign (perhaps) of his knowing that she is with child. He promises to follow, but he will not. He runs to a frozen window that he must break to watch her, already far away on the horizon. A cut to a train that will take Lara to safety abroad (in Mongolia) allows Lara to tell Victor that she is with child and that Zhivago will never leave Russia. She holds the balalaika in her arms (Figure 25). We have just

Figure 25 Parting gift for a child, *Doctor Zhivago*, directed by David Lean, Carlo Ponti/MGM, 1965.

learned that Strelnikov, now returning to his old identity, was arrested while seeking his wife and child and blew out his brains. Many years in the novel are compressed into a single moment when, back in Moscow and quite broken, Zhivago thinks he sees Lara walking on the street. It is a repeated seeing, fused with Zhivago's apparition when, returning from his forced army service, he thought he saw his wife and child walking in the snow. Trying at the film's end to reach the woman for whom he has never given up looking, he collapses from a heart attack. Many attend his funeral.

Back to the first office of oversight, we learn that Lara, having once found Zhivago's half brother, went away having failed to find her lost daughter: *She died, or vanished, Somewhere. . . . in one of the labor camps . . . a nameless number on a list that was afterwards mislaid. That was quite common in those days*. We learn no more about the fate of her first daughter. The half brother admits to having fallen for Lara too. The lost daughter, Tonya, tells now of having gotten lost when a man (Victor) let go of her hand. Would Victor have wanted to lose the daughter born to Zhivago and Lara?

Persons-lost-and-found tie the film's end to its beginning. Finding her identity, she can carry her balalaika with or without a red middle. The color is no longer needed for the self-knowing she has achieved. The end. The industrial office of water works becomes another sort of estranged station stop for the binding and unbinding of human ties. Water works as one sort of powerhouse, while another power is that of electricity, wireless, and, hence, modern communication. When Strelnikov tells Zhivago that personal life is dead in Russia, that history has killed it, we feel the force of a film that wants to rewrite history a half-century later. An outdated form of life, Imperial Russia, is pitted against the trials and tribulations of a new age and adventure that seems to have broken its promise to carve out a desirable track for radical social change.

Despite Oscar nominations and five wins, *best director* went to Robert Wise for *The Sound of Music*, something Lean never forgot (KB 542). Nor did he forget his painstaking work on a score for which Jarre won the Oscar. And then there was the repetition of the Dickensian "dirt hitting the wooden coffin during [a] burial" that Lean showed first (Sragow quoting Spielberg 1985: 26), although Pasternak prepared the scene: of a coffin "closed, nailed, and lowered into the ground. Clods of earth rained on the lid as the grave was hurriedly filled by four spades." The gusts of wind following in the film became winds of time to turn back the clock to reconstruct lives told forward.

Few critics stress enough the musical thread woven by the musical instrument. Few stress enough the theme of inheritance over which one has and doesn't have control. Kenneth Tynan opened his review for the *Observer* (1966) by declaring the "missing link" to be the sound of the novel and ended by pronouncing the film "an orchestra without a conductor." Lean regarded this review as about as cruel as it gets. In 2015, Michael Newton looked back from *Zhivago* to say of *Brief Encounter*: "The whole thing plays like a Chekhov tale set to Rachmaninoff, that music summoning up the vehement feelings concealed in the ordinary day." Assessing "the long and the short of it" in 1966, Gerald Kaufman compared Lean's "third internationally based epic" with Anthony Newley and Leslie Bricusse's 1961 musical, well-titled: *Stop the World—I Want to Get Off*. The musical was short, as Lean's film was long; one cost-effective, the other lavish. Of Lean's first two epics, Kaufman noted their deep flaw, how the characters were nullified for the sake of "a grandiloquent theme or else by vast and overwhelmingly beautiful locations." In *Zhivago*, however, he thought the visual expanse and details heightened rather than dwarfed the human drama. He appreciated the acting when it did not fall into "exhibitionism," and saw in Alec Guinness's role traces of the young Pocket in *Great Expectations*. Kaufman more or less liked Bolt's screenplay and the "plangent nostalgia" in Jarre's "captivatingly lovely—if rather over-employed—theme music." Still, he wondered whether the excessive cost had issued anything finally of real worth (TL: 655).

In 1973, film-music composer Bernard Herrmann recalled Lean saying that "without its wonderful music his film would have been nothing. If that's what he feels about his film, too bad! But do you see what a terrible and really revolting circle it is?" But wasn't this the point, to have a film music inextricable from the film? Herrmann was really chiding a factory line production in Hollywood where producing an independent soundtrack as a "hit" seemed to matter the most (2010: 215).

Pauline Kael disliked the yellow daffodils, "the balalaika music" that, being so tedious, "you could kill the composer," and then the "disgraceful effect" at the end:

the final shot of a rainbow over the huge dam. . . . [T]he banal
suggestion that the suffering has all been for the best and that
tomorrow will be brighter is not only an insult to the audience, it
is a coarse gesture of condescension and appeasement to the
Russians. Would, she asked, Lean and Bolt place a rainbow over
the future of England? (1982: 151–2).

In *The Zhivago Affair*, Peter Finn and Petra Couvée report the
CIA's delight with the film in aiding anti-Soviet propaganda and
in turning the banished novel into "a landmark piece of fiction." If
the people got access to their own censored literature, a literature
promoting universal values of individual rights and respect, they
would be woken up to the tyranny. What better, then, than to
produce concealable pocket editions in every language, especially
a Russian edition, to be distributed for free whenever and wherever
possible! Moscow reeled in fury at the private showings of the film
in diplomatic residences. With Jarre's "instantly familiar" theme, the
new icon of popular culture became "one of the highest grossing
movies of all time" (2014: 255).

Asked whether he considered himself an English filmmaker, Lean
responded with an "of course," but chided the interviewer for playing
to the thought that making big movies made one *American*. If he'd
left England, it had been, as earlier for Coward, mostly to avoid
paying taxes and especially in cases like *Zhivago*, where he'd made
a lot of money! (DL: 109). And an extra tidbit: when Carlo Ponti, who
had helped Lean secure the rights to make the film, recommended
Sophia Loren for Lara's part, he did not get his way. But he did in
1974, when Loren became Laura in his remake of *Brief Encounter*.

The musical red thread is carried by a musical instrument through
bloody lines of battle. Its strings of belonging cannot be cut, whatever
the cuts made by history. If there is a mirror for England still in this
"epic," it is there in what Alan Bennett would show in his British
play of 1983, *An Englishman Abroad*. His title was already a nom
de plume in the production of little red guidebooks where being on
location gave "authenticity" to the description of sites. Yet Zhivago's
gaze, like Lean's camera, surveyed an extensive landscape equally
of conscience and counterfeit. The window-work of revealed truths
and untruths showed broken panes and disabled persons. To whom

and to what Zhivago as an heroic antihero belonged in his times was the unanswered question of his personal-political existence as doctor, poet, critic, husband, father, and lover. Like Lawrence, his figuration was made from Walt Whitman's "Song of Myself" to "contain multitudes." There was, accordingly, no possibility of a resolved ending.

Being his last film not by design but by death, *A Passage to India* came to stand for Lean's *rite of passage* with all the mythmaking invested therein. Proclaiming it among "the most acclaimed, or profitable, or vilified movies of all time," Michael Sragow found less a narrative than a "soundstage" for a woman who, like the country for which she stands, comes to understand the colonizing tactics of a theater for England wherever the English find themselves (1985: 20, 24). The film pits an arranged marriage against a union freely chosen. Freedoms and unfreedoms are framed within a critique of colonizing and colonized nation-states. Dogmatic claims of reason are challenged by the refusal to contain the mystery or the passions that lead to behaviors regarded as inappropriate for an English club. Less the largeness of the themes than the small details allow this film to be read as a testament to Lean's life as a filmmaker. As repetitions and echoes of his previous films, the details reveal his adaptive departures from E. M. Forster's novel. Lean's last film comes full circle back to his first films: an adaptation that, finding its space in the cutting room, opens the door also to a changing room for furniture, fashion, comportment, and thought.

A moon seen in water recalls *Hobson's Choice*; a reference to Tunbridge Wells recalls *Lawrence*; a gramophone with a large horn in the schoolmaster's residence recalls *Ryan's Daughter*. Popular songs and anthems for the pomp and ceremony of British arrivals and departures recall scenes from the early films of crowd celebrations or angry protests, set against local ritual and behavior. Extreme moods mirror hot and cold climates. Train journeys and modes of transportation distance people from their ordinary lives only to keep them recalling proprieties and possessions of home. The allegory that joins the *adventure* on location to the *work of art* is captured in a singularly witty statement from Mrs. Moore (Peggy Ashcroft). Feeling that being in India is not *like home*, she perceives herself always to be, in Forster's words, "facing the footlights" ([1924] 2015: 40). The theological spirit where persons come face-to-face with themselves through walls of shadow and echo is deflated when all the world becomes a stage, first for theater and then for film.

The film could be seen as a courtroom thriller, in full color. A trial, based on a false accusation of *attempted rape*, has not *Madeleine's* inconclusive verdict but a verdict that shifts all blame away from another sympathetic figure of medicine, a falsely accused Indian known as Dr. Aziz (Victor Banerjee). The real target is an abstraction: the English-in-India who display their colonial conceit in claiming to keep the Indians under the rule of their good order. The figures who resist the overwhelming power of English umbrellas are Mrs. Moore, first, and the schoolmaster, Richard Fielding (James Fox), second; but less so, the uneasy son of Mrs. Moore by her first marriage, the magistrate Ronny Heaslop (Nigel Havers), who is to become engaged to Mrs. Moore's traveling companion, a highly resistant Miss Adela Quested (Judy Davis). If the film is another *one woman's story*, then the woman is again a doubled figure, this time of age and youth: Mrs. Moore with her wisdom and kindness, and Adela who doesn't yet know herself.

Adela is seen first purchasing tickets for the passage to India under a tourist advertisement for the Marabar Caves and seen last with a faint smile (as in *Madeleine*) looking out from her window having returned home to England. The echo that frames her adventure translates into a souvenir carried not by a suitcase but by a mind that has come to doubt every familiar way of looking or listening. The echo disturbs ordinary life and common opinion. Yet, falling finally silent, an inexpressible truth remains. The truth is carried less by Jarre's scored music, of which there is little, than by the sounds and silences of winds and waters associated with an ageless mother of nature. Lean blamed finances for his not writing "any music into the script (except in the last bit with the Himalayas). I regret that" (DL: 95). But is more needed? The persistent echo gives the film its frame and form, befitting the combined motif of *reincarnation and destiny*.

This motif enters with the *old Hindu professor* of *philosophy*, Narayan Godbole (Alec Guinness): *the inscrutable Brahmin*. His refusal to engage hands-on in the trial is also his Socratic way of revealing what people do not know beyond what they believe by the evidence of ear and eye. We hear the repetition of all that is, was, and will be, and about waiting for truth to surpass the local contingent or accidental meanings of events: The outcome is already decided. *. . . [D]o what you like but the outcome will be the same.* But the professor is also a little mocked by a wit that is surpassed only by a much greater mockery of the gossiping English in India. That wit comes again, Coward-like, in snippets of pantomime and popular songs that are either mentioned in the script or left uncredited: from John Dalby's "Freely Maisie" to Frederick Weatherly and Haydn Wood's "Roses of Picardy."

Lean worked the uncanny and confrontational through mirrors that estranged Adela and Mrs. Moore in their home away from home. Arriving in India, Adela is unmoved by Ronny and increasingly so, as she learns from Aziz that life can be lived with love. Mrs. Moore is given witty little packages of wisdom to deflate youthful ideas of romance: *Sometimes I think too much fuss is made about marriage. Century after century of carnal embracement, and we're still no nearer understanding one another.* Or, refusing to participate in the sham trial, she says: *The whole of this entertainment is an exercise in power, and the subtle pleasures of personal superiority.* The band strikes up in this moment with "God Save the King."

In 1965, Santha Rama adapted Forster's novel of 1924 into a BBC TV Play of the Month. It took far fewer liberties than Lean did in 1984. Forster's novel pays far more attention to the friendship between the British Fielding and the Indian doctor. Lean frames the film with yet another arrival and departure. The script was again rendered sparse to favor sound and image. Lean remarked: "It's awfully hard when you look back over the really great movies that you see in your life to remember a line of dialogue. You will not forget pictures" (DL: 85; Kennedy 1985: 32).

Yet, here, no pictures work without the soundscape that juxtaposes nature's naturalness with theater's staged artifice. In 1924, the theater of footlights was still as popular as the darkened cinema that separated an audience from life as though in a cave. Forster has Mrs. Moore say: "Life never gives us what we want at the moment that we consider appropriate. Adventures do occur, but not punctually" ([1924] 2015: 18)—only, however, in the dark or in an irregular climate. The film is replete with sunshine and light, as well as the competing sounds of global and local transport: trains, boats, automobiles, bicycles, and animals. A large ship of pomp and ceremony arrives to contrast with the later mournful ship of return, when Mrs. Moore dies all alone, at one with Mother Nature. A loud train of arrival is met with crowd scenes. A local train, wittily named *Marabar Express*, promises an adventure to fuse the new with the old (Figure 26). Monkeys who run and elephants who walk, adorned with bells, contribute to the twists and turns of experience.

With British names and signposts, the roads pave the way to the end of empire and occupation in India's fight for independence. Automobiles speed through cities without concern for those whose lives they cross. Road signs signal, as in *Lawrence*, an opening collision, a speeding car with a bicycle. We do not know yet that the bicycle is ridden by Aziz. His name is spoken first by Adela to Mrs. Moore. Mrs. Moore has already met him in a sacred garden of a mosque. The immediate liking that disconnects Mrs. Moore from the British order lets her tell him about two dead husbands and Aziz to tell her about his wife who died in childbirth.

Figure 26 Marabar Express, *A Passage to India*, directed by David Lean, Thorn EMI Screen Entertainment/Home Box Office, 1984.

Another immediate liking between Aziz and Fielding is staged through the order and disorder of rooms. How, in this furniture-art, the English occupy the regulated rooms, clubs, and streets contrasts with local and more mystical spaces and customs. Spaces of snobbery become spaces of exclusion for those who, in their own country, are made to feel no belonging. Aziz's gestures and words are contrived to be out of sorts. Visiting Fielding near the start, Aziz finds Fielding in the shower mockingly singing from Gilbert and Sullivan's *Mikado* about the nation and majesty that *rules the earth, of The Sun, Whose Rays are all Ablaze*. Told to make himself at home, Aziz observes the furniture and belongings—including a gramophone with a large golden horn (Figure 27). He is intrigued to find a mess: *I always thought Englishmen kept their rooms so tidy. Everything arranged coldly on the shelves is what I thought*.

The mess plays to Mrs. Moore's contrast of *muddles* disliked and *mysteries* preferred. Only Fielding has a comeback: mystery is just a *high-sounding term* for a muddle. Aziz's story ends with a new home far away from the English, caring for two children and the sick. Fielding, returning to England, marries Mrs. Moore's daughter, Stella. She appears at the end silently to take in the Himalayas in one of the rare moments of the scored music. For Forster, the home

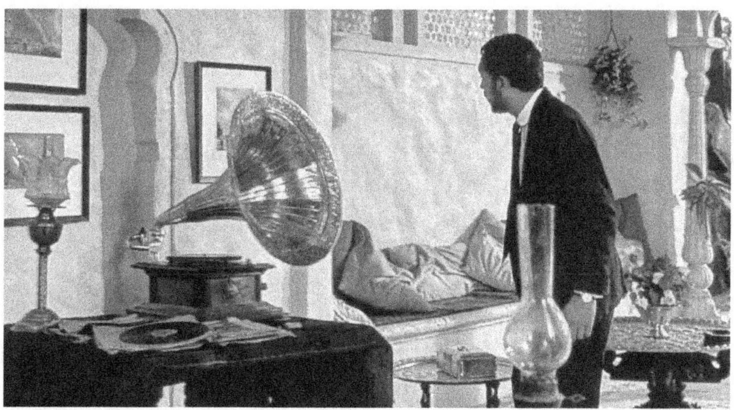

Figure 27 Furniture-art/Gramophone with golden horn, *A Passage to India*, directed by David Lean, Thorn EMI Screen Entertainment/Home Box Office, 1984.

of a free India and of a true friendship between the countries was the "not yet" that inspired him to the novel's last words of hope. Sixty years later, for Lean, the not-yet was still a friendship in the making even after the British had left.

"No event within a film is as significant as the event of film itself" (1981: 207). So wrote Stanley Cavell for cinema's pursuit of happiness. For Lean's film, the event within the bigger adventure is the happening at the Marabar Caves. The Caves advertised in the travel office are seen by Adela again from the window of the arriving train, then from the house where she stays, after which they are described as a *wonder of India*, a perfect destination and site for a picnic. Aziz arranges the picnic trip at great cost and in great detail with the promise that Mrs. Moore and Adela will experience India as the real thing. An early advertising poster for the film mimicked a tourist advertisement authorizing Lean to invite an audience to take a journey with him. The price of entrance to an exotic location raised great expectations that were almost guaranteed to go awry.

Taking the Marabar Express, the party arrives at its destination. To go up the mountain, only some ride by elephants as once royalty rode; most will walk. Entering the caves, the party (and a crowd of many locals) is instructed *to go in quietly. All sounds make an echo, and many sounds create inharmonious effect*. Mrs. Moore recalls *early days* when she *made rather a fool of* herself *in the chamber of horrors*. When asked *what horrors*, she responds: *The waxwork museum*. The wit carries, in Sragow's words, the "bitter theatricality" (1985: 26). In the cultural confrontation, no academic education in metaphysics will touch the mystery of the caves. The comeback in the Caves brings Mrs. Moore no comfort. Hearing her name echoed in conjunction with the echo that has no name, her (Western) faith is shattered. She utters helplessly: *we are merely passing figures in a godless universe*. Her name echoes almost to the end as a shadow over the great lie, Adela's false accusation against Aziz.

When, cycling through fields, Adela finds herself surrounded by erotic antiquities, there are no souvenir shops. The music quickly turns to a screeching of monkeys who pursue her in angry anticipation of the festive masked men who join the crowd to scream at her as she is whisked by car to the court. Unnerved by her bicycle ride, she agrees to marry Ronny. She tells Mrs. Moore: *I feel perfectly ordinary*—at just the moment when she should feel something out of the ordinary. She will break off the engagement. Ronny's gift of white flowers on her arrival comes to stand (as in *Ryan's Daughter*) for something she doesn't want.

Rain and thunderstorms play to the epic strings that unravel Adela's security. Although bored and irritated by the Englishness all around, she agrees to go with Ronny to a Polo match, followed by tea at the club. The script specifies the local band playing (the George Gershwin song of 1924) "Oh! Lady be Good"—which Adela does not want to be in an English way. Ronny's hope that she will play by the rules pushes her, in the heat of the midday sun, toward Aziz. As in *The Passionate Friends*, she moves between the two men who will soon confront each other in court, literally and metaphorically. The confrontation is pushed to its dialectical extreme, in Natalie Hayes's words, between "a West that is all logos" and "an East that is pure eros" (1986: 54).

In the outing to the Marabar Caves, everything is difficult except for the lighthearted moment when, imitating Douglas Fairbanks as Valentino, Aziz hangs off the moving train. With a moment alone outside the caves, A(ziz) & A(dela) discuss the idea of arranged marriage. He takes her hand to guide her. Their hands, prohibited from touching, are shown in a close-up. The bond anticipates the moment when Adela finally withdraws her accusation against Aziz. While she waits by the cave entrance, he smokes a cigarette at a distance. Losing sight of her, he calls her name. It produces an echo: A=A.

A cut to Mrs. Moore shows her waiting at the picnic site; she senses that something terrible has occurred. Another cut shows Adela running down the mountain, having dropped her binoculars, to meet a blindness in the British car that will whisk her away. (Recall the misleading binoculars in *The Passionate Friends*.) The treacherous terrain becomes Adela's terrain of treachery. She arrives home scratched and bloody from the *cactus spines*. Between heat and hysteria, she is encouraged by a gossipy Englishwoman to devise a lie. Adela's disability becomes the echo she cannot erase in her head.

For Lean, the key turns on how Mrs. Moore arrives persuaded that *God is here* but finds her faith "badly shaken" when she perceives the caves as preceding both human existence and God. Lean said that he was moved by the curiosity that first led a human being to drill a hole (DL: 72). Lean's curiosity, far from killing any cat, drove him away from home and then back home. The English closed-mindedness in the film means that, when experiencing the dark and nothingness of the Caves, the English find it all to be featureless and *without interest*. The only thing standing out is the *strange echo*. Unmoved, they rewrite the outing as Aziz's strategy to attack Adela. *A curious place for such an elaborate picnic*, the trial prosecutor remarks in the court, only to get the comeback he wants.

On trial, Aziz is defended for free by a famous lawyer and is supported by an angry crowd who throw stones at Adela. When Mrs. Moore and Fielding declare his innocence, they are accused of disloyalty. The club, from which Fielding now resigns, prohibits Indians. Either the members stand to attention when the anthem plays, or they drink (Indian) tea without conscience when the band plays "Tea for Two" (a First World War song made famous again in 1924). The court is packed. The show trial exhibits anti-Indian scapegoating. Ronny, presiding, stands aside to give charge to his Indian deputy. When darker races are said to be attracted to lighter races, the defense snaps back. A cut shows Mrs. Moore on the boat. Then a cutback to the court where Aziz's crime is presented as premeditated. When the defense walks out, the mob calls for Mrs. Moore. Back on the boat, Mrs. Moore's heart gives its beat over to the oceanic pulse. She is buried at sea. No one in court knows this. Called as a witness, her name finds a stand-in in Adela. The persistent echo in Adela's ear ceases the moment Adela tells the truth.

When, after the trial, Fielding and Adela consider whether she unwillingly made it all up—*Might the whole thing have been an hallucination*—one is reminded of all the anxious dreamscapes of Rosy, Laura, Mary, Jane, and Zhivago. Neil Sinyard (2000) stresses the motif and metaphor of hallucination brought on by the heat of an unfamiliar climate, so that, far away from England's cold climate, the film can be tracked as an overheated "mirage" of "confused states." And though the echo calls out a new name, it comes over as a "distinctive roar" reminiscent of the express train in *Brief Encounter*.

When Mrs. Moore leaves India, Godbole stands discreetly at the train station to signal their mutual recognition. Freed, Aziz departs from the courthouse in celebration and heavy rains. Fielding protects Adela until she can return to England. The last shot is of Adela looking out of the window with raindrops echoing those that fell over the trial. She has just received a letter from Aziz—of understanding. The soft music slightly mocks any film that, in 1984, would turn India into yet another "jewel in the crown" (Elena Oliete-Aldea 2015).

Critics, as always, were divided. Dilys Powell looked back over British cinema in 1987 to make "lean" stand not for Lean's height and stature but, biblically, for "the shrinking of great hopes." The war's aftermath had been a time of gift-giving, she said, when British cinema drove away from its creative and economic dependence on the United States. Despite a great break, he returned with *A Passage*. Unlike Hitchcock and Korda, however, because Lean always did his own thing, he did not spearhead a movement, which is why following the "fat" years of Lean's cinema, "lean years" followed (TL: 13). Across the pond, Harlan Kennedy had already offered an "Old Hollywood proverb": "Inside every Lean movie there is a fat one trying to get out" (1985: 28).

Diana Ketcham thought Lean had sold Forster down the river, thanks to the literary executor, King's College, Cambridge (the provost was a very enthusiastic Bernard Williams), going against Forster's wishes. Lean, Ketcham said, produced so surface a display of "visual splendor" that Forster's "aesthetic negation" that had made Chandrapore into a city of waste, nothingness, and lost meaning was entirely erased. If Adela Quested was carefully named, in my view, to tread, in Forster's view, in the footsteps of every British attempt to comprehend India, then, in Ketcham's view, Lean had missed the road to make "the latest invader" a new and superspectacular cinema of tourism (1985: 17).

Charles Allen took on "the grip of Raj mania." He recalled Salman Rushdie's warning against a glamorous revisionism that made it seem as though the British in India weren't "really as bad as people made out" (1985 TL: 10–11). All the nostalgia, the loving to hate and the hating to love a country, came to match the nostalgia critics were feeling and had so long felt toward Lean. Christopher Cook was more appreciative. He saw an achievement in conveying a world of the past, of clubby pretensions and racial snobbery, that could, nevertheless, still send shock waves through an audience. Was Jarre's score merely "overripe" or deliberately "overripe," to capture Lean's own coming "face-to-face" with his mortality? (1985 TL: 36). Lean received three Oscar nominations for directing, scriptwriting, and editing but he won no Oscar; Jarre was nominated for the brief score—and won.

Of all the critics, Patrick Hederman captured best what I have been seeking in all of Lean's films, that it was through Lean's direction that his film, in general, became a "visible symphony" of which the "keynote" allowed a strange melody" always to return (1985: 336–40). Home, to repeat, is where he cut his keys of analysis.

CODA

Film courts analysis and a criticism that is as unfaithful as it is faithful. The court and the courting make cinema an ongoing trial—inside and out. Lean's films received the harshest condemnation and the strongest praise. Contra criticism's required immediacy, critique calls us to revisit the films over and over again. If one comes away with something different each time, it's a good sign.

Lean's musical signature brings the musical score inside the film. The signature works across his films in repeated motifs. Through the cutting, every shot of a gramophone, radio, or musical instrument contributes to a reeling perspectivism that keeps different and often antagonistic thoughts in play. The images chosen for this book illustrate this particular thread. All the transport to faraway places, at home or far away on location, sustains a furniture-art made from the most familiar things. Carrying forward a wit that Coward invested in the first films, Lean's later films avoid the heavy hand of epic seriousness. To get the wit and to let the wit rescue the films from their often overbearing weight, one must listen in spaces where one feels at first least directed to look. Camera shots can conceal provocations and breaks in convention. For all the romantic visual and musical symphonism of the seamless wholes, the telling details depend often on the wit of a popular song.

Discussing this book with friends, I have often received a whistle—a musical motif—of either approval or disapproval, directed, like a one-liner, at Lean's life's work. My own life's work has always sought a single picture, detail, or line to subvert the overgeneralizations or cold abstractions to which philosophical theory is prone when it bypasses the messy realities of life and practice. When generalizations ring hollow, landscapes of sight and sound reassert themselves to project complex worlds of echo and experience. Life and art imitate each other, though not exactly to converge. Exactness in philosophy comes, as in film, not from copying but from the play between cutting and streaming. Form has always made trouble for the ordinary meaning of words and moods. There is a language of law, well transmuted into a language for film, where *pages* of a *record* tell of the criminal who has *form*. As a whistled tune is no mere whistle, aesthetic analysis exacts from the surface the cracks of a desirable crime that cannot be entirely covered over—or up.

Bibliography

New media resources (repeated access 2022-2024): Amazon's Kindle Books; www.arnoldbax.com; British Film Institute; Columbia University libraries; DavidLeanArchive.com; David Lean Foundation; Gale Primary Sources; Internet Archive; Jstor; Project Gutenberg; Proquest; Scribd; Scripts.com; Walter Goehr, https://archiv.adk.de (Akademie der Künste, Berlin); Youtube.

Documentaries

David Lean: A Self Portrait, Thomas Craven, 1971.
"Camera Three: The Making of a Musical: Do I Hear a Waltz? - 1965," with Arthur Laurents.
Mad About the Boy: The Noël Coward Story, Barnaby Thompson 2023.
Making Waves: The Art of Cinematic Sound, Midge Costin, 2019.
Movie Makers: Noël Coward and Richard Attenborough, #OnThisDay 1971, BBC Archive.
The Kiss in the Tunnel, BFI National Archive, 1899.
Reel Britannia. Terence Davies/Jon Spira, 2022.
Who killed British cinema? Vinod Mahindru & Robin Dutta, 2018.

References

Abbate, Carolyn (2001), *In Search of Opera*, Princeton NJ: Princeton University Press.

Adorno, Theodor W. ([1951] 1970), *Minima Moralia: Reflections from Damaged Life*, E. F. N. Jephcott, trans., New York NY: Verso.

Adorno, Theodor W. ([1955] 1999), "Bourgeois Opera," in R. Livingstone, trans., *Sound Figures*, 15–28, Stanford CA: Stanford University Press.

Adorno, Theodor W. ([1966] 1981), "Transparencies on Film," T. Y. Levin, trans., *New German Critique*, 24–5: 199–205.

Adorno, Theodor W. (2006), *Current of Music: Elements of a Radio Theory*, Frankfurt-am-Main: Suhrkamp.

Agate, James (1945), "At the Pictures: What is the Screen For?," *The Tatler and Bystander*, Nov 28, 178(2318): 260–1.

Agate, James (1948), *Ego 9: Concluding the Autobiography of James Agate*, London: Gerry G. Harrap.

Agee, James (1946), "Brief Encounter," The Nation; repr. (2005), *Film Writing And Selected Journalism*, Aug 31, 250–2, New York NY: The Library of America.

Aldgate, Anthony, and Jeffrey Richards (1986), *Britain Can Take it: The British Cinema in the Second World War*, Oxford: Blackwell.

Allen, Charles (1985), "In the Grip of Raj Mania," *TL*, Jan 24, 113(2893): 10–11.

Anderegg, Michael (1984), *David Lean*, Boston: Twayne Publishers.

Anderson, Lindsay (1957), "Anti-System," *New Statesman and Nation*, Oct 12, 54: 460.

Arendt, Hannah (1973), *The Origins of Totalitarianism*, New York NY: Harcourt Brace Jovanovich.

Arnold, Malcolm (2011), *Malcolm Arnold in Words: A Compilation of his Writings and Interviews*, P. Harris, ed., Buckingham: Queen's Temple.

Arnot Robertson, E. (1947), "Women and the Film," *PFR3*: 31–5.

Ashby, Justine, and Andrew Higson, eds. (2000), *British Cinema, Past and Present*, London: Routledge.

Axelrod, George (1956), *The Seven Year Itch: A Romantic Comedy in Three Acts*, New York NY: Publisher Dramatists Play Service.

Badiou, Alain (2013), *Cinema*, S. Spitzer, trans., Cambridge UK: Polity Press.

Balázs, Béla (1931), *Theory of the Film*, London: Dennis Dobson.

Balcon, Michael (1951), "Ten Years of British Film," *Sight and Sound, Special Issue for the Festival of Britain*: 23–38.

Barr, Charles (1986), "Introduction: Amnesia and Schizophrenia," in Barr (ed.), *All Our Yesterdays, 90 Years of British Cinema*, 1–29, London: BFI.

Barthes, Roland (1977), *Image, Music, Text*, Stephen Heath, trans., London: Fontana Press.

Barton, Ruth (2004), *Irish National Cinema*, London: Routledge.

Basinger, Jeanine (2012), *I Do and I Don't: A History of Marriage in the Movies*, New York NY: Vintage.

Bazin, André (1949), "Le Voleur de Bicyclette: Ou L'épreuve Victorieuse du Néo-Réalisme Italien," *Esprit*, 161(11): 820–32.

Bazin, André ([1967] 1971), *What Is Cinema? Vols. I & II*, H. Gray, trans., Berkeley, California: University of California Press.

Bazin, André (1997), *Bazin at Work. Major Essays and Reviews from the Forties and Fifties*, A. Piette and B. Cardullo, trans., New York NY: Routledge.

Bell, Melanie (2009), *Femininity in the Frame: Women and 1950s British Popular Cinema*, London: Routledge.

Bell, Melanie, and Melanie Williams, eds. (2010), *British Women's Cinema*, London: Routledge.

Benedict, Ruth (1934), *Patterns of Culture*, Boston: Houghton Mifflin.

Benjamin, Walter ([1919] 1996), "The Concept of Criticism in German Romanticism," in M. Bullock and M. W. Jennings (eds.), *Selected Writings vol. 1 1913–1926*, 116–200, Cambridge MA: Harvard University Press.

Benjamin, Walter ([1928] 2008), "To the Planetarium," in M. W. Jennings, B. Doherty, and T. Y. Levin (eds.), *The Work of Art in the Age of Its Technological Reproducibility, and Other Writings on Media*, 58–9, Cambridge MA: Harvard University Press.

Benjamin, Walter ([1939] 2003), "The Work of Art in the Age of Its Technological Reproducibility' (Third Version)," in H. Eiland and M. W. Jennings (eds.), *Selected Writings vol. 4 1938–1940*, 251–83, Cambridge MA: Harvard University Press.

Benjamin, Walter (1999), *The Arcades Project*, H. Eiland and K. McLaughlin, trans. and eds., Cambridge MA: Harvard University Press.

Bergfelder, Tim, and Christian Cargnelli, eds. (2008), *Destination London: German-speaking Emigrés and British Cinema 1925–1950*, New York NY: Berghahn Books.

Besant, Walter, and Henry James (1894), *The Art of Fiction*, Boston: Cupples and Hurd.

Bhabha, Homi (1994), "Of Mimicry and Man: The Ambivalence of Colonial Discourse," in *The Location of Culture*, 85–92, London: Routledge.

Bijsterveld, Karin, and José van Dijck, eds. (2009), *Sound Souvenirs: Audio Technologies, Memory and Cultural Practices*, Amsterdam: Amsterdam University Press.

Black, Joel (2001), *The Reality Effect: Film Culture and the Graphic Imperative*, London: Routledge.

Bolt, Robert (1962), "Clues to the Legend of Lawrence," *New York Times Magazine*, Feb 25: 45, 48, 50.

Bordwell, David (1993), "Film Interpretation Revisited," *Film Criticism*, 17(2–3): 93–119.

Bordwell, David (2017), *Reinventing Hollywood: How 1940s Filmmakers Changed Movie Storytelling*, Chicago IL: University of Chicago Press.

Bordwell, David, and Kristin Thompson (2010), *Film Art: An Introduction*, New York NY: McGraw-Hill.

Boulle, Pierre ([1952] 1954), *Pont de la rivière Kwaï*, Paris: Rene Julliard; tr. (2007), *The Bridge on the River Kwai*, Xan Fielding, London: Fontana.

Bower, Helen (1947), "Some 'Mood Music' Makes Mood Critical," *Detroit Free Press*, Jun 22: 39.

Box, Sydney (1947), "A New Deal for Film Writers," *PFR3*: 49–50.

Briggs, Susan (1981), *Those Radio Times*, London: Weidenfeld & Nicolson.

Brown, Royal S. (1994), *Overtones and Undertones: Reading Film Music*, Berkeley CA: University of California Press.

Brownlow, Kevin (1996), *David Lean*, New York NY: St. Martin's Press.

Buhler, James (2013), "Ontological, Formal, and Critical Theories of Film Music and Sound," in David Neumeyer (ed.), *The Oxford Handbook of Film Music Studies*, New York: Oxford University Press (online).

Canby, Vincent (1970), "Sarah Miles Stars in Lean's 'Ryan's Daughter," *The New York Times*, Nov 10: 54.

Canby, Vincent (1970), "Thoroughly Romantic Rosy," *The New York Times*, Nov 22: 105, 111.

Cassidy, Suzanne (1991), "David Lean, Director, Is Honored In Service at St. Paul's Cathedral," *The New York Times*, Oct 4: 94.

Castelli Louis, and Cleeland, Caryn Lynn (1980), *David Lean: A Guide to References and Resources*, Boston: G.K. Hall.

Caton, Stephen C. (1999), *Lawrence of Arabia: A Film's Anthropology*, Berkeley CA: University of California Press.

Cavell, Stanley ([1978] 2005), "What Becomes of Things on Film," in William Rothman (ed.), *Cavell on Film*, 1–10, Stonybrook NY: SUNY Press.

Cavell, Stanley (1981), *Pursuits of Happiness: The Hollywood Comedy of Remarriage*, Cambridge MA: Harvard University Press.

Cavell, Stanley ([1984] 2005), "What Photography Calls Thinking," in William Rothman (ed.), *Cavell on Film*, 115–34, Stonybrook NY: SUNY Press.

Chapman, James, and Nicholas J. Cull (2009), *Projecting Empire: Imperialism and Popular Cinema*, London: I. B. Tauris.

Chion, Michel (2007), "Mute Music: Polanski's The Pianist and Campion's The Piano," in Daniel Ira Goldmark, Lawrence Kramer, and Richard Leppert (eds.), *Beyond the Soundtrack: Representing Music in Cinema*, 86–96, Berkeley CA: University of California Press.

Christie, Ian (2015), *Doctor Zhivago*, London: BFI.

Cixous, Hélène (1976), "The Laugh of the Medusa," K. Cohen and P. Cohen, trans., *Signs*, 1(4): 875–93.

Clair, René (1972), *Cinema Yesterday And Today*, Stanley Applebaum, trans., New York NY: Dover.

Clarke, Donald (2006), "Close Encounter of the Chaste Kind," *The Irish Times*, Mar 23: 16.

Clapp, James A. (2009), "The Romantic Travel Movie, Italian-Style," *Visual Anthropology*, 22(1): 52–63.

Cole, Hugo (1989), *Malcolm Arnold: An Introduction to his Music*, London: Faber.

Coleman, John (1952), "El Aurens," *New Statesman*, Dec 14, 64: 877.

Combs, Richard (1984), "Films," *TL*, Dec 20, 112(2889): 69.

Combs, Richard (1988), "Master Steven's Search for the Sun," *TL*, Feb 18, 119(3050): 29.

Combs, Richard (1988), "Films on TV," *TL*, Apr 21, 119(3059): 38.

Combs, Richard (1990), "Films on TV," *TL*, Apr 19, 123(3161): 34.

Combs, Richard (1990), "Films on TV," *TL*, Dec 13, 124(3195): 31.

Connor, Edward (1956), "The Sound Track," *Films in Review*, Jan 1, 7(1): 37–8.

Cook, Christopher (1985), "Cinema," *TL*, Mar 28, 113(2902): 36.

Cook, Page (1971), "The Sound Track," *Films in Review*, 22/3: 169–70.

Cooke, Mervyn, ed. (2010), *The Hollywood Film Music Reader*, New York NY: Oxford University Press.

Coward, Noël (1932), *Cavalcade*, London: W. Heinemann.

Coward, Noël (1943), *This Happy Breed, A Play in Three Acts*, London: W. Heinemann.

Coward, Noël (1979), *Still-Life in Plays, The Thirties*, London: E. Methuen.

Crowdus Gary (2001), "The Bridge on the River Kwai," *Cinéaste*, 26(2): 50–1.

Crowther, Bosley (1946), "The Screen," *The New York Times*, Sept 7: 11.

Crowther, Bosley (1951), "Oliver Twist," *The New York Times*, Jul 21.

Crowther, Bosley (1962), "Screen: A Desert Warfare Spectacle," *The New York Times*, Dec 17.

Cuff, Paul (2016), *Abel Gance and the End of Silent Cinema. Sounding out Utopia*, London: Palgrave-Macmillan.

Culshaw, John (1966), "Rachmaninov: The Legacy," *TL*, Mar 3, 75(1927): 328.

Curtis, Carl C. III (2012), "David Lean's Lawrence: 'Only Flesh and Blood.'" *Literature/Film Quarterly*, 40(4): 274–87.

Dalmas, Franck (2014), "A Madame Bovary's Daughter: David Lean's Visual Transliteration of Flaubert." http://journals.openedition.org/flaubert/2335.

Davis, Richard (2001), *Eileen Joyce: A Portrait*, Western Australia: Fremantle Arts Centre Press.

Day, Barry (2004), *Coward on Film: The Cinema of Noël Coward*, Lanham MD: Scarecrow Press.

De la Garza, Armida (2018), "Gendering Irish History on Film A Feminist Geopolitics of Ryan's Daughter (1970)," *Gender And History*, 30(3): 645–65.

De la Roche, Catherine (1947), "A Director's Approach to Film Making," *TL*, Aug 28, 38(970): 337–8.

De la Roche, Catherine (1948), "The Mask of Realism," *PFR7*: 35–43.

De la Roche, Catherine (1949), "The 'Feminine Angle'," *PFR8*: 25–34.

De la Roche, Catherine (1949), "No Demand for Criticism," *PFR9*: 88–94.

DeBona, Guerric (1992), "Doing Time; Undoing Time: Plot Mutation in David Lean's "Great Expectations,'" *Literature/Film Quarterly*, 20(1): 77–100.

Deleuze, Gilles (1986), *Cinema 1, The Movement-Image*, H. Tomlinson and B. Habberjam, trans., Minneapolis: University of Minnesota Press.

Dessem, Matthew (2007), "Brief Encounter," *The Criterion Contraption*, Oct. 2. https://criterioncollection.blogspot.com/2007/10/76-brief -encounter.html.

Dickens, Charles ([1861] 1982), *Great Expectations*, Harmondsworth: Penguin.

Dickens, Charles (1891), *Dickens: American notes; Pictures from Italy; and A Child's History of England*, London: Chapman & Hall.

Doane, Mary Ann (1987), *The Desire to Desire: The Woman's Film of the 1940s*, Bloomington ID: Indiana University Press.

Döhl, Frédéric (2013), "Brief Encounter: Zu David Lean's Film (1945), und André Previns Oper (2009)," *Archiv für Musikwissenschaft*, 70(4): 311–32.

Donnelly, Kevin (2005), *The Spectre of Sound: Music in Film and Television*, London: BFI.

Donnelly, Kevin (2007), *British Film Music and Film Musicals*, London: Palgrave.

Durgnat, Raymond ([1970] 2011), *A Mirror for England: British Movies from Austerity to Affluence*, London: Faber/Bloomsbury.

Dyer, Richard (1993), *Brief Encounter*, London: BFI.

Eisenstein, Sergei ([1944] 1949), "Dickens, Griffith, and the Film Today," in Jay Lehda, trans., *Film Form: Essays in Film Theory*, 195–255, New York NY: Harcourt, Brace and Company.

Eisenstein, Sergei, Pudovkin, Vsevolod, and Alexandrov, Grigori (1928), "A Statement in Sound," in Scott Mackenzie (ed.), (2014), *Film Manifestos and Global Cinema Cultures: A Critical Anthology*, 565–8, Berkeley CA: University of California Press.

Eisler, Hanns, and Adorno, Theodor W. ([1947] 2007), *Composing for the Films*, London: Continuum.

Ellis, John (2000), "British Cinema as Performance Art: 'Brief Encounter,' 'Radio Parade of 1935' and The Circumstances of Film Exhibition," in Justine Ashby and Andrew Higson (eds.), *British Cinema, Past and Present*, 95–109, London: Routledge.

Farber, Manny (1946), "Middle Aged Fling," *The New Republic*, Oct 21: 518–19.

Farber, Manny (2009), *Farber on Film: The Complete Film Writings of Manny Farber*, Robert Polito, ed., New York NY: Library of America.

Farley, Fidelma (2002), "Ireland, the Past and British Cinema: Ryan's Daughter," in Claire Monk and Amy Sargeant (eds.), *British Historical Cinema*, 129–43, London: Routledge.

Farmer, Richard (2016), *Cinemas and Cinemagoing in Wartime Britain: 1939–45*, Manchester: Manchester University Press.

Finn, Peter, and Petra Couvée (2014), *The Zhivago Affair: The Kremlin, the CIA and the Battle Over a Forbidden Book*, New York NY: Knopf/ Doubleday.

Flinn, Caryl (1992), *Strains of Utopia: Nostalgia, Gender, and Hollywood Film Music*, Princeton NJ: Princeton University Press.

Fontanaud, Hadrien (2022), "Lawrence of Arabia (David Lean. 1962), and the Western," in Hervé Mayer and David Roche (eds.), *Transnationalism and Imperialism: Endurance of the Global Western Film*, 118–31, Bloomington IN: Indiana University Press.

Forster, E. M. ([1924] 2015), *A Passage to India*, London: Penguin.

Freud, Sigmund ([1919] 1953), "The Uncanny," in James Strachey (ed.), *The Standard Edition of the Complete Psychological Works of Sigmund Freud, Volume XVII: 1917–1919*, 217–56, London: The Hogarth Press.

Füzi, Izabella (2012), "The Face of the Landscape in Béla Balázs's Film Theory," *Film and Media Studies*, 5: 73–86.

Galsworthy, John ([1918] 1933), *The Forsyte Saga*, New York: Scribner.

Garnet, David (1938), *Letters of T.E. Lawrence*, London: World Books.

Gassner, John (1947), "Expressionism and Realism in Films," *PFR3*: 21–30.

Geraghty, Christine (2008), *Now a Major Motion Picture: Film Adaptations of Literature and Drama*, Lanham MD: Rowman and Littlefield.

Gilliatt, Penelope (1962), "Blood, Sand and A Dozen Lawrences," *The Observer*, Dec 16: 25.

Glavin, John, ed. (2003), *Dickens on Screen*, Cambridge UK: Cambridge University Press.

Godsall, Jonathan (2018), *Reeled In: Pre-existing Music in Narrative Film*, London: Routledge.

Goehr, Lydia ([1992] 2007), *The Imaginary Museum of Musical Works: An Essay in the Philosophy of Music*, Oxford: Clarendon Press.

Goehr, Lydia (2008), *Elective Affinities: Musical Essays on the History of Aesthetic Theory*, New York NY: Columbia University Press.

Goehr, Lydia (2016), "The Domestic Diva: Toward an Operatic History of the Telephone," in Karen Henson (ed.), *Technology and the Diva: Sopranos, Opera, and Media from Romanticism to the Digital Age*, 104–23, Cambridge: Cambridge University Press.

Goehr, Lydia (2021a), *Red Sea-Red Square-Red Thread: A Philosophical Detective Story*, New York NY: Oxford University Press.

Goehr, Lydia (2021b), "Did Bach Compose Musical Works? Thinking with Adorno through Paradigms of Possibility," *New German Critique*, 142: 1–39.

Goehr, Lydia (2022), "Instrumentalizing Music for the Movies. Comedy, Portability, Labor, Critique," in Gianmario Borio (ed.), *The Mediations of Music: Critical Approaches after Adorno*, 125–43, London: Routledge.

Goldmark, Daniel Ira, Lawrence Kramer, and Richard Leppert, eds. (2007), *Beyond the Soundtrack: Representing Music in Cinema*, Berkeley CA: University of California Press.

Goody, Alex (2018), "BBC Features, Radio Voices and the Propaganda of War 1939–1941," *Media History*, 24(2): 194–211.

Gorbman, Carol (1987), *Unheard Melodies: Narrative Film Music*, Bloomington IN: Indiana University Press.

Gordon, Eleanor, and Gwyneth Nair (2009), *Murder and Morality in Victorian Britain: The Story of Madeleine Smith*, Manchester: Manchester University Press.

Gough-Yates, Kevin (1991), "The European Film Maker in Exile in Britain 1933-1945," PhD diss., The Open University, London.

Graffy, Julian (2011), "'But Where Is Your Happiness, Alevtina Ivanovna?': New Debates About Happiness in the Soviet Films of 1956," in Marina Balina and Evgeny Dobrenko (eds.), *Petrified Utopia. Happiness Soviet Style*, 217–38, London: Anthem Press.

Gray, Frances (1987), *Noël Coward*, Basingstoke: Macmillan.

Hajkowski, Thomas (2002), "The BBC, the Empire, and the Second World War: 1939-1945," *Historical Journal of Film, Radio and Television*, 22(2): 135–55.

Halliday, Sam (2013), "Modernism and the Seashell," *Critical Quarterly*, 54(4): 74–92.

Halligan, Benjamin (2022), *Hotbeds of Licentiousness: The British Glamour Film and the Permissive Society*, New York NY: Berghahn Books.

Hammond, Mary (2015), *Charles Dickens's Great Expectations: A Cultural Life, 1860–2012*, London: Routledge.

Hansen, Miriam Bratu (1987), "Benjamin, Cinema and Experience: 'The Blue Flower in the Land of Technology,'" *New German Critique*, 40: 179–224.

Hansen, Miriam Bratu (1993), "Of Mice and Ducks: Benjamin and Adorno on Disney," *South Atlantic Quarterly*, 92(1): 27–61.

Hansen, Miriam Bratu (2008), "Benjamin's Aura," *Critical Inquiry*, 34(2): 336–75.

Hardy, Phil (1987), "Films on TV," *TL*, Jan 8, 117(2993): 26.

Harper, Sue (1992), "The Representation of Women in British Feature Film. 1945–1950," *Historical Journal of Film, Radio and Television*, 12(3): 217–30.

Harper, Sue (2010), "The British Women's Picture: Methodology, Agency and Performance in the 1970s," in Melanie Bell and Melanie Williams (eds.), *British Women's Cinema*, 124–337, London: Routledge.

Haskell, Molly (1974), *From Reverence to Rape: The Treatment of Women in the Movies*, Chicago IL: University of Chicago Press.

Hayes, Natalie (1986), "Review of At the Movies/On Television, by David Lean, et al.," *The San Francisco Jung Institute Library Journal*, 6(4): 51–6.

Hederman, Mark Patrick (1985), "David Lean's 'A Passage to India,'" *An Irish Quarterly Review*, 74(295): 336–42.

Heidegger, Martin (1971), *Poetry, Language, Thought*, Albert Hofstadter, trans., New York NY: Harper.

Henderson, Diana (2019), "Romancing King Lear: Hobson's Choice, Life Goes On and Beyond," in Victoria Bladen, Sarah Hatchuel, and Nathalie Vienne-Guerrin (eds.), *Shakespeare on Screen: King Lear*, 125–39, Cambridge: Cambridge University Press.

Herrmann, Bernard (2010), "A Lecture on Film Music (1973)," in Mervyn Cooke (ed.), *The Hollywood Film Music Reader*, 209–22, New York NY: Oxford University Press.

Hetherington, S. J., and Mark Brownrigg (2006), *Muir Mathieson, 1911-1975: A Life in Film Music*, Dalkieth: Scottish Cultural Press.

Higson, Andrew (1989), "The Concept of National Cinema," *Screen*, 30(4): 36–47.

Higson, Andrew (1995), *Waving the Flag: Constructing a National Cinema in Britain*, Oxford: Clarendon.

Higson, Andrew, ed. (1996), *Dissolving Views: Key Writings on British Cinema*, London: Cassell.

Hillman, Roger (1995), "Narrative, Sound, and Film: Fassbinder's The Marriage of Maria Braun," in L. Devereaux Leslie and Roger Hillman (eds.), *Fields of Vision: Essays in Film Studies, Visual Anthropology, and Photography*, 181–95, Berkeley CA: University of California Press.

Hinton, Stephen (1989), *The Idea of Gebrauchsmusik. A Study of Musical Aesthetics in the Weimar Republic (1919–1933)*, with particular reference to the works of Paul Hindemith. New York: Garland.

Hinton, Stephen (2012), *Weill's Musical Theater: Stages of Reform*, Berkeley CA: University of California Press.

Hoare, Philip (1995), *Noël Coward: A Biography*, London: Sinclair-Stevenson.

Hodson, Joel C. (1994), "Who Wrote Lawrence of Arabia? Sam Spiegel and David Lean's Denial of Credit to a Blacklisted Screenwriter," *Cinéaste*, 20(4): 12–18.

Hodson, Joel C. (1995), *Lawrence of Arabia and American Culture*, Westport, CT: Greenwood.

Hoeckner, Berthold (2007), "Transport And Transportation In Audiovisual Memory," in Daniel Ira Goldmark, Lawrence Kramer, and Richard Leppert (eds.), *Beyond the Soundtrack: Representing Music in Cinema*, 163–83, Berkeley CA: University of California Press.

Honan, William (1989), "David Lean, 81, Is at It Again, Working on Brando and Conrad," *The New York Times*, Oct 17: 69, 76.

Horkheimer, Max ([1936] 1982), "Egoism and the Freedom Movement: On the Anthropology of the Bourgeois Era," *Telos*, 21: 10–60.

Horkheimer, Max, and Theodor W. Adorno ([1944] 1981), *Dialektik der Aufklärung. philosophische Fragmente*, Rolf Tiedemann, ed., Frankfurt-am Main: Suhrkamp.

Horkheimer, Max, and Theodor W. Adorno (2002), *Dialectic of Enlightenment: Philosophical Fragments*, E. F. N. Jephcott, trans., Stanford CA: Stanford University Press.

Horowitz, Gregg (2012), "A Made-to-Order Witness: Women's Knowledge," in Katalin Makkai (ed.), *Vertigo*, 112–38, London: Routledge.

Huckvale, David (2022), *The Piano on Film*, Jefferson NC: McFarland & Co.

Huntley, John (1947), *British Film Music*, London: Skelton Robinson.

Huntley, John (1947), "Notes on Film Music," *PFR 3*: 15–17.

Huntley, John (1948), "British Film Music," *PFR6*: 94–5.

Huntley, John (1949), "The Music of 'Hamlet' and 'Oliver Twist'," *PFR8*: 110–16.

Huntley, John (1969), *Railways in the Cinema*, London: Ian Allan.

Hurtgen, Charles Livermore (1962), "Film Adaptations of Shakespeare's Plays," PhD diss., University of California, Berkeley CA.

Jackson, Kevin (2007), *Lawrence of Arabia*, London: BFI.

James, Clive (1970), "Radio," *TL*, Apr 23, 83(2143): 563.

James, Clive (1971), "Reasonably well met by moonlight," *TL*, Sept 30, 86(2218): 456.

James, Henry (1909), *Italian Hours*, Boston & New York: Houghton, Mifflin (online).

Jenkins, Brian (2019), *Madeleine Smith on Trial: A Glasgow Murder and the Young Woman Too Respectable to Convict*, Jefferson NC: McFarland & Co.

John, Juliet (2005), "Fagin, the Holocaust and Mass Culture; or, Oliver Twist on Screen," *Dickens Quarterly*, 22(4): 204–23.

John, Juliet (2010), *Dickens and Mass Culture*, New York NY: Oxford University Press.

Johnson, Ian (2005), *William Alwyn: The Art of Film Music*, Woodbridge: Boydell Press.

Jung, Carl (1933), *Modern Man in Search of A Soul*, New York NY: Harcourt, Brace and Company.

Kael, Pauline (1963), "Circles and Squares," *Film Quarterly*, 16(3): 12–26.

Kael Pauline (1970), "Bolt and Lean," *The New Yorker*, Nov 21: 116–18.

Kael, Pauline (1982), *5001 Nights at the Movies: A Guide from A to Z*, New York NY: Picador/Henry Holt.

Kaplan, E. Ann, ed. (1978), *Women in Film Noir*, London: BFI.

Kaplan, E. Ann, ed. (1990), *Psychoanalysis and Cinema*, London: Routledge.

Karpf, Anne (1990), "Radio Review," *TL*, Dec 6, 124(3194): 47.

Kaufman, Gerald (1966), "The Long and Short Of It," *TL*, May 5, 75(1936): 655.

Kaufman, Gerald (1983) , "On Location," *TL*, Sept 1, 110(2824): 19.

Keller, Hans (2006), *Film Music and Beyond: Writings on Music and the Screen, 1946–59*, Christopher Wintle, ed., London: Plumbago.

Kennedy, Harlan (1985), "I'm a Picture Chap," *Film Comment*, 21(1): 28–32.

Ketcham Diana (1985), "'A Grandiose Muddle," *The Threepenny Review*, 22: 17.

Kirkley, Donald (1946), "Brief Encounter," *The Sun*, Oct 25: 16.

Kittler, Friedrich A. (1999), *Gramophone, Film, Typewriter*, Geoffrey Winthrop-Young and Michael Wutz, trans. and ed., Stanford CA: Stanford University Press.

Koch, Gertrud (1982), "Why Women Go to the Movies," *Jump Cut*, 27: 51–3.

Koch, Gertrud (1985), "Ex-Changing the Gaze: Re-Visioning Feminist Film Theory," *New German Critique*, 34, 139–53.

Kracauer Siegfried (1949), "The Mirror up to Nature," *PFR9*: 95–9.

Kracauer, Siegfried (1960), *Theory of Film: The Redemption of Physical Reality*, New York: Oxford University Press.

Kracauer, Siegfried (1995), *The Mass Ornament: Weimar Essays*, Thomas Y. Levin, trans. and ed., Cambridge MA: Harvard University Press.

Kracauer, Siegfried (2012), *Siegfried Kracauer's American Writings: Essays on Film and Popular Culture*, Johannes von Moltke and Kristy Rawson, eds., Berkeley CA: University of California Press.

LaFave, Kenneth (2017), *Experiencing Film Music: A Listener's Companion*, New York NY: Rowman & Littlefield.

Landy, Marcia (2000), "The Other Side of Paradise: British Cinema from an American Perspective," in Justine Ashby and Andrew Higson (eds.), *British Cinema: Past and Present*, 63–79, London: Routledge.

Langhamer, Claire (2006), "Adultery in Post-war England," *History Workshop Journal*, 62: 86–115.

Lant, Antonia Caroline (1991), *Blackout: Reinventing Women for Wartime British Cinema*, Princeton, NJ: Princeton University Press.

Larsen, Egon (1950), *Spotlight on Films: A Primer for Film-Lovers*, London: Max Parrish & Co.

Laurents, Arthur (1954), *The Time of the Cuckoo: A Comedy in Two Acts*, New York NY: Samuel French.

Lawrence, T. E. ([1922] 1935/1997), *Seven Pillars of Wisdom: A Triumph*, London: Wordsworth.

Lean David (1947), "Brief Encounter," *PFR4*: 27–35.

Lean, David (1947a), "Film Director," in Oswell Blakeson (ed.), *Working for the Films*, 27–37, London: Focal Press.

Lean, David, and Organ, Steven, ed. (2009), *David Lean: Interviews*, Jackson MS: University of Mississippi Press.

Lean, Sandra (2001), (with Barry Chattington), *David Lean: An Intimate Portrait*, London: Universe.

Leech, Clifford (1948), "Dialogue for Stage and Screen," *PFR6*: 97–103.

Lejeune, C(aroline) A(lice). (1945), "The Films," *The Observer*, May 13 and Nov 25: 2 & 2.

Lejeune, C. A. (1947), *Chestnuts in her Lap 1936-1946*, London: Phoenix House.

Lejeune, C. A. (1955), "Love in Venice," *The Observer*, Oct 2: 9

Lejeune, C. A. (1958), "Brief Encounter," *The Observer*, Dec 14: 14.

Lennon, Peter (1983), "The Vortex to Vega," *TL*, Mar 17, 109(2803): 33.

Lennon, Peter (1986), "Documentary," *TL*, Apr 10, 115(2955): 29–31.

Lessing, Gotthold Ephraim ([1766] 1984), *Laocoön: An Essay on the Limits of Painting and Poetry*, Edward Allen McCormick, trans., Baltimore MD: Johns Hopkins University Press.

Light, Alison (1991), *Forever England: Femininity, Literature and Conservatism between the Wars*, London: Routledge.

Lindgren, Ernest (1951), "William Alwyn," *Sight and Sound*, 19/10: 19–20.

London, Kurt (1936), *Film Music, A Summary of the Characteristic Features of its History, Aesthetics, Technique; and Possible Developments*, London: Faber & Faber.

Low, David (1952), *Low's Company. Fifty Portraits*, with verses by Helen Spalding and L.A.G. Strong, London: Methuen.

Ludwig, Emil (1946), "The Seven Pillars of Hollywood," *PFR1*: 90–5.

Macfie, Alexander Lyon (2007), "Representations of Lawrence of Arabia: From Said's Orientalism (1978), to David Lean's film (1962)," *Journal of Postcolonial Writing*, 43(1): 77–87.

MacGowan, Douglas (2007), *The Strange Affair of Madeleine Smith: Victorian Scotland's Trial of the Century*, Edinburgh: Mercat.

Mack, J. E. (1976), *A Prince of Our Disorder: The Life of T.E. Lawrence*, Boston/Toronto: Little, Brown and Company.

Mackay, Robert (2000), "Leaving Out the Black Notes: The BBC and 'Enemy Music' in the Second World War," *Media History*, 6(1): 75–80.

Mackay, Robert (2000a), "Being Beastly to the Germans: Music, Censorship and the BBC in World War II," *Historical Journal of Film, Radio and Television*, 20(4): 513–25.

Mackay, Robert (2006), "'An Abominable Precedent': The BBC's Ban on Pacifists in the Second World War," *Contemporary British History*, 20(4): 491–510.

Mackay, Robert (2006a), "'No Place in the Corporation's Service": The BBC and Conscientious Objectors in the Second World War," *Media History*, 12(1): 37–46.

Mackendrick, Alexander (1954), "A Film Director and His Public," *TL*, Sept 23, 52(1334): 482f.

Mackenzie, Scott, ed. (2014), *Film Manifestos and Global Cinema Cultures: A Critical Anthology*, Berkeley CA: University of California Press.

Malraux, André (1939), pub. 1940 "Esquisse d'une psychologie du cinéma," [online]; "Sketch for a Psychology of the Moving Pictures," in Susanne, K. Lang (ed.) (1958), *Reflections on Art: A Source Book of Writings by Artists, Critics, and Philosophers*, 317–27, Baltimore MD: Johns Hopkins Press.

Malraux, André (1947), *Le Musée Imaginaire*, Paris: Albert Skira.

Manvell, Roger ([1944] 1950), *Film*, London: Pelican.

Manvell, Roger (1947), "Film Music," *PFR3*: 10–14.

Manvell, Roger (1955), *The Film and The Public*, Harmondsworth, Middlesex: Penguin.

Margalit, Avishai (2017), *On Betrayal*, Cambridge MA: Harvard University Press.

Mathieson, Muir (1947), "Developments in Film Music," *PFR4*: 41–6.

Maxford, Howard (2000), *David Lean*, London: Batsford.

Maxwell, Fiona (2018), "All the Window's a Stage: Theatricality and Show Window Display, 1897–1917," *Ezra's Archives*, 8(1): 1–18.

Mazey, Paul (2020), *British Film Music: Musical Traditions in British Cinema, 1930s–1950s*, London: Palgrave.

McFarlane, Brian (1992), "David Lean's 'Great Expectations'—Meeting Two Challenges," *Literature/Film Quarterly*, 20(1): 68–76.

McFarlane, Brian (2014), *Screen Adaptations: Great Expectations*, London: Bloomsbury.

McFarlane, Brian (2015), *Twenty British Films: A Guided Tour*, Manchester: Manchester University Press.

McFarlane, Brian (2019), *The Never-ending Brief Encounter*, Manchester: Manchester University Press.

McInnis, Peter S. (2020), "From Kankakee to Venice: Postwar American Travel Consumerism in David Lean's Summertime (1955)," *Film & History: An Interdisciplinary Journal*, 50(2): 47–59.

McKee, A(lison) L. (2000), "Art or Outrage? Oliver Twist and the Flap over Fagin," *Film Comment*, 36(1): 40–1, 43–5.

McKee, Alison L. (2021), "To Have and to Hold: The Possessive Spectator, The Spinster Narrative, and Katharine Hepburn in David Lean's Summertime (1955)," *Journal of Film and Video*, 73(2): 26–45.

McQuiston, Kate (2013), *We'll Meet Again: Musical Design in the Films of Stanley Kubrick*, New York: Oxford University Press (online).

Merleau-Ponty, Maurice ([1945] 1964), "The Film and the New Psychology," in Hubert L. Dreyfus and Patricia Allen Dreyfus, trans., *Sense and Non-Sense*, 48–62, Evanston IL: Northwestern University Press.

Metz, Christian (1991), *Film language: A Semiotics of the Cinema*, Michael Taylor, trans., Chicago IL: University of Chicago Press.

Mill, J. S (1869), *The Subjection of Women*, London: Longmans (online).

Millar, Gavin (1970), "Films," *TL*, Dec 17, 84(2177): 856.

Monk, Claire, and Amy Sargeant, eds. (2002), *British Historical Cinema: The History, Heritage and Costume Film*, London: Routledge.

Moraitis, Catherine (2001), *The Art of David Lean: A Textual Analysis of Audio Visual Structure*, PhD diss., Bloomington IN: Indiana University Press.

Morley, Sheridan ([1969] 1985), *A Talent to Amuse: A Biography of Noël Coward*, New York NY: Doubleday.

Morton, Lawrence (2010), "Composing, Orchestrating, and Criticizing (1951)," in Mervyn Cooke (ed.), *The Hollywood Film Music Reader*, 327–40, New York NY: Oxford University Press.

Moscrop, Andrew(2011), "Doctor Zhivago," *British Medical Journal*, 343(7813): 47.

Mulvey, Laura (1975), "Visual Pleasure and Narrative Cinema," *Screen*, 16: 6–18.

Mulvey, Laura (2006), *Death 24x a Second: Stillness and the Moving Image*, Chicago IL: University of Chicago Press.

Murphy, Robert (1989), *Realism and Tinsel: Cinema and Society in Britain, 1939–1949*, London: Routledge.

Murphy, Robert, ed. (2013), *British Cinema: Critical Concepts in Media and Cultural Studies, 4 vols*, London: Routledge.

Murray-Schafer, R. ([1977] 1994), *The Soundscape. Our Sonic Environment and the Tuning of the World*, Rochester VT: Destiny Books.

Neame, Ronald (2003), *Straight from the Horse's Mouth*, Lanham MD: Scarecrow Press.

Neilson Baxter, R. K. (1949), "The Man with the Box Brownie," *PFR9*: 82–7.

Neumeyer, David, ed. (2013), *The Oxford Handbook of Film Music Studies*, New York NY: Oxford University.

Newton, Michael (2015), "Loved but not lost: David Lean's *Brief Encounter* and *Dr Zhivago*," *The Guardian*, Nov 13.

Nietzsche Friedrich (1997), *Untimely Meditations*, D. Breazeale ed., R. J. Hollingdale, trans., 57–124, Cambridge UK: Cambridge University Press.

Nietzsche, Friedrich (1999), *The Birth of Tragedy and Other Writings*, Raymond Geuss and Ronald Speirs eds., Cambridge: Cambridge University Press.

Nietzsche, Friedrich (2001), *The Gay Science: With a Prelude in German Rhymes and an Appendix of Songs*, Bernard Williams ed., Cambridge: Cambridge University Press.

Nietzsche, Friedrich (2005), *The Anti-Christ, Ecce Homo, Twilight of the Idols: And Other Writings*, Aaron Ridley and Judith Norman eds., Cambridge: Cambridge University Press.

Norgate, Matthew (1944), "Film Guide," *TL*, Jun 1, 31(803): 609.

Norris, Geoffrey (1976), *Rakhmaninov. The Master Musicians Series*, London: J.M. Dent.

O'Brien, Kate ([1934] 1990), *The Ante-Room*, New York NY: Vintage Books.

O'Flynn, John (2022), *Music, the Moving Image and Ireland. 1897–2017*, London: Routledge.

O'Neill, Michael, Mark Sandy, Mark, and Sarah Wootton, eds. (2012), *Venice and the Cultural Imagination: "This Strange Dream upon the Water,"* London: Routledge.

O'Rawe, Des (2005), "Venice in Film: Postcards and Palimpsests," *Literature-Film Quarterly*, 33(3): 224–32.

Oakes, Philip (1990), "Branch Line: Stoking Passions," *TL*, Sept 27, 124(3184): 10.

Oliete-Aldea, Elena (2015), *Hybrid Heritage on Screen: The "Raj Revival"in the Thatcher Era*, London: Palgrave.

Orr, John (2010), "David Lean: The Troubled Romantic and the End of Empire," in J. Orr (ed.), *Romantics and Modernists in British Cinema*, 64–85, Edinburgh: Edinburgh University Press.

Orwell, George (1936), *Keep The Aspidistra Flying*, London: Gollancz.

Orwell, George (1971), *The Collected Essays, Journalism and Letters of George Orwell, vol. 2*, Sonia Orwell and Ian Angus, eds., Harmondsworth, Middlesex: Penguin.

Paganoni, Maria Christina (2010), "From Book to Film: The Semiotics of Jewishness in 'Oliver Twist.'" *Dickens Quarterly*, 27(4): 307–20.

Palmer, Christopher (1980), "Film Music," in Stanley Sadie (ed.), *The New Grove Dictionary of Music and Musicians* 6th edn, 549–53, New York NY: Oxford University Press.

Palmer, Russell (1948), *British Film Music*, London: Skelton.

Pasternak, Boris (1958), *Doctor Zhivago*, Max Hayward and Manya Harari, trans., London: Collins.

Perkins, V. F. (1972), *Film as Film*, Harmondsworth: Penguin.

Perkins, Roy, and Martin Stollery, eds. (2004), *British Film Editors: The Heart of the Movie*, Berkeley CA: University of California Press.

Pettitt, Lance (2000), *Screening Ireland: Film and Television Representation*, Manchester: Manchester University Press.

Phillips, Gene D. (2006), *Beyond the Epic: The Life and Films of David Lean*, Lexington KY: University Press of Kentucky.

Powell, Dilys (1987), "British Cinema," *TL*, Jan 29, 117(2996): 13.

Pratley, Gerald (1974), *The Cinema of David Lean*, Cranbury NJ: A. S. Barnes; London: Tantivy.

Price, Hollie (2021), *Picturing Home: Domestic Life and Modernity in 1940s British Film*, Manchester: Manchester University Press.

Prokosch, Mike (1971), "Films. A Tale Told by an Idiot. RYAN'S DAUGHTER at the Charles Cinema till Doomsday," *The Harvard Crimson*, Jan 1.

Puckett, Kent (2017), *War Pictures. Cinema, Violence, and Style in Britain, 1939–1945*, New York NY: Fordham University Press.

Quéval, Jean (1950), "France looks at British Films," *Sight and Sound*, Jul 1, 19: 198–200.

Quéval, Jean (1954), "Néo-cinéma" 1-17, and "En Grande-Bretagne" 101-13, André Bazin, et. al. Cinema 53. A travers le monde, Paris: Editions du Cerf.

R.M. (1945) "Monthly Bulletin," *BFI*, Dec 31, 12(144): 145.

Rance, Nick (1998), "'Victorian Values' and 'Fast Young Ladies': From Madeleine Smith to Ruth Rendell," in Gary Day (ed.), *Varieties of Victorianism: The Uses of a Past*, 220–35, Basingstoke: Macmillan.

Rattigan, Neil (2001), *This Is England: British Film and the People's War, 1939–1945*, Madison, WI: Fairleigh Dickinson University Press.

Rehding, Alexander (2006), "On the Record," *Cambridge Opera Journal*, 18(1): 59–82.

Reisz, Karel (1953/1966), *The Technique of Film Editing*, London: Focal Press.

Remes, Justin (2014), "Serious Immobilities: Andy Warhol, Erik Satie and the Furniture Film," *Screen*, 55(4): 447–59.

Rhode, Eric (1962), " Two-and-a-half Pillars of Wisdom," *TL*, Dec 20, 68(1760): 1055.

Richards, Jeffrey, and Dorothy Sheridan eds. (1987), *Mass-Observation at the Movies*, London: Routledge.

Richards, Jeffrey, and Jeffrey Hulbert (1984), "Censorship in Action: The Case of Lawrence of Arabia," *Journal of Contemporary History*, 19(1): 153–70.

Ross, Alex (2007), *The Rest Is Noise: Listening to the Twentieth Century*, New York NY: Farrah, Straus and Giroux.

Rowan, Paul Benedict (2020), *Ryan's Daughter: The Making of an Irish Epic*, Lexington KY: University Press of Kentucky.

Roy Clifton, N. (1983), *The Figure in Film*, Newark NJ: University of Delaware Press.

Ruskin, John (2010), *The Works of John, Vol. 18: Sesame and Lilies; the Ethics of the Dust; the Crown of Wild Olive; with Letters on Public Affairs 1859–1866* (online).

Said, Edward (1978), *Orientalism*, New York NY: Vintage.

Sandall, Roger (1963), "Lawrence of Arabia by Sam Spiegel, David Lean," *Film Quarterly*, 16(3): 56–7.

Santas, Constantine (2008), *The Epic in Film: From Myth to Blockbuster*, Lanham: Rowman & Littlefield.

Santas, Constantine (2012), *The Epic Films of David Lean*, London: Scarecrow.

Sarris, Andrew (1970), "Notes on the Auteur Theory in 1970," *Film Comment*, 6(3): 6–9.

Sartre, Jean-Paul (1974), "Motion-Picture Art (1931)," in Michel Rybalka and Michel Contat (eds.), *Selected Prose: The Writings of Jean-Paul Sartre, vol. 2*, 53–9, Evanston, IL: Northwestern University Press.

Scheuer, Philip (1946), "Coward's 'Brief Encounter" Moving Marital Drama," *Los Angeles Times*, Oct 19: A5.

Schickel, Richard (1984), "A Superb Passage to India," *Time*, Dec 31, 124(07).

Shandley, Robert R. (2009), *Runaway Romances: Hollywood's Postwar Tour of Europe*, Philadelphia PA: Temple University Press.

Shaw, George Bernard (1903), *Man and Superman. A Comedy and A Philosophy*, New York: Brentano.

Shaw, George Bernard (1947), "Shaw on Radio Music," *The Musical Times*, 88(1247): 9–10.

Shepard, Jim (2003) "Grab Your Hankies, All You Women (and Democrats)!" Jun 1, (online).

Shklar, Judith N. (1984), *Ordinary Vices*, Cambridge MA: Harvard University Press.

Sigal, Clancy (1984), "Other Highlights," *TL*, May 17, 111(2858): 35.

Silver, Alain (1974), "The Untranquil Light: David Lean's 'Great Expectations,'" *Literature/Film Quarterly*, 2(2): 140–52.

Silver, Alain, and James Ursini ([1974] 1991), *David Leans and his Film*, Hollywood CA: Silman-James Press.

Silverman, Kaja (1988), *The Acoustic Mirror. The Female Voice in Psychoanalysis and Film*, Bloomington IN: Indiana University Press.

Silverman, Steven M. (1989), *David Lean*, New York NY:: H.N. Abrams.

Simmel, Georg ([1911] 2002), "Das Abenteuer," *Philosophische Kultur. Gesammelte Essais*, 11–28, Leipzig: Klinkhardt; (1997), "The Adventure," in David Kettler, trans., David Frisby and Mike Featherstone (eds.), *Simmel on Culture: Selected Writings*, 221–32, London: Sage.

Simmel, Georg ([1913] 2007), "The Philosophy of Landscape," *Theory, Culture & Society*, 24(7–8): 20–9.

Sinyard, Neil (1998), "Home and Englishness in the Films of David Lean," (online).

Sinyard, Neil (2000), "Lids Tend to Come Off: David Lean's Film of E. M. Forster's A Passage to India," in Robert Giddings and Erica Sheen (eds.), *The Classic Novel: From Page to Screen*, 147–62, Manchester: Manchester University Press.

Slobin, Mark E. ed. (2008), *Global Soundtracks. Worlds of Film Music*, Middletown CT: Wesleyan University Press.

Smith, A. Duncan (1905), *Trial of Madeleine Smith*, Toronto: Canada Law Book Co.

Smith, Adrian (2010), "The Dawn of the Jet Age in Austerity Britain: David Lean's The Sound Barrier (1952)," *Historical Journal of Film, Radio and Television*, 30(4): 487–514.

Smith, Grahame (2003), *Dickens and the Dream of Cinema*, Manchester: Manchester University Press.

Smyth, J. E (2016), "Review of Brief Encounter," *Cinéaste*, 41(4): 53–4.

Sontag, Susan ([1964] 2018), *Notes on Camp*, Harmondsworth: Penguin.

Sragow, Michael (1985), "David Lean's Right of "Passage,'" *Film Comment*, 21(1): 20–7.

Street, Sarah (2009), "'Another Medium Entirely': Esther Harris, National Screen Service and Film Trailers in Britain. 1940-1960," *Historical Journal of Film, Radio and Television*, 29(4): 433–48.

Street, Sarah (2010), "'In Blushing Technicolor': Colour in Blithe Spirit," *Journal of British Cinema and Television*, 7(1): 34–52.

Swynnoe, Jan G. (2002), *The Best Years of British Film Music. 1936–1958*, Rochester NY: Boydell Press.

T. M. P. (1945), "Ectoplasmic Highjinks of Noel Coward Tale, 'Blithe Spirit,' Mark Return of the Winter Garden to the Cinema Fold," *The New York Times*, Oct 4: 27.

Tanitch, Robert (1989), *Guinness*, New York NY: Applause Theatre Book.

Tanner, Michael (2007), *Troubled Epic: On Location with Ryan's Daughter*, Cork: Collins.

Thompson, David (2008), "Unhealed Wounds," *The Guardian*, May 10.

Thorau, Christian (2019), "'What Ought to be Heard': Touristic Listening and the Guided Ear," in Christian Thorau and Hansjakob Ziemer (eds.), *The Oxford Handbook of Music Listening in the 19th and 20th Centuries* (online), New York NY: Oxford University Press.

Thornley, John (1989), "A Brave New World. Music for the British Sound Cinema, 1930–55," *TL*, Nov 30, 122(3142): 46–7.

Todd, Ann (1980), *The Eighth Veil*, London: William Kimber.

Truffaut, François (1978), *The Films in My Life*, Leonard Mayhew, trans., New York NY: Simon & Schuster.

Truss, Lynne (1989), "Ireland," *TL*, Nov 9, 122(3139): 50.

Tunley, David, Rogers, V., and Meher-Homji, C. (2017), *Destiny: The Extraordinary Career of Pianist Eileen Joyce*, Melbourne: Lyrebird Press.

Turner, Adrian (1994), *The Making of David Lean's Lawrence of Arabia*, London: Dragon's World.

Tynan, Kenneth (1966), "Zhivago–the missing link," *The Observer*, May 1: 25.

Vanel, Hervé (2013), *Triple Entendre: Furniture Music, Muzak, Muzak-Plus*, Urbana: University of Illinois Press.

Vargas, A. L. (1949), "British Films and their Audience," *PFR8*: 71–6.

Vaughan Williams, Ralph (1986), *National Music and Other Essays*, London: Oxford University Press.

Vermilye, Jerry (1978), *The Great British Films*, Secaucus NJ: Citadel Press.

Wartenberg, Thomas E (2006), "Beyond Mere Illustration: How Films Can Be Philosophy," *The Journal of Aesthetics and Art Criticism*, 64(1): 19–32.

Watt, Ian (1959), "Bridges over the Kwai," *TL*, Aug 6, 62(1584): 216–18.

Webster, Wendy (2003), "Domesticating the Frontier: Gender, Empire and Adventure Landscapes in British Cinema. 1945–59," *Gender and History*, 15(1): 85–107.

Weinberg. Herman G. (1959), "Coffee, Brandy, and Cigars," *Film Culture*, 20: 86–91.

Wells, H. G. (1913), *The Passionate Friends*, New York NY: Harper.

Wharton, Edith (1905), *Italian Backgrounds*, New York NY: Scribner.

White, Rebecca (2012), "Representations of Venice in Daphne Du Maurier's Don't Look Now and Nicolas Roeg's Screen Adaptation," in Michael O'Neill et al. (eds.), *Venice and the Cultural Imagination: "This Strange Dream upon the Water,"* 157–70, London: Routledge.

Whitebait, William (1944),"The Movies," *The New Statesman and Nation*, May 27, 27(692): 352.

Whitebait, William (1945), "The Movies," *The New Statesman and Nation*, Apr 14, 29(738): 239–40.

Whitebait, William (1946), "The Movies," *The New Statesman and Nation*, Feb 9, 31(781): 100.

Wiebe, Heather (2024), *Mobilizing Music in Wartime British Film*, New York: Oxford University Press.

Williams, Melanie (2014), *David Lean*, Manchester: Manchester University Press.

Williams, Tony (2000), *Structures of Desire: British Cinema, 1939–1955*, Stonybrook NY: SUNY Press.

Wilson, David (1966), *Letter to Editor*, *Hi Fi/Stereo Review*, July edition: 12.

Wimmer, Leila (2009), *Cross-Channel Perspectives. The French Reception of British Cinema*, Bern: Peter Lang.

Winnington, Richard (1947), "Critical Survey," *PFR2*: 16–24.

Wittgenstein, Ludwig (1922), *Tractatus-Logico-Philosophicus*, London: Routledge & Kegan Paul.

Wittgenstein, Ludwig (1980), *Culture and Value*, G. H. von Wright, ed., Chicago IL: University of Chicago Press.

Wollenberg, H. H. (1948), "Round the World's Studios," *PFR6*: 40–4.

Wollenberg, H. H. (1948), "Round the World's Studios," *PFR7*: 91–5.

Woolf, Virginia (1926), "The Cinema," *The Nation & Athenaeum*, Jul 3: 381–3.

Wright, Adrian (2008), *The Innumerable Dance: The Life and Work of William Alwyn*, Woodbridge: Boydell Press.

Yagoda, Ben (2019), "Flames of Passion" in "Brief Encounter," (online).

Zambrano, A. L. (1974), "'Great Expectations.' Dickens and David Lean," *Literature/Film Quarterly*, 2(2): 153–61.

Žižek, Slavoj (1997), *The Plague of Fantasies*, London: Verso.

Index of Names and Titles

FILMS, FILMMAKERS, THEATER PLAYS

MUSICALS, POPULAR SONGS